DATE DUE

DEMCO, INC. 38-2931

Chinese Export Porcelain

Cover illustration: Lotus bowl, c. 1760. Diameter, 15½ inches. Courtesy Elinor Gordon.

ANTIQUES Magazine Library

Chinese Export Porcelain

AN HISTORICAL SURVEY

Edited by Elinor Gordon

Main Street/Universe Books

New York

Articles included in this volume are printed exactly as they appeared in the following issues of *The Magazine* ANTIQUES.

Part I. Lowestoft, What Is It?: I, Misapprehensions, March, 1928; II, Several Whys and Wherefores, May, 1928; III, Centres of Manufacture and a Classification, November, 1928; IV, Biblical and Floral Designs, March, 1929; V, Genre Designs, June, 1929; VI, Ship Designs, August, 1929.

Part II. Quality in Oriental Lowestoft, December, 1937; Lowestoft China, July, 1947; Crosscurrents in China Trade Porcelain, January, 1974; Chinese Porcelain Interchange, February, 1957; Oriental Porcelain Frivolities, May, 1966; Imitations of Chinese Lowestoft, October, 1933; The Yesterday and Today of Oriental Lowestoft, June, 1931.

Part III. Design Sources of Early China Trade Porcelain, January, 1972; Western Ceramic Models for China Trade Porcelain, November, 1956; Chinese Porcelain Figures of Westerners, February, 1961; Porcelain as Room Decoration in Eighteenth-Century England, December, 1969; Dutch Decorators of Chinese Porcelain, February, 1932; German and English Decorators of Chinese Porcelain, March, 1932.

Part IV. Lowestoft: Exclusively American, April, 1932; American Eagle Lowestoft, June, 1930; State Arms on Chinese Lowestoft, October, 1930; The Cincinnati and Their Porcelain, February, 1930; American Ship Lowestoft, June, 1931; The Commodore Decatur Punchbowl, April, 1932; A Lost Set of Eighteenth-Century Oriental Lowestoft, October, 1938.

Part V. Chinese Armorial Porcelain, August, 1928; Introduction to Heraldry, December, 1952; Collecting Armorial Export Porcelain, December, 1952; Fitzhugh and FitzHughs in the China Trade, January, 1966; The Canton Pattern, August, 1975; The Rose Medallion and Mandarin Patterns in China Trade Porcelain, October, 1967.

First Edition
Fourth printing, June 1979

Library of Congress Catalog Card Number 75-39887

ISBN 0-87663-252-5, cloth edition
ISBN 0-87663-923-6, paperback edition

Published by Universe Books, 381 Park Avenue South, New York City 10016. Produced by The Main Street Press, 42 Main Street, Clinton, New Jersey 08809.

Printed in the United States of America

Cover design by Lawrence Grow

Contents

Introduction

Chinese export porcelain has attracted the interest of a growing number of collectors on a worldwide basis in re-recent years. Auction houses in London, the European continent, and the United States regularly schedule sales devoted exclusively to the ware. Those attending such events may be astonished by the ever escalating prices being brought for items as diverse as a seventeenth-century coffee pot made for the Dutch market and a much less spectacular Canton or Nanking blue-and-white garniture sent to America in the early years of the nineteenth century. In 1786 George Washington purchased a 302-piece set of export ware for $150. Only twenty years ago Chinese export pieces of good quality might be had for reasonable sums. Today one *must* know both the market for such porcelain and something of the china's history and particular qualities in order not only to compete for prizes but to survive the rough and tumble pursuit of profit.

While export ware itself dates back to the early part of the sixteenth century, interest in it seems largely to have disappeared during the second half of the nineteenth century, a period when its importation to various Western countries virtually came to a halt. So much so was this the case that a major English authority on porcelain, William Chaffers, in his first edition of *Marks and Monograms on European and Oriental Pottery and Porcelain* (1863), erroneously and absurdly identified this porcelain as having been made at a small factory in Lowestoft, England. This attribution was made despite the fact that hundreds of thousands of pieces, still existing at the time, had been imported into England for many years prior to 1756 when the little Lowestoft works were established. The factory ceased to exist in 1802.

Chaffers' erroneous attribution had one unfortunate effect. It was accepted as the gospel truth. Consequently, this pure Chinese porcelain has been called Oriental Lowestoft or Chinese Lowestoft for almost one hundred years, causing considerable confusion to layman and novice collector alike. The reader of this volume will find these terms used again and again by writers of the 1920s, 30s, and 40s. They, however, were merely following established form and knew the porcelain to be Chinese. Today the term *Chinese export porcelain* is considered an accurate one since the porcelain was made in China, it was made for export, and it is a true hard paste ware. This term has been adopted by such leading international auction galleries as Christie's and Sotheby's of London, Switzerland, and Hong Kong, Sotheby-Parke-Bernet in the United States, and by leading collectors, and a number of prominent writers. Hopefully, use of this designation will become standard, eventually putting an end to the confusion caused, first, by the unbiquitous Mr. Chaffers.

One must realize that at no time did this porcelain have a generic name in the manner of Bow, Chelsea, Spode, or Meissen, porcelains which took the name of the factory or town where made. Before the advent of Chaffers, export ware was referred to as India Company china in England. In France it is still referred to as *porcelain de la Compagnie des Indes,* and in Holland as *chine de commande.*

Correction of Chaffers' major error and many smaller ones was long in coming in North America and Great Britain. If we disregard the privately printed books by V. Griggs in 1887 and I.A. Crisp in 1907, which were catalogues of their personal collections, and the Sir Algernon Tudor-Craig book in 1925, solely on armorial porcelain of the eighteenth century, it is evident that writers of original treatises were notably silent. References to export ware were generally limited to a few paragraphs in books devoted to Chinese porcelain in general by such authorities as S. V. Bushell, W. B. Honey, and V. G. Gulland. Not until the publication in 1954 of J. A. Lloyd Hyde's *Oriental Lowestoft* did the subject receive the extensive treatment it so seriously needed.

One authority in the field, however, had intended to publish an important new book in the 1930s. This was Homer Eaton Keyes, editor of *The Magazine* ANTIQUES from its founding in 1923 until his death in 1938. Over the years he contributed a series of articles, thirteen in number, covering almost all aspects of this porcelain. A group of six articles, "Lowestoft—What Is It?" began appearing in 1928, and these fundamental primers of Chinese export ware perform a most useful service today. They are reprinted as the first section of this book. It is a tribute to Keyes' sagacity, insight, and wit that they remain, today, along with his other contributions on the subject, almost without exception as valid as when written over forty-five years ago.

Any discussion of Chinese export porcelain must begin with at least a short history of its manufacture, design, and distribution over the centuries. Probably no objects have served more usefully as a link between Eastern and Western cultures since the Middle Ages. *China*, of course, is a term which entered our vocabulary with hard paste porcelain in the sixteenth century and has unconsciously absorbed a thousand different meanings.

The manufacture of porcelain goes back a number of centuries. It was made at different locations in China but it is recorded that Emperor Woeng Wu (1368–98) of the Ming dynasty selected the town of Ching-tê Chên on the P'oyang River in the province of Kiangsi, to build kilns for the manufacture of porcelain for the royal house. In time other private factories grew up around the royal establishment and the town was to become known as "The Porcelain City." Ching-tê Chên was fortunately located because it was surrounded with all the necessary elements for the making of fine porcelain. In the river bed was an excellent quality of white clay (kaolin); in the hills a good quality of feldspar (petuntse) for the glaze, abundant ferns, the ashes of which were mixed with the petuntse to harden the glaze, and pigments for the porcelain. Also in the hills were coal and wood to fire the kilns. In addition, the location on the P'oyang river, near P'oyang lake, gave the town access through a series of waterways and overland trails to some of the major seaports, including Canton, about four hundred miles to the southeast.

Over the years the importance of Ching-tê Chên grew until in the eighteenth century it is said to have boasted around 3,000 kilns and a population of a million persons. In some ways the city can be compared with the auto manufacturing center of Detroit. Everyone was engaged in some aspect of the porcelain industry. A type of production line was developed in which each individual had one specific task to perform in the manufacture of a single piece. Father Francois Xavier d'Entrecolles, a Jesuit missionary, who was the first Westerner to describe the details of porcelain manufacture, states in letters written in 1712 and 1722 that one piece might pass through fifty or sixty hands before its completion.

Export of the ware began fairly early. From very early times there are records of individual pieces of porcelain, probably made at Ching-tê Chên which found their way to Rome and the Middle East. These probably arrived via the Old Silk Route or were carried by adventurous trading junks. Among the early owners of Chinese porcelain were Marco Polo (1252–1324), the Duke of Normandy (1363), and the Doge of Venice, Pasquala Maliprero (1461). A steady flow of exports, however, did not begin until the arrival of Portuguese merchants at Canton in 1517. When barred from the ports of Ningho and Chuan, the Portuguese established a trade post at Macao. Since 1557 this coastal city has been their private possession. In 1596 the Dutch reached Bantam, and in 1598 a Dutch fleet of eight ships sailed to trade with the Far East. The British East India Company was set up in 1599 and established at Bantam in 1620. In 1698 the first French ship traded with the Far East.

In 1699 the port of Canton was finally opened to foreign trade by the Emperor Kang Hsi and the English established the first hong, or factory, on a narrow sand spit in the Pearl River along the waterfront. They were followed by the French in 1728, the Dutch in 1729, the Danes in 1731, Swedes in 1732, together with the Austrians, Russians, Indians, Armenians, the Spanish Manila Company, and finally the Americans in 1784. The largest number of hongs at any one time was thirteen. They were two or three stories high with the first floor reserved for business and the storing of merchandise while the second and third floors were used for living quarters for the staff. No women were allowed at the hongs and this restriction lasted until after the Opium Wars in 1841.

All business with the Chinese, including the rental of the various hongs, was conducted through individual hong merchants. These men, who never numbered more than ten or eleven at any particular time, belonged to an association called the Co-hong. They were responsible to the Emperor for the conduct and transactions of the individual foreign traders as well as the personal conduct of the individual crew members. In the early days of trading all foreigners had to leave Canton at the end of the trading season. Most went to Macao to await the next season, an event determined by the monsoon trade winds.

At first with the Portuguese, Spanish, and Dutch merchants all the porcelain exported was of the blue and white variety and the forms were largely of Chinese origin. It wasn't long, however, before the trading nations began to order forms which complied with European usage. These nations supplied the Chinese potters with wooden models as well as actual European items in silver, pewter, faience, etc., to be copied in porcelain. As early as 1639, records of the Dutch East India Company show, an order for 25,000 items was to be made from wood models supplied by the Dutch. Even before special European forms were ordered, however, special decorations on the blue and white porcelain were requested by the foreigners. The decoration of a celestial globe, a favorite device of King Manuel I (1469–1521), was put on an ewer made for him. In several Portuguese collections are found early primitive examples of the national arms, including the arms of King Sebastian (1557–87) which appear four times on a border of a blue and white dish. Such pieces would seem to qualify as the earliest armorial objects known. The use of individual coats-of-arms and initials, sometimes in a cypher design, came to be one of the most desired forms of decoration. Such diverse personalities as Catherine the Great, Thomas Jefferson, DeWitt Clinton and his wife, General Knox, and members of the English royal family, the liveried companies of London, and prominent families of Brazil and Mexico all had porcelain decorated with their personal arms, initials, or other devices. In addition, the Chinese made large quantities for their neighbors in the Far East such as Siam, Burma, the Philippines as well as the Middle Eastern countries. Pieces with Arabic script included in the decoration are not uncommon.

Much Chinese export porcelain survives today in near perfect condition largely because of the extraordinary number of pieces shipped to the major European countries and, after 1784, directly to America. These literally run into the millions. T. Volker in his publication of the records of the Dutch East India Company, 1602–1682, concludes that on a conservative basis approximately twelve million pieces were imported during this period by the Dutch alone. The opening of Canton to Western traders in 1699 prompted a tremendous increase in the volume of exported porcelain, and this flow continued unabated until near the close of the eighteenth century. In America importations increased sharply after the Revolutionary War and again after the War of 1812. In Europe, however, the volume of trade steadily declined during the nineteenth century, and virtually came to an end as far as both North Americans and Europeans were concerned when the town of Ching-tê Chên was destroyed and most of the inhabitants slaughtered during the T'aip'ing rebellion in 1853. The town and the kilns were later rebuilt, but it never again attained its prominent position in the manufacture of porcelain.

Visitors as diverse in outlook and distant in time as scholar J. A. Lloyd Hyde and Mrs. Edward Boehm, widow of the creator of the Boehm porcelains, have traveled to Ching-tê Chên in the twentieth century. Hyde relates his 1931 search for old export ware and craftsmen capable of producing similar porcelains in this volume (pp. 74–75). Mrs. Boehm visited the old porcelain city in January of 1975, and has reported that porcelain is still being made there in a limited way. No visitors to China in modern times, however, have been able to uncover a treasury of unexported export ware.

The principal cause of the decline in the trade is due to the gradual takeover of the porcelain business by English and continental factories. The secrets of Chinese production were mastered, in particular, by German and Dutch craftsmen. They were in a good position to satisfy the European and North American customers on two counts—that of taste and promptness of delivery. Orders taken by the East India companies would generally be two years or longer in filling. English and continental manufacturers either carried the items in stock or could supply them on short notice at competitive prices.

It was no simple matter, however, for the Europeans to copy the glazes and the colors so carefully developed by the Chinese. Up to the latter part of the seventeenth century almost all the export porcelain was of the blue and white variety. After the kilns at Ching-tê Chên were burned down by warring factions in the year 1675, they were rebuilt by the Emperor K'ang-hsi and placed in charge of an accomplished manager, T'sang Ying-hsüan.

Under his supervision new colors were developed for decoration, the outsanding being *famille verte* (green), and the porcelain reached a very high quality. K'ang-hsi was succeeded as emperor in 1723 by his son Yung-Chêng who reigned until 1735. During this period the colors *rouge-de-fer* and gold were developed and the quality of the porcelain reached an even higher level. Yung-Chêng in turn was succeeded by Ch'ien-lung (1736–1795). It was during the early part of his reign that the beautiful *famille rose* colors and decoration were perfected. Some of the finest quality porcelain was made around the middle of this century.

At the same time, however, during the height of the Western trade, ship captains and managers (or super cargoes) were instructed to purchase pieces of heavier quality to reduce breakage in shipping. Concurrent with this change to heavier (and poorer) porcelain, the quality of decoration began its decline. The coarse heavy porcelain, often with crudely decorated designs, bore little resemblance to that of fine egg shell quality and meticulous decoration.

New designs were introduced at the end of this period and during the early part of the nineteenth century. Among them was the so-called Fitzhugh design in blue, green, orange, brown, mulberry, gold, black, yellow, and combinations of colors, and the Rose Medallion design in which a piece is largely covered with large floral medallions in rose, greens, and blues. Other designs introduced at this time include the Mandarin in which the floral medallions enclose Chinoiserie designs in colors similar to those of Rose Medallion, and a design of overall flowers, birds, and butterflies in shades of orange and brown which today is referred to as the Sacred Bird and Butterfly design. A variant on this is the Cabbage Leaf and Butterfly design which contains large enamel green leaves and colorful butterflies. The first half of the nineteenth century also saw the manufacture of vast amounts of blue and white designed ware, currently referred to as Canton and/or Nanking. Recent information on these increasingly popular and valuable wares bring this volume to a close (pp. 157–170).

Although this historical sketch is necessarily limited, the various articles included in *Chinese Export Porcelain* expand in great detail various points barely touched on, and present a thousand-and-one additional bits of useful and interesting informration. The anthology is divided into five sections, and brief comments on the articles found in four of these sections will be found at the beginning of each. Homer Eaton Keyes' classic articles defining and explaining the different forms and designs of export porcelain, which follow, need no further introduction.

I   Lowestoft, What Is It?

I. *Concerning a Number of Misapprehensions*

By The Editor

Note. In offering a series of brief articles on so-called Lowestoft porcelain, I wish to assume no garments of superior wisdom; nor do I lay claim to the discovery of any hitherto hidden sources of information. For some years past, however, I have been interested in the curious stylistic vagaries which are manifest in the decoration of those porcelains which were manufactured in China for the sole purpose of finding a foreign market. These vagaries, though apparently rather shocking to many connoisseurs, I have found exceptionally fascinating.

It was my first intention to concern myself solely with examples of porcelain in which they occur. Having learned, however, that even such obviously Oriental products — to say nothing of others less readily identifiable — are still attributed by many persons to the English porcelain factory at Lowestoft, I found myself virtually compelled either to abandon a topic of no small interest or else to bring it into relation with the larger subject by treating it as part of a discussion of Chinese foreign-market porcelain in general. I have been encouraged to undertake the latter course primarily by my friend Edward A. Crowninshield, who has made long and careful study of the porcelain in question. To Mr. Crowninshield, therefore, I am indebted for much preliminary assistance and for the offer of more to come. Sir Algernon Tudor-Craig, whose work on Chinese Armorial Porcelain, though recently published, has already become a standard work of reference, has likewise promised to examine portions of the manuscript before its sins of omission and commission have assumed the fixity of printed type. The field is perilous, but, backed by two such doughty champions, who would not venture to invade it? H. E. K.

ALTHOUGH much has been said and written about Lowestoft porcelain, a great many persons still harbor extremely muddled notions of the subject. This, no doubt, is due to the rather usual and, perhaps natural, human assumption that the name of an article is inevitably indicative of its materials, its source, or both. Yet no assumption could be further from the truth.

This is the case with the so-called Lowestoft porcelain. Most of the ware which still passes under that name probably never even traveled through the

Fig. 1 — English Lowestoft Saucer (*eighteenth century*)

little English town of Lowestoft; much less was it manufactured there, or anywhere else in England. It is, in fact, a Chinese product — as Chinese as bird's-nest soup and pigtails. And this should ordinarily be apparent to anyone with half an eye, who will take the trouble to make effective use of that fraction of normal vision.

But if such Lowestoft porcelain is not English and not of Lowestoft, how did it ever acquire so inept a name? Nobody seems to be quite sure. Where did the Welsh

rabbit get its name? In matters of this kind, perhaps, one guess is as good as another; but, in the case of the porcelain under discussion, the following circumstances may afford a helpful clue to a satisfactory answer.

At the outset it should be borne in mind that the first importation of Chinese porcelains into Europe, on a really large commercial scale, appears to have been made by the Dutch East India Company, which, during the seventeenth century, dominated trade with the Orient just as

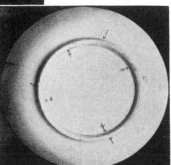

Authenticated by Bernard Rackham of the South Kensington Museum. Soft paste porcelain decorated with pseudo-Chinese designs in red, blue, and gold. The under side shows bluish flecks in the glaze, and a distinct bluish line is observable at the points indicated in the illustration by the arrows.

Brought to the editor by Samuel W. Woodhouse, Jr.

Fig. 2 — ENGLISH LOWESTOFT TEAPOT, CUP, AND SAUCER
The teapot carries a decoration similar to that shown in Figure 1. The cup and saucer are a fine quality of Lowestoft.
Owned by the Pennsylvania Museum.

the Portuguese had dominated it in the sixteenth century and as the British did in the eighteenth.* The little fishing town of Lowestoft, situated as it was on the east coast of England, offered a convenient port of entry for goods shipped from Holland. Hence the name of this town may easily have become associated with the goods for which it served as a primary distributing centre.†

Again, from 1756 to 1807, or thereabouts, a porcelain factory maintained a not too flourishing existence in Lowestoft. When that factory's fortunes began to wane, one, at least, of the former employees turned china merchant in place of china manufacturer. This individual was a man named Robert Allen. He is said to have opened a shop, where he set up a kiln and painted and fired articles which he procured from Rockingham and other places. No doubt he likewise took toll of the Chinese wares that passed through his native town; for, upon a Chinese teapot decorated with a very Oriental interpretation of the crucifixion, he inscribed his name *Allen, Lowestoft,* just as any Boston, or New York, or Chicago dealer in glass or china would be likely to have his name placed on ware imported from Europe or made to his order in New York, New Jersey, Ohio,

or any other of the great pottery states of America.*

Perhaps, in future centuries, students of ceramics will try to build a theory of the American pottery industry on the assumption that plates and other utensils — actually of French manufacture but bearing the imprint of Gilman and Collamore of New York — were made in this country. If so, they will be no more foolish in their acceptance of fallacious documentary evidence than were those who accepted Robert Allen's inscription on a Chinese teapot as proof that the piece was an English product; or than the collector who proudly displayed, as a bit of Canadian ware, a Staffordshire blue and white platter bearing the trade-mark of a firm of Montreal distributors.

Documentary evidence, it should be remembered, even that of inscribed names and dates, affords a very untrustworthy reliance in identifying objects of art. In the long run, it is style, material, texture, and certain indefinable, yet, to the trained eye, almost unmistakable, aspects of technique — the so-called *internal* evidence of the thing itself, rather than the external evidence of documents or inscriptions — that really count.

Be that as it may, the discovery of the Robert Allen teapot, and its acceptance by various writers as proof that specimens of similar ware had either been made, or, at the very least, decorated in the town of Lowestoft, helped to fix an already widely applied name for such ware in general. An error once disseminated is only with great difficulty corrected. That is why so many persons, today, still labor under the delusion that all so-called

*It was not long before the British trade in this field equalled and outdistanced that of the Dutch. The Portuguese brought in the first sea-borne porcelain from China about 1518. Toward the close of that century, however, Portuguese fleets had been swept from the map by the Dutch. The Dutch East India trade, in turn, declined severely soon after 1730. On this point see *China and Europe* by Adolf Reichwein, New York, 1925.

†Sir Algernon Tudor-Craig doubts that there is any foundation of fact for the repeated statements that Lowestoft was a port of entry for shipments from Holland. That an obscure and tiny fishing village should have been thus utilized seems to him out of the question. He is inclined to view the tradition of Lowestoft's association with Chinese porcelain as entirely mythical, and to pin sole responsibility for its origin upon the unfortunate Chaffers, who, in an effort to identify the source of specimens of various hard paste porcelains the texture and type of which were beyond his understanding, finally hit upon the idea of attributing all such pieces to Lowestoft.

*Even Frederick Litchfield in his *Pottery and Porcelain*, p. 229, though he recognizes the fabric of this teapot to be Oriental, falls into the error of accepting Allen as the decorator of the piece. The teapot in question, which is in the Schreiber Collection in the South Kensington Museum, is illustrated in ANTIQUES, Vol. I, p. 254. Concerning this particular piece, Sir Algernon Tudor-Craig writes that he believes the Allen signature to be "a forgery made in order to bolster up the ridiculous theory of Lowestoft ware in Chaffers."

Lowestoft china was made in the English seaport town whose name it bears.*

And even those who are able to distinguish — almost at a glance — between Oriental porcelain and English porcelain, and who know that most so-called Lowestoft is not from the town of Lowestoft at all, are at a loss for some distinguishing term by which they may, in casual speech, distinguish between the ware actually made in Lowestoft and that Oriental ware which was variously imported into England, the European countries, and the early American states. So they have come to speak of *English Lowestoft* when they refer to the local English product; and of *Chinese Lowestoft* when they refer to that of China.

Sometimes, again, these Chinese wares are designated under their accepted French term as *Compagnie des Indes* porcelain; sometimes — when the decoration justifies the term — as *Chinese armorial ware;* sometimes, by the rather awkward entitlement of *Chinese foreign-market* porcelain. One may take his choice of epithets; but since, in time, most names lose their basic significance and become no more than identifying symbols, it seems sensible, because easiest, to identify all those porcelains which were made in China expressly for export to Western markets, as Chinese Lowestoft.† In the discussion of the purely native types of Chinese porcelain, it is advisable to stick to the nomenclature devised by the connoisseurs of such ware.

To the student or collector already familiar with the subject, all this explanation must seem a very wordy and very elementary statement of well-known facts. Unfortunately, however, the facts, while well known to a few, are still obscure to the many. And it seems, more-

over, necessary to follow the obvious yet a little further in order to clear the approach to some discussion and analysis of Chinese Lowestoft as such. In short, a few sentences as to the true English ware actually made at Lowestoft are in order.

ENGLISH LOWESTOFT

For an extended discussion of English Lowestoft porcelain the reader is referred to an article by Frederick Litchfield, the well-known expert of porcelains, which appeared in Volume I, page 252, of ANTIQUES.* No attempt will here be made to cover the same ground. Suffice it to say that, as early as 1757, the town of Lowestoft boasted a pottery, where, in due course, a considerable quantity of porcelain was produced. Some of this, it is said, was shipped to Holland, while the rest was probably absorbed by the English market. That any of it was exported to America seems doubtful. Specimens of this Lowestoft ware have been identified in certain instances by inscriptions upon them — as in the case of mugs and inkwells bearing the device *A Trifle from Lowestoft*, dated teapots marked with the initials of their owners, and certain plates of powdered blue ground in one of whose white reserves appears a representation of the church at Lowestoft.

All of this porcelain is of the so-called soft paste variety. The texture of the earlier pieces is said to resemble that of the porcelain of Bow, while, in later years, there is a closer resemblance first to Worcester porcelain and later to the bone porcelain of Staffordshire. It is important, however, to observe that, in the case of English Lowestoft porcelain, the glaze has a decidedly bluish tinge and that this blue color is clearly observable wherever the glaze has settled thickly in crevices and within the bottom rim of pieces (*Fig. 1*).†

Fig. 3 — ENGLISH WORCESTER TEAPOT; ENGLISH LOWESTOFT CUP
The difficulty of distinguishing between Worcester and English Lowestoft is here exemplified. The Worcester teapot is superior to the cup in both glaze and potting. But the superiority is not readily discernable by the casual observer.
Owned by the Pennsylvania Museum.

---

*This error, it should be stated, is more common to American than to English collectors. The latter know only one kind of Lowestoft, their own native product. Some of them, to be sure, have been inclined to confuse certain Chinese pieces with the native product, and in so doing have muddled the whole matter of identifying the English ware. But the paradoxical American term *Chinese Lowestoft* is virtually unknown in England.

†Note particularly the words "made in China expressly for export to Western markets." They are all-important; for it is only to the Chinese porcelains whose form and decoration display obvious and clearly marked departures from Oriental traditions that the term Lowestoft is applicable. Such porcelains were produced at the order of European trading companies, and the character of their design was dictated by the commercial requirement of pleasing a European, rather than an Asiatic taste.

*The two books best calculated to convey a clear idea of Lowestoft china are Sir W. R. Spellman's *Lowestoft China*, London, 1907, and Frederick Arthur Crisp's *Catalogue of Lowestoft China*, London 1907. The latter is illustrated with excellent color plates.

†The Lowestoft pottery produced no earthenware. An easy way of determining whether a piece of tableware is of earthenware or porcelain is to hold it against strong light. Only if translucent may the piece be classified as porcelain. This test will dispose of the claims of many pieces of early blue and white

Fig. 4 — ENGLISH LIVERPOOL CUP AND SAUCER
Long considered to be English Lowestoft until identified as Liverpool porcelain by P. Entwistle, F. R. A. I., of the Liverpool Museums.
Photograph by courtesy of Samuel W. Woodhouse, Jr.

The decoration is diverse in character. In many instances it is applied in an underglaze blue, and gives evidence of emulation of Chinese motives. But Frederick Litchfield in his *Pottery and Porcelain*, plate 42, opposite page 224, pictures three teapots in enamel colors, one of which shows a strongly Oriental type of decoration, another an apparent imitation of the magenta colored Meissen ware of Germany, and yet another, large medallions, somewhat after the Oriental manner, within which bloom plump English roses and other flowers.

Various writers, borrowing optimistically one from another, have perpetuated the fable that a scattered rose pattern relieved by festoons of flowers and bordered with fine dotted lines is the one most characteristic of English Lowestoft decoration. Nothing could be further from the truth. Such patterns are far more likely to occur on New Hall porcelain — a ware distinguishable by the milky whiteness of its glaze and the clear, almost metallic, color of its enamel decoration — than on true English Lowestoft.*

As for the marks on English Lowestoft, a number are pictured in Mr. Litchfield's article in ANTIQUES, already referred to. They are of a rather nondescript aspect. Many of them are obvious imitations of the marks of other factories; others are equally obvious imitations of

Chinese characters. Apparently the factory was never sufficiently proud of its product to give it a distinctive and unmistakable label.

So much by way of preliminaries. We have seen that there was, in the English fishing village of Lowestoft, a porcelain factory which was in operation for something over half a century. We have seen that this village may easily have been a port of entry for Chinese porcelain imported from the Orient *via* Holland. And we have seen, further, that, partly for this reason, many persons have confused the imported Chinese wares with the locally made wares and have identified both types as Lowestoft.

Having thus hurriedly cleared the ground, we may very well forget that any such ware as English Lowestoft ever existed. Examples of this English Lowestoft are very rarely encountered outside of a few museums. And as to their correct attribution—whether to Lowestoft, to Worcester, to Bow, or to some other establishment — even museum directors are often at a loss.* Occasionally a few pieces of English Lowestoft come into the hands of dealers; but, in such instances, they are quickly snapped up by specializing collectors.

The possibility of finding enough of such ware for actual table use today is almost as remote as that of finding the tableware of the Lotus eaters.

Chinese Lowestoft, on the other hand, was imported into all European countries, into England, and even into the United States, in vast quantities. It appeared in the form of huge dinner services, tea sets, sets of plates, cups and saucers, presentation bowls, tankards, and innumerable other individual items. Of these importations sufficient quantities remain intact, even today, to supply considerable dinner services for those who can

*See ANTIQUES, Vol. XIII, p. 33.

Fig. 5 — ENGLISH NEW HALL TEAPOT
Even in the photograph, the shining and impeccable whiteness of this piece — characteristic of New Hall porcelain — is apparent. The sprigs of roses, the fine dotted line, and the diamond pattern on a rosy field are the features which the novice loves to pounce upon as evidences of true English Lowestoft. As a matter of fact, they occur far more frequently on New Hall and Bristol china than on that of Lowestoft.
Owned by Mrs. L. B. Rantoul.

Staffordshire earthenware to affiliation with the wares of Lowestoft. Exceptionally thick and heavy pieces of true porcelain may fail to transmit even a strong light; but in the case of cups, saucers, small plates and bowls, the test is adequate.

*Spellman observes, concerning one of his illustrations, that it shows "one of the few soft paste pieces bearing the Lowestoft rose." This rose pattern appears on Bristol as well as on New Hall china.

pay the price; while plates in half dozens, individual platters, teapots, bowls, small sets of cups and saucers, and various single pieces, in good condition, are procurable at sums varying according to the rarity and popularity of their patterns. While, therefore, we are forgetting that there was such a porcelain as English Lowestoft, let us be sure to remember that, even as early as the eighteenth century, China was so far commercialized as to manufacture porcelain to please the peculiarities of European and American taste; and that, by virtue of custom if not of strict exactitude, this is the ware most commonly known in America as Lowestoft.

It is this Chinese ware, its types, and its mode of decoration that will be the subject of subsequent discussions.

NOTE

In the attribution of Chinese porcelains to the Lowestoft factory Richard Chaffers appears to have been the chief offender. In his *Marks and Monograms on Pottery and Porcelain* (edition of 1876) he consumes many pages in an effort to prove, both by citations of hearsay evidence and by considerations of the character of Chinese pottery forms and pastes, that Lowestoft manufactured a hard paste porcelain of almost precisely the type produced in China. He claims, however, to be able to discover differences between the texture of the Chinese ware and his so-called hard paste Lowestoft. It would have been impossible, he further observes, for Chinese porcelain to be profitably imported into England in the face of the prohibitive English duties then in force.

Of the insignificant value of hearsay evidence little need be said. On the basis of such evidence, bits of Staffordshire earthenware have been credited to the Bennington factories in Vermont. Mr. Chaffers' assumption that he could differentiate between a mythical hard paste produced at Lowestoft and Chinese hard paste offers only one more example of the human genius for self-delusion. The best authorities now agree that *no* hard paste porcelain was made at Lowestoft. The texture of Chinese European-market porcelain, however, varies considerably in different examples. This fact, no doubt, contributed to Mr. Chaffer's confusion.

It is frequently stated that Chinese porcelain blanks were imported into Continental countries — notably Holland — and into England, where they received their decoration at the hands of local artists. J. G. A. N. de Vries in his book *Porselein*, page 80, is authority for the statement concerning this practice in Holland. In his introduction to Sir Algernon Tudor-Craig's notable work *Armorial Porcelain of the Eighteenth Century*, Sir Henry Farnham Burke presents an opposite view, to the effect that some English porcelain blanks were sent to China to receive their decoration.

Such statements are likely to cause considerable misapprehension. It is yet to be shown conclusively that sets of household porcelain were imported in blank from China for express purpose of receiving decoration at the hands of European artists. Individual pieces of Chinese ware, and perhaps small sets, either blank or bearing sparse patterns in one or more colors, were, however, not infrequently touched up by European china painters. Special reasons may likewise have prompted the owners of large Chinese sets occasionally to order decorative amplifications of already existing patterns. Sir Algernon Tudor-Craig cites, in this connection, a plate, once in his possession, bearing the arms of Lord Gamber, which, though "certainly of Chinese manufacture (c. 1775), including the rose diaper border, had the arms added in England after 1810, as they bore the coronet and supporters of Lord Gamber, who was not created a peer until that date." The plate in question is believed to have been part of a large service.

The practice of enhancing the value of simple Oriental pieces with many-colored additions over the glaze is unbeautifully characterized as "clobbering." But, as Hannover, in his *Pottery and Porcelain* (Vol. II, p. 168), observes, "these falsifications, if we may call them so, of early times hardly play any noteworthy part in the European antique market of today." Clobbering, however, is by no means a lost art. The eagerness with which collectors seize upon early Chinese export wares showing certain types of decoration offers a temptation which present-day artists more skilled of hand than scrupulous of heart are not always able to resist.

Fig. 6 — ENGLISH NEW HALL CUP, SAUCER, AND TEA PLATE
These pieces are part of a set to which belongs the teapot illustrated in Figure 5. The whiteness of the ware and the enamel-like quality of the decoration are characteristic, and should obviate confusion with true English Lowestoft.
Owned by Mrs. L. B. Rantoul.

II. *Several Whys and Wherefores*

By HOMER EATON KEYES*

IN a previous discussion, an attempt was made to relieve some current confusion as to the significance of the term Lowestoft. It was pointed out that, during the latter part of the eighteenth century, at the tiny English fishing village of Lowestoft, there was operating a porcelain factory, only an insignificant quantity of whose product survives today; yet that, by some curious trick of circumstance, the name of this establishment has, for years, been quite indiscriminately applied to a great variety of porcelains which were manufactured in China especially for the English, Continental, and American markets.

Question now arises as to how the Chinese came to make these export porcelains, and how a people apparently so unenterprising in many commercial matters succeeded in flooding Europe with its products.

We need not seek far to find answer. In the industrial arts, and in certain specialized lines of agricul-

Fig. 1 (above and below) — TURKISH-MARKET PORCELAIN (*eighteenth century*)
Made in China and decorated with Arabic symbols to please the Turkish trade.
Owned by Miss Caroline Carter

ture, the Chinese were, from very early times, extraordinarily proficient. Emerson may be unduly optimistic in asserting that high achievement, even in the making of mousetraps, will suffice to establish a pathway of eagerness to one's door; yet he was fundamentally correct. History is silent as to the mousetraps of China, but it is filled with accounts of other products of this mysterious realm: silks, lacquers, bronzes, cunning carvings in ivory, and, above all, porcelain — to say nothing of those staple yields of the soil, rice and tea.* These things were luxuries which appealed to the folk of all foreign lands. China had but to offer such merchandise, and traders from afar were quite ready to call for it and to carry it promptly home.

Land routes connecting China with India, Persia, Siam, and eastern Europe

*Continued from the March number of ANTIQUES. Copyright, 1928, by Homer Eaton Keyes. All rights reserved.

*The Chinese, it will be recalled, were making fine and beautifully decorated porcelains at a time when Europeans in general had not yet progressed beyond a rather coarse type of earthenware for household use. And, as Sir Algernon Tudor-Craig observes, "pottery figures were made in China when Britons were painting in woad."

Fig. 2 — DUTCH-MARKET PORCELAIN (*c. 1690*)
Chinese blue and white porcelain representing the destruction of a house during a revolt in Rotterdam.
Owned by the Ryks Museum, Amsterdam

were opened to commerce no one knows how long ago. And the astute Chinese were, at all times, prepared to manufacture wares calculated to appeal to the national taste of any and all customers. Special types of porcelain were turned out for Indian, Persian, and Siamese markets; and, to beguile the Turkish fancy, cups, saucers, and plates were covered with lengthy inscriptions in Arabic characters, or in what would pass for them (*Fig. 1*).*

China and its wonders, however, first became familiar to Europeans in general through the writings of that adventurous Venetian Marco Polo, who, about the year 1280, visited the court of the Great Khan himself, and thereafter remained with that potentate as friend and confidential adviser for a period of some seventeen years. Marco Polo traveled widely through the Khan's dominions, and, upon returning to Italy, wrote copiously of his observations and experiences. Even today the *Travels of Marco Polo* is considered a narrative of absorbing interest. More than two hundred years later (1515), during the great seafaring days which followed close upon Columbus' discovery of America, the Portuguese navigator Vasco da Gama found his way to the Chinese coast *via* the Cape of Good Hope. By 1542 the Portuguese were in command of the Asia-European coastal trade from the Persian Gulf to Japan.

This domination was, however, soon shattered by the enterprising Dutch, who literally drove the Portuguese from the seven seas, capturing, it is said, during the first half of the seventeenth century, no less than three hun-

dred Portuguese vessels.* Meanwhile the English, in their turn, were slowly gaining on the Dutch, and, by the close of the first quarter of the eighteenth century, had succeeded in surpassing their Continental neighbors in the East Indian trade.

The Portuguese were, doubtless, pioneers in the importation of considerable quantities of Chinese porcelains into Europe. But the Dutch appear to have been the first to commercialize these wares on a large scale and to insist upon dictating the shapes of different pieces and the nature of their decoration. Vast shipments of Chinese tableware were carried to Europe by the Dutch, who were able to offer this merchandise at a price which shortly made it an article not merely of luxury, but of daily necessity even in ordinary households. "Blue porcelain from the Orient was cheaper than any other manufactured, certainly cheaper than the common English earthenware."†

More expensive and more calculated to appeal to the taste of wealthy customers were those Chinese porcelains whose decoration, applied over the glaze, sparkled with a variety of brilliant colors. De Vries tells us, in considerable detail, of how, in various Holland cities large and small, the merchants of chinaware were equipped either with stocks of Chinese porcelains or with samples from which the customer might select a design to be carried out on tea or dinner sets made to his special order. Indeed, the great majority of the orders for porcelain which went forward from Holland to China stipulated the nature of the decoration to be applied.

They even stipulated the forms of various pieces. The Chinese tea drinkers used cups without handles. Europe

*Reichwein, *op. cit.*
†de Vries, *Porselein.*

Fig. 3 — GERMAN-MARKET ARMORIAL PORCELAIN (*1708-1720*)
Made and decorated in China for the House of Wittelsbach.
Owned by the Bavarian National Museum, Munich

*Hannover, *Pottery and Porcelain*, Vol. II, pp. 19 and 162. Reichewein, *China in Europe.*

19

Fig. 4 — EUROPEAN-MARKET ARMORIAL PORCELAIN (*1763*)
Chinese porcelain decorated in China probably for a wedding gift. The small size of the items of the set tends to intensify the scale of the decorations upon them.
Collection of Edward Crowninshield

preferred its drinking vessels to be equipped with ears. Thereupon the ears were added.* Europe liked landscapes, figure subjects, baskets of flowers, sprinklings of bright blossoms far better than "outlandish dragons" on its table services. The landscapes and the flowers were provided, and the dragons disappeared. Europe craved forms already familiar in domestic earthenware. China obediently supplied the demand. Europe, furthermore, was pleased with tableware which bore portrayals of local scenery, repetitions of popular paintings and engravings, pictures illustrating wellknown tales and legends — whether ancient or modern — religious pictures, depictions memorializing places, persons, and events, or scenes of that shipping which was bringing such vast wealth to the merchants of Holland

and of England alike. And, when members of the aristocracy discovered that, for quite reasonable sums, they could secure from China great dinner services emblazoned throughout with family crests and coats of arms, they ordered such equipment by the shipload.

And, to repeat: whatsoever Europe ordered, the patient and versatile Chinese did their best to produce.

Fig. 5 — EUROPEAN-MARKET PORCELAIN (*eighteenth century*)
Chinese bowl picturing the judgment of Paris. Juno, Venus, and Minerva, in the order named, are on display in a beauty contest in which the prize is a golden apple. Based, doubtless, on a print from a painting by Rubens, the depiction shows a Chinese attempt to emulate the somewhat exuberant Flemish ideal of female pulchritude. *Owned by Mrs. W. Murray Crane.*

The porcelain known today as Chinese Lowestoft is that whose form and design were thus particularly specified by European and, later, by American buyers, and whose manufacture took place in China in accordance with these specifications.

The earliest example of this Europeanized Chinese ware, of which I find notice, is a blue and white plate, now in the Ryks Museum at Amsterdam. This piece of porcelain,

*Few Chinese tea cups were equipped with handles before 1740, and the majority continued without handles through the eighteenth century. When coffee cups were supplied to special order, they were made for use with the outfit of saucers intended for the tea cups. Thus, twelve coffee cups and twelve tea cups would have but twelve saucers among them.

though sometimes described as picturing a fire in Amsterdam, more probably represents the destruction of the dwelling of Jacob van Zuglen, October 5, 1690, during a revolt in Rotterdam. Though bearing a false date mark of 1621–27, it must be virtually contemporary with the event which it celebrates (*Fig. 2*).*

Among surviving specimens of armorial dinner sets produced in the Orient at European behest, the plate of Figure 3 is likewise to be accepted as early. The illustration is from an original in the Bavarian National Museum at Munich. The combined arms, which completely cover the field and even trespass on the rim of this plate, are those of Count Theodor Eustach von Sulzbach and his wife Maria Eleanore von Hessen-Rheinfels-Rothenburg. The noble pair were married in 1692; but the Count did not come into enjoyment of his full authority and entitlement until 1708. The Countess died in 1720. It is between 1708 and 1720, therefore, that the armorial service of which this specimen was once a part must have been ordered — doubtless through agents of the Dutch East India Company.†

A mighty service it was. General Director Halm of the National Museum writes that, after more than two centuries of vicissitude, some forty soup plates, three plates similar to the one illustrated, and perhaps ten small plates remain as gorgeous reminders of a past magnificence. Their borders and cartouches are executed in ruddy gold, the arms themselves in rose, purple, green, blue, and black.

Sir Algernon Tudor-Craig in his *Chinese Armorial Porcelain* (p. 11) illustrates a Sino-English plate of similar period (*c. 1710*) displaying the arms of Somers. Here again the armorial design occupies the entire field of the piece.

Such an arrangement seems to be characteristic of

Fig. 6 — EUROPEAN-MARKET ARMORIAL PORCELAIN (*eighteenth century*)
Chinese porcelain decorated in China. The border is quite in Chinese style. The centre shows Mercury and Neptune, classical divinities respectively of commerce and of the seas, supporting the cypher of the owner, who was evidently interested in sea-borne trade.
Collection of Edward Crowninshield

the earlier armorial porcelain. This wealth of colored decoration inevitably tended to obscure rather than to enhance the character of the ware which it so generously enveloped. Later in the eighteenth century — certainly after 1750 — armorial cartouches were usually reduced in size, and borders were simplified to suit the more austere taste inculcated by the classical revival. This observation, however, is, I surmise, rather more applicable to porcelain made for the English market than to that manufactured for the delectation of the Dutch, who appear to have cherished a fondness for lush and rather heavy decorative enamel overlays upon their tableware.

It is with this circumstance in mind that I suspect the tea set pictured in Figure 4 of having been made for a Continental rather than an English bridal couple. Each piece of this set bears the date *1763* and the cypher of the contracting parties, above which two cherubic visitants, modishly clad in Chinese raiment, support a coronet.* The borders give evidence of a painstaking effort to imitate the deft Rococo scrolls and diaper patterns of the French porcelain of Sèvres; but the slow-handed conscientiousness of their delineation has robbed them of that spontaneous grace and sprightliness which is the very essence of Rococo.

The Oriental china painter's touch is incomparably delicate and precise in tracing forms familiar to native decorative traditions. Birds, flower sprays, gnarled tree

---

*See de Vries *op. cit*, p. 14, and Münsterberg, *Chinesische Kunstgeschichte*, Vol. II.

†Sir Algernon Tudor-Craig calls attention to a Nankin blue jardinière, of 1693, showing the arms of Johnson impaling Lovelace, which he believes to be the earliest armorial piece manufactured in China.

*Every piece of Chinese ware bearing a flying figure of any kind is liable to be hailed in America as connected in some way with the Order of the Cincinnati. In most instances such attributions of special meaning are absurd. The design of the Cincinnati china is very specific in its totality. The flying figure which it displays is, however, used, in one form or another, on many Chinese pieces which have no more relation to the Order of the Cincinnati than to the Ku Klux Klan. As will later be noted, a similar confusion of mind exists concerning Chinese porcelains whose decoration includes the representation of an anchor. Specimens thus decorated are, by no means, invariably to be associated with the State of Rhode Island.

Fig. 7 — Europen-Market
Porcelain (*late eighteenth or
early nineteenth century*)
Chinese bowl picturing the port of
Canton with the warehouses of
foreign trading companies and the
national flags of foreign conces-
sionaires. The accompanying Chinese painting, though much later in
date than the bowl, gives a clue to
the latter's pictorial intention.

branches, clouds, sinuous dragons, fishes, medallion outlines, and geometric repeats it renders with unerring and
exquisite lightness. It frequently becomes hesitant,
uncertain, and sometimes a trifle heavy when constrained
by the necessity for duplicating foreign patterns, whose
elements had even less meaning for the Oriental wielder
of the brush than is conveyed to an American by the
hieroglyphics of a Chinese laundry check. We have
some evidence of this in the happily composed, freely
executed, and typically Chinese floral border shown in
Figure 6; whereas the classic figures of Mercury and
Neptune, who support the cypher in the field of the
plate, quite obviously occasioned the artist an extremity
of woe.

It is, however, just such stylistic discrepancies that
appeal to the lover of these European-market Chinese
wares. They are, indeed, the earmarks of genuineness,
testimonials to the authenticity of many fragile souvenirs of spacious days when the great merchant fleets of
England and of Holland fared forth, with sails full blown,
on two and three-year voyages into the magical East,
to return at length deep-freighted with shining splendors
from perfumed littorals of romance.

* * *

In this chapter, even while overstepping the limits of
space allotted to me, I have yet omitted much material
that should have been included. In the main, however, I
have perhaps succeeded in indicating something of the
general character of the Chinese porcelains which were
produced for the European market. I hope, too, that I
have made clear the fact that the designs for such porcelains were, in the main, dictated from Europe by European factors, though the fabric of the ware itself is Chinese,
the technical methods employed in its decoration Chinese, and many of the decorative elements Chinese; so that
the resultant product becomes a kind of Sino-European
hybrid — a hybrid, however, in whose obvious ancestral
diversity resides a potent element of charm, a strangely
exotic appeal to the imagination.

At another time I shall have more to say concerning
where and how this porcelain was produced and concerning its various adornments.

III. Centres of Manufacture, and a Classification

By HOMER EATON KEYES*

IN the two previous chapters of this series we have tried to give a clear general outline of the nature of so-called Chinese Lowestoft porcelain; to explain how this ware came by its unfortunate and misleading name; and to differentiate between this distinctively Chinese product — which, during the eighteenth century was shipped in great quantities to all parts of the civilized world — and the true English Lowestoft ware which, during a period of fifty years or so, was manufactured in a relatively small way in an unimportant East Anglian town.

It may now be well to say a word concerning the centres where this Chinese porcelain was produced, and the ports through which it was forwarded to overseas markets. After that, some attempt at a classification of the special designs made for European consumption will be in order. The topic of American-market designs will later occupy a chapter or two of its own.

All authorities appear to be in agreement as to the place where Chinese Europeanized porcelain for the foreign trade was produced. This was the city of Ching-tê Chên, in the Province of Kiang-si. The reason for the development here of the porcelain industry is found in the very simple circumstance that the district abounded in china clay, one of the two chief ingredients of porcelain. The other ingredient, *petuntse*, or china stone, came to the factories by boat from Ch'i-mên, some seventy miles distant.† Ching-tê Chên, furthermore, though an inland city, was situated on the Ch'ang River and was thus connected by water routes not only with Peking but with the chief ports of the Empire.‡

In its palmy days, Ching-tê Chên was, we learn, quite the traditional hive of industry. Every one of its inhabitants, from infant to octogenarian, found employment in the porcelain factories. John Robinson, quoting from contemporary writings,

Fig. 1 — SAMPLE PLATE (c. 1790)
Four different patterns, each numbered, are shown on the one plate. From such sample plates, in the hands of his local crockery merchant, the customer could select whatever design pleased his fancy, with reasonable certainty that, six months or a year later, the goods would be delivered as ordered. This illustration offers ample evidence that the so-called "American Lowestoft" pattern was a well-recognized stock design.
From the Victoria and Albert Museum, London

informs us that, two hundred years ago, the town had a population of over a million, and that the atmosphere of the place was murky with the smoke of three thousand kilns.*

Though the history of Ching-tê Chên as a centre of the porcelain industry goes back to early times, the town's most flourishing period extends from the reëstablishment of the factories by the Emperor K'ang Hsi — about the year 1680 — to the close of the eighteenth century, when a decline in porcelain manufacturing set in. In 1837, when this decline was well under way, the population of the place had been reduced by fifty per cent, while the number of kilns had fallen to five hundred. In 1853, during the T'ai P'ing rebellion, the city and all its great *fabriks* were laid in ruins.

Certain of the factories of Ching-tê Chên were, it appears, an imperial property and were operated under management designated by no less a person than the Emperor of China, himself. Here were produced the finest of wares, intended primarily, if not exclusively, for court use. Private establishments turned out more commercial articles for the outside markets of Asia, Europe, and, eventually, of America.

There were, to be sure, other porcelain centres than Ching-tê Chên. The town of Tê-hua in the Province of Fukien was noted for its marvelous white porcelain, the famous *blanc de Chine*, whose delightful texture and unsullied purity of tone delighted seventeenth- and eighteenth-century Europe. Save, however, for a few quite extraordinary figures, the products of Tê-hua have little or no place in our present discussion.† At Ho-nan and in communities to the west of Canton, porcelain factories were in operation; and, while these establishments appear not to have essayed manufacture of the finest grades, it is far from impossible, as Robinson shrewdly observes, that they contributed to the supply of coarser export wares.‡

Another point upon which most writers agree is that, while the potteries of Ching-tê Chên commanded the services of highly skilled painters, the bulk of the European-market porcelain made in China received its decoration at the chief Chinese port

*Continued from the May number of ANTIQUES. Copyright, 1928, by Homer Eaton Keyes. All rights reserved.

†For a full discussion of this, see Chapter I of R. L. Hobson's *The Later Ceramic Wares of China*, 1925.

‡H. B. Morse, author of *Chronicles of the East India Company Trading to China*, states that porcelain made in Ching-tê Chên was transported by the Meiling Pass to Canton for shipment to Europe. The exact route appears to have been down the Peh River, across Poyang Lake, up the Kan Kiang River, to the approach to the Meiling Pass. Then, after a bit of land transportation, shipments again took to the water, by way of the North River, to Canton.

*Blue and White "India-China," published in *Old-Time New England*, January, 1924.

†See ANTIQUES, Vol. XIV, pp. 213 et seq.

‡Robinson *op. cit.*, p. 110. See also the map accompanying A. L. Hetherington's *Pottery and Porcelain Factories of China*.

Fig. 2 (Left)—Dutch-Market Armorial Dish (*c. 1730*)
A large specimen bearing the arms of the Holland city of Groeningen.
From the Ryksmuseum, Amsterdam

Fig. 3 (Right) — English-Market Armorial Plate (*c. 1750*)
Bearing the arms of Gifford. An exceptionally well-decorated piece, on which the painting enhances the character of the porcelain without concealing it.
From the collection of Sir Algernon Tudor-Craig

of shipment — Canton.* There would be excellent reasons for such an arrangement. The Oriental warehouses of the European trading companies were, for the most part, during the eighteenth century, concentrated at Canton. In the same city were stationed the various company representatives. It must have been more convenient for all parties concerned to have fulfillment of the often exacting and easily misunderstood foreign requirements supervised as directly as possible by a responsible foreign agent. Even so, errors were bound to occur; and the Chinese artists' misinterpretations or too literal renderings of patterns supplied by European designers occasionally caused serious complications.†

In the case of standard patterns, of which there were many, the danger of mistakes by the artists, and of dissatisfaction on the part of customers, was minimized by the expedient of supplying the china merchants of England and the Continent with

sample plates, upon each of which several different pattern slices were segmentally arranged and carefully identified by number. A few of these plates are to be found in public collections in England and on the Continent. That illustrated (*Fig. 1*) is reproduced by permission of the authorities of the Victoria and Albert Museum.*

Very little would be gained by an attempt to treat more exhaustively the topic of the sources of the European-market porcelain of China, or the methods of its transportation to the Occidental market. Interest really centres in the ware itself and in the designs with which it was decorated.

To offer a minutely defined classification of these designs might be possible, but it would be scarcely profitable. Six categories will suffice, though any one of them might easily be many times subdivided. We shall identify these categories as those of Armorial designs, Mythological designs, Religious designs, Genre designs, Shipping designs, and Floral designs. Each of these terms we shall apply very broadly; each we shall discuss briefly, leaving to the accompanying illustrations the chief task of elucidation.

ARMORIAL DESIGNS

Armorial designs seem to mark almost the first attempts of the Chinese so to Europeanize their porcelain as to extend its

---

*Burton, in his *General History of Porcelain*, speaks of the metal enamelers of Canton as turning their talents to the decoration of export porcelain, and of "the Canton style" as specific and recognizable. Some decoration of porcelain, it is thought, may have been undertaken at the ports of Amoy and Shanghai.

†A typical, and often cited, case is that of an armorial design upon which the European artist, instead of supplying a detailed color study, had indicated the proper heraldic colors by writing their names in the spaces designated. Thereupon, the faithful Chinese copyist completed his decoration in the outline form submitted, including the directions, "red here," "blue here," and so on, with which the designer had expressed his wishes. Sir Algernon Tudor-Craig has some plates of this kind.

*The purchaser of specially made china had to exercise a good deal of patience, since an interval of from six months to a year between order and delivery was the normal expectation.

Fig. 4 (Left)—Dutch-Market Armorial Plate (*c. 1750*)
This piece will probably qualify as pseudo-armorial, since no actual arms are indicated, a cypher taking their place. A plate with different border, but showing almost precisely the same elaboration of flags and naval insignia surrounding the central cartouche, is illustrated in de Vries' *Porselein*. In the latter instance, however, the cartouche is occupied by the arms of the Ver-Huel family.
From the collection of Miss Mabel Choate

Fig. 5 (Right) — English-Market Plate (*1791*)

Fig. 6 — DUTCH-MARKET PLATE (c. 1750)   Fig. 7 — EUROPEAN-MARKET PLATE (c. 1750)
Both plates depict *The Judgment of Paris*. That of Figure 6, in brilliant color, shows the interpretation of the subject most frequently employed on Chinese ware. The borders surrounding this theme show considerable variation. Here we have medallions with shipping scenes. The representation of Paris and the rival goddesses shown in Figure 7 is rarely encountered. It offers an example of the painted-in-ink technique, with touches of color on the flesh. The border, likewise, in penciled lines and gold, gives evidence of an attempt to emulate French designs of the period.
From the collection of Edward A. Crowninshield

foreign utilization. Sir Algernon Tudor-Craig, in his recent article in ANTIQUES, wherein he discusses the borders in Chinese armorial porcelain, cites a blue and white jardinière of the year 1693–5, bearing the arms of Johnston impaling Lovelace. This he believes to be the earliest known example of its type.* But thereafter such designs, not only in the simple early blue and white, but in colors enhanced with gold, were multiplied in great profusion. The dinner service made for the noble Bavarian house of Wittelsbach, a specimen of which was pictured in ANTIQUES for May, 1928,† offers an early example of this more elaborate form of decoration.

Armorial porcelain was made, apparently, for customers in every European state; and quantities of it survive today in still colossal

Fig. 8 — EUROPEAN-MARKET CUP AND SAUCER (c. 1750)
Orpheus. Clearly illustrating the painted-in-ink style of decoration based on engravings. Here, as frequently occurs, the flesh is lightly tinted. The flowing scarf of Orpheus is a fine, deep red; the tree is green; border, black, edged with gold.
From the collection of Edward A. Crowninshield

dinner services and in dainty sets for afternoon tea. To the expert in heraldry the date of a piece of such porcelain is usually revealed by the character of its heraldic devices. The average American collector who is ignorant of such abstruse sign language will, however, be able to fix satisfactorily approximate dates for his finds by studying the different kinds of borders illustrated by Sir Algernon Tudor-Craig in his article already referred to; and by bearing in mind that, on plates made previous to 1750 or 1760, the coat of arms often occupies a relatively large part of the field, whereas, after this latter date, such decoration undergoes a material shrinkage in its proportions, so that a liberal expanse of the porcelain field is left exposed.

With this consideration in view, we should have no hesitation in assigning the large plate bearing the arms of the Dutch City of Groeningen (*Fig. 2*), to the first half of the eighteenth century, even without the evidence of the border, which bespeaks a date not far from 1730. An English-market plate, of the year 1750, bearing the arms of Gifford (*Fig. 3*), displays far more restraint in its decorative handling,

*See ANTIQUES, Vol. XIV, p. 124. An important exception is the underglaze blue plate bearing a representation of the Rotterdam Riot, which is cited in ANTIQUES, Vol. XIII, p. 385. Examples of this plate occur in the Ryksmuseum, Amsterdam; the Victoria and Albert Museum, London; and the Dresden Museum. The author of these notes has recently acquired a remarkable cup and saucer showing the same design.

†See ANTIQUES, Vol. XIII, p. 385.

a circumstance due in part to its later period, in part to the apparent fact that the English taste leaned less to florid and overloaded tableware than did that of the Dutch. A fine Dutch pseudo-armorial plate is, however, shown in Figure 4.

The ultimate refinement of armorial design, reached during the last decade of the eighteenth century, is well illustrated in the plate of Figure 5, showing the arms of Chadwick. On the back of each piece of the set to which this plate belongs, are inscribed the words, *23 March 1791*. Later on we shall encounter this type of decoration on Chinese porcelain made for the American trade, which became active after the Revolutionary War.

Little more need here be said of Chinese armorial porcelain. Those who wish to pursue the subject in greater detail should make acquaintance with Sir Algernon Tudor-Craig's book, *Armorial Porcelain of the Eighteenth Century*.* But it may be added that, in general, the Chinese makers appear to have lavished more intelligent and painstaking effort on their armorial services than upon any other of their foreign-market porcelains. Many surviving examples of the type display really exquisite workmanship, combined with an impeccable balance of design. Such examples occur with sufficient frequency to enable almost any persevering collector to acquire a series illustrative of the style of each successive decade of the eighteenth century. Tea sets and complete dinner services, of excellent quality, are likewise obtainable, though they are rapidly becoming scarce.

Mythological Designs

The gods, goddesses, and heroes who played so important a rôle in European art of the seventeenth century were infinitely multiplied by the diligence of contemporary engravers, who thus supplied the Chinese decorators with an endless variety of themes for the embellishment of export porcelains. In many instances the Oriental artists imitated not only the form, but the technique of the engravings which served them as models,

*Century House, London, 1925.

Fig. 9 — EUROPEAN-MARKET PLATE (*c. 1750*)
Shepherd and Sleeping Nymphs. The small size and relatively dainty treatment of the penciled pictorial design, as well as the character of the border, distinguish this plate and that of Figure 7 from the majority of their type.

Fig. 10 — DUTCH-MARKET PLATE (*c. 1750*)
Representing the goddess *Cybele*. Painted-in-ink technique within an orange-red circle; gold spearhead border. One of a set of eight.
From the author's collection

copying, with conscientiously delicate and accurate brush strokes, every line and cross-hatching which the graver's burin had cut in the original sheet of copper. Not infrequently they touched with a faint bloom of tint the faces and nude bodies of the characters portrayed. Occasionally, too, they abandoned the black-and-white technique and wrought their pictures in full enamel color, with attempts at light and shade effects in the European style.

The mythological subjects depicted are innumerable. Among these, *The Judgment of Paris*, which frequently occurs — usually in color — on teapots, bowls, and plates, was a favorite. All the Chinese versions of this theme appear to be based on the same engraving after Rubens; but they vary greatly in their quality of craftsmanship. The three nude goddesses who compete for the golden apple never failed to give the artist considerable trouble; but, whereas some of the delineations of those Olympian ladies and the shepherd connoisseur are passable, others are almost ludicrously grotesque. One example of this subject, decorating a bowl, was reproduced as Figure 5, on page 386 of ANTIQUES for May.* Two other versions are shown here in Figures 6 and 7, each with a different border.

A cup and saucer, quite unusual in its carefully wrought border of butterflies, represents Orpheus lustily plucking harmony from his lyre (*Fig. 8*). Here, again, decorative skill is inadequate to the task of depicting the nude human form. Orpheus is as boneless as an oyster and not dissimilar to that unambitious bivalve in bodily conformation. But his beauty is redeemed by the delicacy of the brush strokes with which he is delineated, and by the deft touches of color which are applied lightly to his body and, with heavier richness, to his flowing scarf and to the tree which careens on the hilltop beside him. Virtually the same border, by the way, impartially surrounds a *Baptism of Christ* which adorns a plate in the Victoria and Albert Museum.

Rather more skillfully

*See ANTIQUES, Vol. XIII, p. 386.

handled is the *Shepherd and Sleeping Nymphs* of Figure 9, with its French type of border quite similar to that shown in Figure 7. Again, the plate of Figure 10, representing Cybele in her car drawn by jungle beasts, possesses a good deal of charm. In this piece, the border around the penciled central design is a rich orange-red enhanced with gold tracing. The rim shows the familiar spearhead design, in gold outlined with brown. Apparently the Chinese painter of Cybele labored under the impression that he was portraying a scene of Christian rather than pagan significance, for he has endowed the mythological goddess with a Madonnalike aspect, and has encircled her head with a nimbus.*

A full-colored mythological design, whose subject appears to be a swift conference between Jupiter and Vulcan, is shown in Figure 11. Here the picture spills over on the rim of the plate and is enclosed in a narrow but elaborate edging of gold.

The list might be almost indefinitely extended. The examples illustrated and described will, however, sufficiently indicate the general character of the category as a whole. Apparently, such decorations were more popular on the Continent than in England. At any rate, many more specimens are to be found among the early porcelains displayed in the shops of Holland than in similar English establishments.

In producing this class of porcelain, the Chinese decorators were not always at their best. Unused to depicting the nude human figure, whose correct delineation was the touchstone of proficiency among European painters of the late Renaissance, they usually bungled their attempts even to copy the engraved prints which were supplied to ease the anguish of original composition. Hence, in this work they seldom achieved beauty in the classic sense. Yet they almost never allowed the quality of interest to elude them, and their technique usually remains exquisite even where their draftsmanship is faulty. So

Fig. 11 — European-Market Plate (c. 1750)
Probably representing *Jupiter and Vulcan*. In full color. The large and somewhat complicated design occupies both centre and rim of the plate. The border is of gold edged with red.
From the collection of Edward A. Crowninshield

large and so important was their output of mythological designs, that no collection of Chinese Lowestoft may be considered complete unless it includes one or more examples of the type.*

As for the dates of these designs, we may, in any specific instance, perhaps hazard no more than a guess. To the technique employed in carefully following the black-and-white details of European engravings, the Chinese applied the term *painting-in-ink*. A list of decorations used on imperial porcelain between 1729 and 1732, carefully compiled by Hsieh Min, Governor of the Province of Kiang-si, mentions this style of work, which, however, was, probably, perfected not long after the year 1722.† The Victoria and Albert Museum owns a European-market painted-in-ink plaque with an allegorical scene commemorative of a marriage, which is dated 1741.

Evidently, then, the Chinese-painted imitations of engravings preceded, by many years, the transfer printing process whose exploitation was begun, about 1756, by Sadler and Green of Liverpool. Indeed this meticulous hand work of the Chinese decorators may have stimulated Occidental potters to their invention of an inexpensive mechanical method of producing similar effects on earthenware, porcelain, and enamel.‡ Once the Western mechanism of transfer work was fully developed, not even the low-priced skill of the East could compete with it. We are, therefore, fairly safe in assuming that few, if any, Chinese plates in imitation of engraving were produced much after the close of the third quarter of the eighteenth century. The majority of examples encountered probably belong in the decade between 1750 and 1760.

*It should be borne in mind that no one artist undertook the entire decoration of a piece of Chinese porcelain. Each element of a design was often applied by a separate specialist.

†W. B. Honey, *Guide to the Later Chinese Porcelain*, Victoria and Albert Museum, London, 1927, pp. 56, 74, 77.

‡In his book *Transfer Printing on Enamels, Porcelain, and Earthenware*, William Turner elaborates this theory at some length.

*If the figure represented is Ariadne instead of Cybele — as seems possible — the halo would be explained; for Ariadne possessed a crown of stars, which subsequently became a heavenly constellation.

Postscript Note. — An interesting and valuable letter from a correspondent in China, who signs himself *G. A. R. Goyle*, though written from the standpoint of recent observation, sheds considerable light on some problems of old Chinese porcelains. Ching-tê Chên is still a centre of porcelain manufacture, though sadly declined from the status of earlier days. Says our correspondent:

"I was last in Ching-tê Chên in the spring of 1926. There were about 120 kilns working and the product went from the very finest to the very coarsest in all varieties. I hold that this must have been equally the case about 1800, when Ch'ien Lung had scarcely closed his eyes (he died in 1795), and when there were still several thousand kilns active in Ching-tê Chên. Then, as now, the merchants from all over the vast empire went there yearly and ordered the ware *according to the taste of their districts*. The Chinese merchant who orders porcelain exercises a rigorous examination on the spot, and accepts only the best. The rejected ware is sold by auction and finds ready buyers at greatly reduced prices.

"Under such circumstances, the crafty Cantonese becomes suddenly very lenient in his examination, and takes what he thinks is at all saleable at Canton. The foreigner is not now as exacting as the Chinese buyer, and there is no reason to assume that he was more particular in the eighteenth century.

"How orders were handled in China in the eighteenth century, I cannot say. The procedure today would be to get in touch with a porcelain shop, say in Canton. The shopkeeper, who goes once a year to Ching-tê Chên, or who, if his turnover is large, has a representative there, gladly takes any orders for sufficient quantities of porcelain. Delivery requires about eight months."

IV. *Biblical and Floral Designs*

By HOMER EATON KEYES

IN the previous installment of this series, we offered the following tentative classification of Chinese Lowestoft porcelain: Armorial designs, Mythological designs, Biblical designs, Floral designs, Genre designs, and Shipping designs. Of these six classes, we considered the first two. We may now turn our attention to the third and fourth.

BIBLICAL DESIGNS

Concerning Chinese European-market porcelain bearing Biblical designs, a good deal of nonsense has been written.† It has been assumed that this ware was produced under the supervision of the Jesuit missionaries in China and that it was primarily intended to serve the lofty purpose of converting the Oriental heathen, or, at least, of reënforcing and educating the faith of those who had been persuaded to embrace Christian doctrines. There may be some soul stimulation in imagining an enlightened Chinese family reverently pouring tea from a pot ornamented with painted-in-ink illustrations of Scriptural events or, each morning, absorbing spiritual and physical nourishment from a breakfast service spread with saintly illuminations. But there is no evidence to support the belief that anything of the kind ever happened. Indeed, it is hardly necessary more than to present such a situation in words to recognize its absurdity.

Hence, we may as well dismiss the notion that Biblical pictures on Chinese porcelain bore any closer relation to Chinese thought and custom than did armorial and mythological designs. We may equally well abandon the misleading term *Jesuit China*, so frequently applied to ware thus piously decorated. Our only evidence that the Jesuit missionaries among the Chinese were at all interested in such ware or, indeed, possessed any knowledge of it, appears to be an ecstatic memorandum of Father d'Entre-

colles, and our knowledge that two Jesuit priests were, for a time during the early eighteenth century, attached to the Imperial Court in a vain attempt to impart European principles of painting to the Chinese.*

Scenes from the Bible were commonly used to decorate Dutch fireplace tiles as well as all kinds of earthen tableware and household utensils made by local potters on Dutch soil. They likewise appear extensively on the creamware imported into Holland from English factories. Their employment by merchants of the East India Company to extend the European sale of Chinese porcelain was merely a commercial matter of course. Indeed, the entirely nonsectarian character of most of the Biblical designs perpetuated seems to imply a shrewd intention to appeal as widely as possible to Christian susceptibilities and hence to avoid arousing specific denominational prejudice.

The majority of Biblical designs on Chinese porcelain — though by no means all — appear to have been executed in fine black penciling, in imitation of the copper engravings from which they were derived. This circumstance has given rise to another perverse and irritating error: namely, that technique and topic are both of Jesuit inspiration, and that the term *Jesuit China* is, therefore, applicable to all pieces wrought in the black-and-white manner — whatever

Fig. 1 — EUROPEAN-MARKET PLATE (*c. 1750*)
Representing the Birth of Venus. Painted-in-ink technique. One of the finest examples of its type, displaying little or none of the bodily distortion usually characteristic of Chinese attempts to delineate the nude. The black-and-white method employed is the same as that used on most of the plates bearing Biblical scenes.
From the Edward A. Crowninshield collection

their subject. Since we have already shown that the Jesuit fathers probably had no connection with the Biblical porcelain, we need hardly argue their complete innocence of responsibility for the painted-in-ink depictions of undraped goddesses and nymphs, and of scenes from the scandals of Boccaccio, which bulked large among the porcelains stowed in the holds of Dutch merchantmen homeward bound from the East.

That Chinese Biblical porcelain was produced in large sets or services may likewise be doubted. The Dutch people have always shown a fondness for displaying individual specimens of ornamental earthenware and porcelain on walls or shelves — often in substitution for paintings.

† ANTIQUES must confess to culpability in this respect. In the issue for October, 1922, the Attic states that the Jesuit missionaries used Biblical porcelain among other methods of teaching. Such errors come from too ready acceptance of "the authorities."

* On this point in general, see W. B. Honey's *Guide to the Later Chinese Porcelain*, among publications of the Victoria and Albert Museum.

Fig. 2 — EUROPEAN-MARKET SMALL TRAY (*c. 1750*)
Representing the Crucifixion. Not so crude in execution as it seems at first glance; but a most unpleasant interpretation of the subject.
By permission of the Ryksmuseum, Amsterdam

Fig. 3 — EUROPEAN-MARKET PLATE (*c. 1750*)
Representing the Nativity of Christ. Such pieces are popularly known as "Jesuit China," but without any apparently sound reason.
By permission of the Ryksmuseum, Amsterdam

Evidence that they occasionally employed Chinese Biblical plates as protective icons comes from Edward A. Crowninshield, who reports finding a framed example, bearing a representation of the Crucifixion, which long hung above the bed-head in a Dutch sleeping room. Similar pieces were doubtless used with mixed decorative and religious intent; and Biblical plates were, at times, pressed into service on the table. Teapots, and a few small trays ornamented with Scriptural scenes likewise occur, but other utensils to match are extremely rare.* Hence our doubt that they were ever extensively produced by the Chinese potters.

It is this Crucifixion which most frequently appears on Chinese Biblical porcelain. Usually the scene is represented, as in Figure 4, with Christ on the cross, flanked by the two thieves, the two Maries slightly in the rear at the left, John the Disciple at the right; and, in the foreground, a group of soldiers casting large dice for the garments of the Saviour. In so far as information is available, the engraving from which this decoration was borrowed has not been specifically identified.

Fig. 4 — EUROPEAN-MARKET PLATE (*c. 1750*)
Representing the Crucifixion. Perhaps the most usual of the Biblical designs copied by the Chinese on porcelain for the European market. It occurs on teapots as well as plates. One such teapot, marked, on the bottom, with the name of Allen of Lowestoft, is partly responsible for the myth that ware of this kind was made in England. See ANTIQUES, Vol. I, p. 254.

Two quite different versions appear on two small plates, or trays, in the Ryksmuseum in Amsterdam. In one of these the figure on the cross is unmistakably that of a woman. In the other (*Fig. 2*) we have a grisly interpretation of that grisliest of originals, Matthias Grünewald's terrible Crucifixion, now in the Colmar Museum.*

Other scenes from the life of Christ which appear on Chinese porcelains are the Baptism, of which an example may be found in the Victoria and Albert Museum, London; the Nativity (*Fig. 3*); and the Resurrection (*Fig. 5*).†

Of this last design, De-Vries ‡ notes a variant form, in which three small figures of Dutch sailormen appear inappropriately in the background. Their presence, he says, is explained by modern French collectors on the ground that the original design for

*A covered cup and saucer with the Resurrection is noted by Honey, *op. cit.*, p. 68.

* Another of Grünewald's versions of this painting shows only the Virgin Mary and Saint John beside the cross. This may be the one followed by the Chinese limner.
† The Old Testament is represented in the Victoria and Albert Museum by a plate depicting the Finding of Moses. Jacob and Rachel plates also occur.
‡ DeVries, *Porselein*.

Fig. 5 — EUROPEAN-MARKET PLATE

Representing the Resurrection. It is to be observed that the plates pictured in Figures 3, 4, and 5 all have the same border. But a Baptism of Christ in the Victoria and Albert Museum has a border of butterflies.

By permission of the Ryksmuseum, Amsterdam

Fig. 6 — EUROPEAN-MARKET PLATE (*c. 1760*)

Perhaps classifiable in the Biblical category, though many portrait plates without religious significance occur. This and Figures 1, 2, 3, 4, and 5 are wrought in the painted-in-ink technique.

the plate carried instructions for including *les trois Maries* in the scene; and that, this being read as *les trois marins* by some clerk insufficiently acquainted with the Scriptures but fully cognizant of the popularity of seagoing episodes, instructions in kind were given to the Chinese draftsman. Be the story true or false, most of these Resurrection plates portray no spectators other than an imperturbable angel and a group of benumbed centurions.

Probably in the category of Biblical, or religious, designs should be included such plates as that cited by De-Vries, bearing a portrait of Jan Van Leyden as head of the Anabaptists, and similar plates showing a bust of Martin Luther, or some other eminent divine, framed in a medallion below which occurs a more or less appropriate Biblical representation (*Fig. 6*).

Fig. 7 — EUROPEAN-MARKET PLATE (*c. 1750*)

A scene from the career of the Prodigal Son; qualifying in the category of Biblical designs because of its theme rather than in deference to its decorum. Painted in colors.

From the collection of Miss Mabel Choate

the unfortunate experience of Susanna with the Elders, and the pre-prohibition excesses of Noah gave painters of the Renaissance an excuse for expressing their carnal complexes in monumental pictures whose sensuous implications are but thinly veiled beneath a pretense of pious purpose. Even the esteemed Doolittle, our early New Haven engraver, might have had difficulty in avoiding censorship of some among his Prodigal Son series had he been unable to invoke the sponsorship of the Scriptures for his more indelicate depictions.

Similarly the Dutch-market Chinese plate of Figure 7 qualifies in the category of Biblical designs because of its theme and in spite of its treatment. Quite possibly one of a series of six or more, it portrays the Prodigal Son

Another kind of Biblical design on Chinese porcelain calls for some preliminary apology. By no means all the artists who have undertaken to illustrate Scriptural or Apocryphal events have approached their task with any profoundly religious intent. Salome's dance before Herod,

divesting himself of his wealth among evil companions. Viewed by itself, it seems hardly calculated to implant righteous aspirations in the heart of youth. We may therefore hope that, in conjunction with others of the set, it once pointed an inescapable lesson of the melancholy and degrading outcome of dissolute prodigality. In the same order of designs is the handsome teapot of Figure 8, whereon Joseph flees the wiles of woman with an enduring pertinacity that well might stimulate the lyre of Keats to yet another ode.

The assembling of a representative group of Chinese Lowestoft specimens bearing Biblical designs should properly appeal to the ambition of the collector. The range of available subjects might prove somewhat brief as well as narrow; but in that very circumstance reside elements of attractiveness. One may always hope to complete a small category; yet, in the case of the one under discussion, the hope will not be so easily fulfilled as to impair the zest of search.

Fig. 8 — EUROPEAN-MARKET TEAPOT (*c. 1750*)
Representing Joseph and the wife of Potiphar. Another Biblical theme whose intent is open to question.

gold, or black and gold. In the latter case it has been assumed that the original owners were in mourning at the time of purchasing their tableware. Quite possibly this is true. The donning of habiliments of grief has often been carried to great lengths.

Lowestoft floral designs are dainty, charming, and entirely obvious — attributes which account for their wide popularity and for their extensive imitation, particularly by modern French manufacturers. No one with a reasonably developed sense of textures in

FLORAL DESIGNS

Floral Chinese Lowestoft may be dismissed with a word and an illustration (*Fig. 9*). Most of it is, or appears to be, a perfectly frank and unmistakable imitation of English models which were, no doubt, sent to China to be copied by Oriental artists. The patterns are, in the main, those made familiar to us by the so-called cottage china of Bristol, New Hall, and, to some extent, Lowestoft — sprigs of roses, a rose diaper border, and floral festoons, occasionally bordered with fine dotted lines in black. At times, the flowers are disposed in tiny silhouette bouquets painted in blue and porcelain is likely to mistake the French imitations for old Chinese originals; but it is sometimes very difficult to identify the source of the rose-sprigged and garlanded tea sets which pass under the somewhat vague entitlement of Lowestoft in near-antique shops at home and abroad. Some of these are, without much question, attributable to New Hall; some to Bristol; few, if any, to the English factory of Lowestoft; and a good many to the *fabriks* of clever Frenchmen.

* * *

This brings us to the topic of Genre designs, the most varied, the most interesting, and the least appreciated of the categories of Chinese European-market porcelains.

Fig. 9 — CHINESE LOWESTOFT SAUCERS — TYPICAL FLORAL PATTERNS
That in the middle of the group is executed in black and gold. *Owned by Mrs. Archibald M. Crossley*
The other two display the familiar colors of the *famille rose. Owned by the Editor*

V. Genre Designs

By Homer Eaton Keyes

THE dictionary, we may regretfully observe, defines the word *genre*, in its application to painting, as: "A style or subject matter . . . dealing realistically with scenes from everyday life as distinguished from historic, heroic, romantic, or ideal themes."

For the purposes of this discussion, it will be necessary to extend this definition to embrace many additional subjects — in fact, almost all subjects, historical, romantic, or plainly episodic, in which the treatment is intended to be essentially naturalistic. Such a liberty may constitute an unpardonable sin against the immortal Noah, but it is the unavoidable alternative to stringing out categories to an excessive degree of attenuation.

Under the head of genre, therefore, will come those rare seventeenth-century Chinese porcelains painted in underglaze blue with a representation of the riot in Rotterdam. Hitherto this scene has been mentioned only as occurring on plates. Its recent discovery on a cup and saucer, of the finest eggshell fabric, constitutes an event of sufficient importance to be worth memorializing with

* Continued from the March number of ANTIQUES. Copyright, 1929, by Homer Eaton Keyes. All rights reserved.

Fig. 1 — DUTCH-MARKET CUP AND SAUCER (*c. 1690*)
Decorated with a representation of the riot in Rotterdam. Compare with Fig. 2, p. 385, Vol. XIII of ANTIQUES.
Author's collection

an illustration (*Fig. 1*).

An early and well executed set of plates included within the same elastic category offers a series of cartoons satirizing the era of excessive speculation which swept Europe during the early eighteenth century. The colors are an underglaze blue and a green, intensified with rich overglaze applications of crimson enamel and lines of gold. Each plate carries a verse or two of satirical rhyme. To American collectors, perhaps the most enticing member of this series will be the one here illustrated, whereon a glib stock salesman invitingly enquires, "Who bids on Utrecht or New Amsterdam?" (*Fig. 2*).

Another unusual plate, in full colors, which belongs on the borderland between history and genre, quite obviously pictures Benjamin Franklin at the Court of France. The artist apparently felt himself incapable of mastering a composition of more than two figures; but, in zealous deference to the wise Philadelphian's reputed prowess with the ladies, he portrays four damoiselles jealously gazing down from four medallions set in the border of his design (*Fig. 3*).

It has already been remarked that many of the paintings

Fig. 2 — DUTCH-MARKET PLATE (*early eighteenth century*)
Painted in underglaze blue and green, with overglaze touches of crimson and gold.
Author's collection

Fig. 3 — EUROPEAN-MARKET PLATE (*late eighteenth century*)
Apparently portraying Franklin at court, but compare with plate XLII of Williamson's *Book of Famille Rose*.
From the collection of Miss Mabel Choate

Fig. 4 — PILGRIMS OF CYTHEREA (*1708*)
Reproduced from a French engraving by Bernard Picart. From a similar print, the large dish pictured on the Cover was later copied.

The rim bears gilt scrollwork edged with red. The original engraving from which this piece of work was taken is here reproduced in Figure 4. It is a fairly well known work of the French artist Bernard Picart; and, besides the date *1708*, carries the inscription:

PELERINS DE L'ISLE DE CITHERE

Que ces Pelerins Sont hureux.
Qu'ils font un voyage agreable.
Amour conduit leurs pas, Bacchus marche avec eux.
Qu'a Cithere ils auront bon liet et bonne table.

Amatory scenes, some highly romantic, some vulgar, were popular. Like the Pilgrims of Cytherea, the figures on the cup and saucer of Figure 5 appear to have been inspired by a French original. Figure 6, from a plate in full color, is perhaps worth including here, since some critics hold that it represents the great French sentimentalist Jean Jacques Rousseau gallantly picking cherries for Madame de Warrens. On the other hand, it may be no more than an idyl of a Dutch orchard.

In Figure 7, most delicately executed, love goes a-fishing, apparently with unbounded success, though the majestic size of her trophy seems to rouse no uncontrollable excitement in the breast of the décolleté *pêcheuse*. Similar scenes frequently occur in needlework panels and in paintings of the period. In this cup and saucer, it may be observed, we have an example of that pure genre in which the Dutch so delighted. We have another in the saucer of Figure 8,

executed on Chinese European-market porcelain were derived from engravings. Some were likewise taken from specially made drawings. De Vries mentions Pronk, draftsman for the East India Company, who supplied the sketches for a distinguished series of plates depicting the City of Amsterdam, and who, likewise, made numerous water-color drawings to serve as models for more commonplace themes.*

In a number of other instances it is possible to identify the original painting or engraving which served the Chinese decorator. A brilliant example of this was pictured in ANTIQUES for May, 1928.† The really superb fourteen-inch dish reproduced on this month's Cover offers yet an-

Fig. 5 — EUROPEAN-MARKET CUP AND SAUCER (*mid-eighteenth century*)
Painted-in-ink technique. Doubtless derived from one of the innumerable French prints of the day. Unusual in the complete absence of borders.
From the collection of Miss Mabel Choate

Fig. 6 (below) — DUTCH-MARKET PLATE (*mid-eighteenth century*)
Cherry picking. By some, supposed to represent Jean Jacques Rousseau.
Author's collection

other illustration. As even the reduced version testifies, the centre of the dish bears an exceptionally well wrought painted-in-ink portrayal of a loving pair pursuing a pilgrimage under the guidance of a torch-carrying Eros. Here and there light touches of delicate pink suffuse the flesh tones with warmth. Surrounding this central panel occurs a wide chrysanthemum border in white enamel, framed by the familiar mid-eighteenth-century spearhead—or, as De Vries calls it, fleur-de-lis— pattern, in gold and red.‡

* De Vries, *Porselein*, p. 7.
† See ANTIQUES, Vol. XIII, No. 5, Frontispiece.
‡ De Vries, *Porselein*.

whereon a wide-trousered Dutchman, with his luggage beside him, directs the effort of some boatmen who are about to convey him to one of the waiting vessels in the outer harbor.

The foregoing designs are all essentially Continental in character. The next two (*Figs. 9 and 10*), a pitcher showing a harvest scene, and details from a punch bowl which is enlivened with fox-hunting episodes, suggest an appeal to English taste. Mr. Fox, being the protagonist of the life-and-death drama of this bowl, is given the emphasis of exaggerated size. The microscopic hounds are more clearly visible on the actual bowl than in the engraving. The subject was so completely unfamiliar to Oriental experience as to be beyond the grappling powers of a Chinese artist. Much the same thing may be said of the hunt elaborated on the teapot, with cup and saucer, of Figure 11. In this instance, the victim is probably a wild boar about to be penetrated with a spear. But we should not care to insist upon this identification of the beast.

One of the most fascinating of genre Chinese designs appears on the miniature tea set illustrated in Figures 12 and 13 Evidently dating from the late eighteenth or early nineteenth century, this set bears a colored reproduction of Bartolozzi's mezzotint after William Hamilton's picture *Playing at Marbles*. The fortunate possessor of this rare little set likewise owns a copy of the engraving which inspired its decoration (*Fig. 14*).

Another more than ordinarily exquisite bit of Chinese work is the small porcelain box shown in Figures 15 and 16. The sides of

the box are delicately marbled. Within a gold circlet on the lid, an auburn-haired youth in red coat and green trousers holds a song bird on his upraised hand. Touches of gold enrich his costume. Toilet articles of this kind are not often encountered in Sino-European porcelain. Like some of the enamels on metals, which display a technical excellence unapproached by the great majority of export porcelains, such bijoux must have been produced to special order, by artists of higher skill than those thought competent to decorate the ordinary run of commercial pictorial wares.

Fig. 8 — DUTCH-MARKET CUP AND SAUCER (*mid-eighteenth century*)

The wide variations in the quality of Sino-European wares is probably to be accounted for primarily by variations in cost. Armorial porcelain, obviously, was made to personal order and for the gratification of families usually able to pay for the best, and invariably certain to insist upon receiving their money's worth. Some of the pictorial wares, likewise, must have been intended to satisfy a cultivated artistic taste, and hence were executed with corresponding nicety and at an appropriate price.

We know, however, that the Dutch merchants were thrifty traders. De Vries* cites a letter from the management of the East India Company, complaining of the charges exacted by the Chinese factors, and threatening to make future purchases in England — probably of English earthenware. The same author observes that other criti-

Fig. 9 (below) — ENGLISH-MARKET JUG (*c. 1790*)
In full color, representing a harvest scene. The damsel leaning on the hamper recalls contemporary figures of Hope supported by an anchor.
From the collection of Edward A. Crowninshield

*Op. cit.

34

Fig. 10 — DETAILS FROM PUNCH BOWL (*late eighteenth century*)
Besides these interesting depictions of a harried fox, the bowl is decorated with medallion portraits.
From the collection of Mrs. W. Murray Crane

cisms were many, and that the shapes and sizes of porcelain utensils were carefully stipulated, with a view to keeping down packing costs. Hence it seems fair to conclude that, when he made a close bargain with his European principals, the Chinese agent gave in return no more than he was paid for, and that he seldom received a remuneration that justified employment of the most skillful workers or the finest materials obtainable.

Examples in the wide category of genre might be multi-plied indefinitely. The popular literature of the day, including the tales of Boccaccio (*Fig. 17*), added its quota of subjects to the Chinese artist's catalogue, just as some years later it suggested themes for the engravers of transfers in England and in France.*

The personal taste of a merchant or sea captain, again, might dictate the nature of the design on porcelain of his special ordering, as in the curious armorial teapot of

*See ANTIQUES, Vol. XI, pp. 210–211.

Fig. 11 — EUROPEAN-MARKET TEAPOT, CUP, AND SAUCER (*late eighteenth century*)
Representing a hunting scene.
From the collection of Edward A. Crowninshield

Fig. 12 — ENGLISH-MARKET MINIATURE TEA SET (*late eighteenth or early nineteenth century*)
A partial set decorated with a scene taken from a Bartolozzi print.
From the collection of Miss Mabel Choate

Figure 18, which shows the owner's house in elevation, but the terrace, entrance path, and shrubbery in flat plan. Sometimes the designs are wrought in full color; sometimes, again, in painstaking emulation of the technique of the European engravers on metal. Sometimes the workmanship is exquisite; sometimes it is relatively coarse and ungainly. But, whatever its failures in the essentials of draftsmanship, it is always interesting, always decorative. And examples are fairly plentiful. Those who like fine old porcelain for actual use may still find cups and saucers, full tea sets, and series of plates in pictorial designs, often at prices which betray an unaccountable lack of appreciation for one of the most intriguing types of porcelain ever produced.

As for the collector of single specimens, he will discover at his disposal a sufficient range of subjects and styles to maintain his interest for an almost indefinite period. First-rate items are occasionally to be encountered in the American market, still more frequently in London, and most frequently of all in Holland. Indeed, the supply still available in the cities of the latter country suggests the likelihood that, during the eighteenth century, Chinese pictorial porcelains were made chiefly at the behest of Dutch merchants for primary shipment to Dutch ports, whence, in the course of time, many pieces have filtered through various trade channels into France, England, and America.* This state-

* Denmark and Sweden were likewise heavy users of Chinese porcelain bearing European designs. De Vries cites complaints of the Dutch East India representatives concerning the advantageous terms given by the Chinese to Scandinavian merchants. Hannover, in Volume II of his *Pottery and Porcelain*, mentions several valuable services commemorating important events in Danish and Swedish history. Examples of these are in the museums of Copenhagen and Stockholm.

Fig. 13 — TEAPOT FROM SET ABOVE
Shown for purposes of comparison with the accompanying print, which its decorative scene closely follows.

Fig. 14 — PLAYING AT MARBLES
A mezzotint by Bartolozzi, after a painting by William Hamilton.
From the collection of Miss Mabel Choate

Figs. 15 and 16 — EUROPEAN-MARKET TOILET BOX AND LID (*late eighteenth century*)
Marbled sides in grays and red. Lid in full color.
Author's collection

ment, however, should be viewed only as a general surmise; though, besides the evidence already cited, it finds support in the widespread Dutch fondness for pictorial ceramics of all kinds and in our very full knowledge of the organized efforts of the Dutch East India Company to keep Chinese artists supplied with interesting designs. Post-Revolutionary American taste appears to have inclined largely to ship decorations and to pseudo-heraldic designs. As we shall later observe, when ex-

Fig. 17 (right) — DUTCH-MARKET PLATE (*mid-eighteenth century*)
Illustration from Boccaccio.

tended pictures appear on American-market porcelain from the Orient, they usually take the forms of landscapes or urban views. Yet, after all, no great importance attaches to the question of the specific auspices under which the Chinese produced their porcelains. Let it suffice that we be able to identify this Oriental craftsmanship and appreciate its attributes of excellence.

Fig. 18 (below) — DUTCH-MARKET TEAPOT (*eighteenth century*)
Depicting a mansion with its gardens, partly in elevation, partly in plan.
From the collection of Edward A. Crowninshield

VI. *Ship Designs*

By HOMER EATON KEYES

Illustrations from the collection of Edward A. Crowninshield

OF ship and shipping designs on Oriental porcelain made for the English and Continental trade very little need be said. The topic will call for more extended treatment when we reach the discussion of American-market wares. So much of the wealth of Europe in the seventeenth century was derived from sea-borne commerce, so many important families owed their position to prowess in the merchant service or in the navy as to create an inevitable demand for nautical symbols on table services and occasional pieces of household porcelain.

One of the handsomest designs of this kind—of special moment because its accompanying inscription bears an unmistakable date—pictures the ship *Vryburg*, under command of Captain Jacob Rÿsik.† No doubt the Dutch Captain, himself, supplied the drawing for the Chinese copyist and insisted upon careful regard for accuracy in detailing the masts, sails, and rigging of his vessel. The result is perhaps the closest approximation of ship portraiture known to Chinese porcelain (*Fig. 1*).

During the early nineteenth century we find Oriental painters on glass and canvas achieving no small reputation as delineators of American and European sailing craft. But the rise of a purely pictorial branch of marine art was accompanied by a corresponding decline in the verisimilitude of ship pictures executed on porcelain. These latter, indeed, rapidly degenerated to the point where they became

little better than symbolic outlines individualized as to their nationality only by an overwhelming flag.

Not improbably the native merchants in the Chinese trading ports maintained stocks of ready-decorated ship wares for sale to foreign seamen. If so, they were but paralleling the habit of the potters of Staffordshire and Liverpool, who turned out great quantities of bowls and pitchers printed with transfer pictures of smart-looking vessels that needed but to be flagged and labeled at the purchaser's behest to become accepted portraits of pet craft.

Fig. 1 — THE SHIP *Vryburg* (*1756*)
Dutch-market Chinese plate exemplifying the best that Oriental artists accomplished in the portrayal of ships on porcelain.

The purely general, or symbolic, nature of the majority of the ships that float on Chinese porcelain is well demonstrated in the illustrations of Figures 2, 3, 4, 5, and 6. Of these, the designs on the cup, saucer, and tea caddy in Figure 2 are, on the whole, the most carefully drawn and display the greatest anxiety on the artist's part to achieve some semblance of a ship with wind in her sails and visible means of support for her tall masts. If his success was but moderate, it surpasses the usual accomplishment of the time.

* * *

At this stage of our discussion, nothing would be gained by an attempt to differentiate between the ship-pattern porcelain made for the European market and that sold to the captains of American merchantmen in the Far Eastern trade. It will be recalled, however, that, while from the seventeenth century on, the English and Continental East India Companies had maintained active business contacts with China, America's participation in Oriental commerce

† Probably one of a set, since the same subject is illustrated by DeVries in his *Porselein.*

38

Fig. 2 — Cup, Saucer, and Tea Caddy (late eighteenth century)
The American flag at the stern of these vessels places the porcelain in the category of American-market ware. The workmanship is far above the usual level attained in "ship Lowestoft."

did not begin until well after the close of the Revolutionary War; or, to be exact, until 1784, when the ship *Empress of China* sailed out of New York harbor on her voyage to Canton.

By that time foreign-market Chinese porcelains had been commercialized to meet an increasingly general and often indiscriminating demand. Apparently the careful supervision of design and workmanship which the Dutch East India Company had exercised until well through the decade of 1750 began to relax as the eighteenth century drew toward its close. The Chinese market had grown to be everybody's market. Furthermore, the porcelain and earthenware of England were offering formidable competition, even on Dutch soil, to Oriental wares.

Fig. 3 — Chinese Plate (late eighteenth or early nineteenth century)
The huge American flags betoken an American vessel. The detail should be compared with that in Figure 1.

All of these circumstances working together could lead to but one result — that of deterioration in the quality and variety of the designs employed by the Chinese artists, and, often, in the grade of the porcelain itself. There were, of course, exceptions to this ruling tendency. As we shall later discover, some splendid services and special presentation pieces were turned out in China to meet American requirements. A number of very pleasing armorial designs were likewise executed subsequent to the year 1790. Delightful pictorial sets appear at even later dates. But, in general, after 1780, or thereabouts, the old-time picturesque and manifold gorgeousness of Chinese Lowestoft rapidly yielded to stock forms of prettiness, to which an aspect of special significance was easily imparted by the addition of an eagle, a pseudo-armorial device, or a symbolic ship.

In assembling ship Lowestoft, most collectors prefer to acquire specimens depicting vessels of their own country. Since, however, in the vast majority of instances, the ships are much alike, while their flags materially differ, the acquisition of the largest possible variety of the latter emblems might prove both interesting and profitable.

In the ship category, likewise, may properly be included a number of pieces in which ships are but an incidental part of the design. DeVries, for example, cites and illustrates a plate, across whose surface is spread a highly animated Dutch whaling scene, wherein sailing craft, small boats, icebergs, polar bears, and excited birds and mariners circle in wild confusion about a vastly spouting leviathan.

Fig. 4 — CHINESE TANKARD *(late eighteenth or early nineteenth century)*
Delightful in color; and in general, daintily executed, despite the summary delineation of the ship. Ship tankards are rare.

Harbor scenes likewise occur, their middle distance filled with merchant craft, their foregrounds clogged with the bulky figures of Dutch traders (*Fig. 6*). We have, too, several Chinese versions of that scene dear to the heart of the Staffordshire potters — *The Sailor's Farewell* — in which is pictured a youth hastily disengaging himself from the clutches of his sweetheart, while his ship impatiently awaits him in the offing (*Fig. 7*).

Ships and shipping symbols also enter into the designs on armorial and presentation porcelain. It would be impossible to catalogue them all, though, somewhat later, when we reach the consideration of American historical Lowestoft, we shall illustrate some notable examples of ship decorations, at least one of which, in importance and in quality of execution, not only equals but surpasses the portrait of the Dutch *Vryburg*.

Fig. 5 (*left*) — CHINESE CUP AND SAUCER *(late eighteenth century)*
The floral border suggests some of the favorite Bristol designs. A British flag signalizes the nationality of the vessel.
Fig. 6 (*centre*) — DUTCH-MARKET CUP *(c. 1770)*
The delicately painted decoration somewhat in the Meissen manner brings this piece into the category of ship porcelain.
Fig. 7 (*right*) — THE SAILOR'S FAREWELL *(c. 1770)*
A favorite European motive interpreted by a Chinese decorator.

II General

The seven articles appearing in this second section vary widely in their content and should add greatly to the reader's knowledge of the background history of Chinese export porcelain. The first, "Quality in Oriental Lowestoft," by Homer Eaton Keyes, could very well be considered an extension of the six-part series presented first in this volume, and written in 1928–29. The objects illustrated in this later, 1937 article are from the collection of the late Martin Hurst which, prior to its sale, was considered outstanding for quality.

It is interesting to note that, at the time this article was written, export ware was commonly referred to as "Oriental Lowestoft," just as it had been in the 1920s. Throughout the article Keyes refers to "Lowestoft," a term now reserved for porcelain made at Lowestoft, England. He also refers to a "curdled potato soup" glaze used on large platters. This glaze today is almost universally called "orange peel." The reference to the early terms used in these articles is not made in criticism but, rather, is intended to point out the differences in terminology over the years.

Quality is never simple to define, and Keyes admits this difficulty with his usual good humor. He writes of the allure of decoration and advises that "from time to time, the iconographic enthusiast should close his mind against other demands and devote himself to pondering examples of Lowestoft solely in terms of their quality." The particular ingredients to be measured are, in his words, "brilliance in drawing," "purity of color," and "care in the execution of details." As Keyes is the first to admit, however, "it is, of course, useless to attempt to describe such subtleties in words."

Perhaps the most important contribution in this article is the destruction of the theory, commonly held even today, that all ware decorated with a blue border and gold stars was made exclusively for the American market. Keyes points out that this was a design commonly used in porcelain shipped to England, the continent, and the Near East several years prior to the first shipments to America. "Its golden stars," he writes, "are more likely to have been snatched direct from heaven's overspreading dome than from the flag of the new-born American republic."

The second article, "Lowestoft China," by Mrs. Jacques Noel Jacobsen deals solely with the manufacture of china at Lowestoft, England, and for this reason may seem out of place in an anthology of articles such as this. Because of the erroneous use of the English name in respect to the Chinese ware, however, it is well for the reader to know how this mislabeling occurred, as well as to know just what English Lowestoft china is, and how it was produced.

"Crosscurrents in China Trade Porcelain," by Clare LeCorbeiller, Associate Curator of Western European Art at the Metropolitan Museum of Art,, sheds recent scholarly light on the complex origins and development of export porcelain designs before their virtual standardization after the beginning of the nineteenth century. Mrs. LeCorbeiller's article is suitably followed by Carl C. Dauterman's "Chinese Porcelain Interchange." Dauterman demonstrates that Western forms of porcelain and its decoration were greatly influenced by contacts with the Chinese and that, conversely, certain developments and technological advances in Western countries at the same time greatly affected design and decoration in China. He describes how Andrea Cassius, a Dutch physician's assistant, created a new color called "purple of Cassius" in the third quarter of the seventeenth century. This pigment was adopted by the Chinese and used, after 1720, as a rose color in their *famille rose* ware. Porcelains of this hue were to dominate the decorative palette during the middle and later years of the eighteenth century, and on into the 1800s.

Pamela C. Copeland possesses one of the finest collections of Chinese export figures in the United States, consisting largely of animals. In her article, "Oriental Porcelain Frivolities," she describes a number of these pieces with special emphasis on the dates of manufacture and figurative details of different periods. The objects illustrated, including some Japanese pieces, cover a period of over two hundred years, from the middle of the sixteenth century through the middle of the nineteenth century. Collectors, in particular, can profit from a close reading of this article. Mrs. Copeland freely admits her errors in selecting pieces for the collection, and argues persuasively that the development of a good eye for form and proportion and a skeptical mind as to attribution is a must for the collector. She offers some valuable information on the methods used in modeling figures which the porcelain connoisseur entering the market will find useful for identification purposes.

Homer Eaton Keyes' "Imitations of Chinese Lowestoft" should be read and reread by every collector of Chinese export porcelain. Only the use of such a term as "Chinese Lowestoft" in this article written forty-two years ago is outdated. The imitators, more active today than ever before, were well known to Keyes and he explains many of their tricks. In particular, he warns against those "most dangerous imitations . . . achieved by removing the decoration from genuine old pieces of Oriental ware and substituting a rarer design that materially enhances their apparent value." As Keyes states at the beginning of his article, "Imitation is said to be the sincerest form of flattery: but it is likewise one of the insincerest means of commercial exploitation."

The last article in this section is "Yesterday and Today of Oriental Lowestoft" by J. A. Lloyd Hyde, an outstanding authority who has traveled all over the world in pursuit of knowledge on this subject. In 1954 Hyde published the first book devoted solely to Chinese export porcelain. About this time a change in the terminology was gradually taking hold and the book, of necessity, carried three titles for identification purposes: *Oriental Lowestoft, Chinese Export Porcelain,* and *Porcelain de la Cie des Indes.* The only term not embraced by Hyde, China trade porcelain, has only recently been superseded by the more inclusive Chinese export porcelain

His article, written in 1931, gives a number of interesting sidelights on the manufacture and decoration of porcelain based, in part, on three trips he made to China between 1929 and 1931. These took him to Canton, Macao, Hong Kong, and Shanghai. Hyde searched there for leftover items made for the American and European markets during earlier periods, but he was largely unsuccessful and found none of the armorial design variety. He also found that while Chinese porcelain produced in 1930 generally was of mediocre quality, it was still possible to order objects fashioned with skill. It was, however, necessary to search for someone to decorate them.

Hyde's observations, confirmed by other visitors during the twentieth century, are useful; some of the historical background information has been revised in recent years. At the time Hyde wrote this article the China trade had not been as well researched as it has been today. Hyde states that when the British East India Company lost the Chinese monopoly in 1833, so-called "Oriental Lowestoft" was no longer manufactured, and that twenty years later (1853) the kilns at Ching-tê Chên were destroyed during the T'aip'ing rebellion. It is now established that the kilns were rebuilt in 1864. Records in the possession of The Museum of the American China Trade, Milton, Massachusetts, as well as United States Custom records, show that the quantity of porcelain exported to America after the kilns were rebuilt was at a rate almost equal to the preceding years and continued to around 1884 when Japanese porcelain makers began to dominate the foreign market.

Quality in Oriental Lowestoft

By HOMER EATON KEYES

Note. For most of the illustrations accompanying the following discussion, I gratefully acknowledge the generous coöperation of William Martin-Hurst, Esquire, of Roehampton, England. Mr. Martin-Hurst has accumulated an exceptional collection of *famille rose* porcelains, among which he has included several foreign-market examples, not because they represent their particular type of ware, but because they deserve recognition as worthy specimens of eighteenth-century Chinese ceramic art. Their selection, in short, has been determined solely on the basis of excellence and without regard for associational considerations. The pieces here illustrated were photographed specially for An-TIQUES by Thomas Fall of London. It will be observed that nearly all of them are credited to a period prior to the 1750 decade. The export porcelain made subsequent to that period is usually less elaborately and intricately decorated. Though its enameled designs are still deftly and delicately executed, they incline to sparsity. Hence, while the articles upon which these later decorations appear are often charming for domestic use or for grouping in cabinets, they yield few specimens individually so significant as to appeal to the specializing connoisseur. After 1800 elaboration is again in evidence on Chinese export wares, but it is usually elaboration of a coarse and slap-dash type in which the old-time refinement of pattern and technique yields place to bolder and cruder effects more easily achieved.

This generalization is open to the contradiction offered by occasional late items of rare distinction and high excellence; but in its wider applications it may, I feel sure, be accepted.

— *H. E. K.*

QUALITY, though a word on every tongue, eludes satisfactory definition. All the more difficult is the capturing of its subtle connotations. Hence when we speak of *quality* in oriental Lowestoft, we must pick our sustaining phrases with care and enunciate distinctly, lest we be misunderstood. To most persons oriental Lowestoft is oriental Lowestoft — all out of the same pot and all of equal merit, though, for reasons of taste or sentiment, certain types of decoration may be considered more desirable than others.

For the average American collector one group of Lowestoft and one only has any significant appeal. That is the one which exhibits a blue border dotted with gilt stars, and therewith a central medallion in blue and gold depicting either a pseudo-armorial shield surmounted by two enamored doves, or, alternatively, a blue and gold urn, or a floral spray.

Porcelain adorned with the sundry variations of such motives is widely believed to have been specially dedicated to the patriotic citizens of the United States. Unhappily, the facts do not accord with the tradition. This blue and gold ware was, in its day, quite as widely used in England and on the Continent as in America. It even found its way into the bazaars of northern Africa and the Near East, where today its surviving fragments are being retrieved for export to the United States. Its golden stars, I surmise, are more likely to have been snatched direct from heaven's overspreading dome than from the flag of the new-born American republic. Having made its first appearance in the 1780's, by which time supreme excellence was becoming the exception rather than the rule in the commercial output of Chinese ceramic factories, it cannot vie in quality with the earlier export wares of the Orient.

The claim of blue and gold Lowestoft upon the affections of Americans is based on other attributes. For one thing, the ware, if not decoratively impressive, possesses the counter-balancing appeal of daintiness and refinement, both in its form and in the handling of its ornamental motives. It is immediately recognizable, and, in general, is an eminently safe purchase for the neophyte. But a still more potent consideration endears the ware

Fig. 1 — ARMORIAL PLATES (*1723–1735*)

a. Arms of Bliss impaling Bliss. Period of Yung Chêng, during whose reign occurred the transition from the *famille verte* to the *famille rose* type of decoration. Finely diapered borders often interrupted by medallions enframing floral designs are characteristic. So, too, are heavily mantled armorial designs so large as almost to fill the centre of the plates on which they appear. The diapered border here is executed in sepia and gold. The rest of the decoration is in brighter hues. *Diameter,* 10 ¾ in.

b. Arms of Izard. *Famille rose* coloring

to Americans. It is to be remembered that, since direct trade relations between the United States and China were not under way prior to 1784, this blue and gold represents the type of oriental porcelain most frequently brought or sent home as gifts or as merchandise by our seafaring ancestors, our traders, and our business and consular envoys in the Far East. No wonder that surviving examples, haloed with such precious associations, are among the most revered of American penates. They deserve to be. The sentiment that prompts their cherishing is something to be praised and encouraged. It is never to be belittled or criticised, except in those instances where its virtuous essence becomes tainted with blind prejudice. However, fond though we may be of our "American Lowestoft," I fear that we must in all honesty admit that a large proportion of it fails to deserve top rating — either in its fabric or in the element of the skill and care employed in its decoration. Our armorial eagles, for example, are, for most part, ungainly sparrows. Our ships, save for a few vessels anchored in donation punchbowls, are but Chinese junks to whose sterns the stars and stripes have been appended. Even George Washington's famous and almost priceless Cincinnati items are but common Canton ware glorified by a none too competently portrayed figure of Fame.

To this general rule, of course, notable exceptions may be cited. Among these are two extraordinary punchbowls whose outward adornment consists of a careful copy of a Cincinnati membership certificate. Then, too, we have the magnificent Decatur bowl with its almost miraculously perfect transcript of a Saint-Memin profile, illustrated and discussed elsewhere in this issue. Several of the punchbowls pictured and described by Doctor Woodhouse in ANTIQUES for February 1936, and the late but magnificent piece bestowed by the Turkish Sultan upon the American naval architect, Henry Eckford (ANTIQUES for June 1931, *p. 446*), are likewise to be highly esteemed. Outside of this group the artistically distinguished pieces of porcelain made in China for the American market might almost be counted on the fingers of one hand.

In making this statement I am anxious to be neither misunderstood nor misinterpreted. I am endeavoring simply to emphasize the difference between what is historically, and, to some extent, sentimentally important, and consequently of high monetary value, and that which is in its own character meritorious.

At this point, however, I must confess to some embarrassment. It would, I surmise, be hard to discover a serious student of Chinese porcelains, as such, who sees good in any of the eighteenth-century oriental wares specially made for export to foreign lands. These wares, the pundits contend, are neither Chinese nor European. Instead they are, virtually without exception, but mongrel products unworthy of serious consideration by persons of æsthetic sensibility.

The measure of truth in this unkindly dictum is perhaps large. No one who has even a casual acquaintance with the finer examples of *famille rose* porcelain of the type produced in China for the Emperor Ch'ien Lung and his entourage will contend that the foreign-pattern products equal the best of wares made for domestic consumption. Nevertheless, two points in favor of the so-called mongrel items may pertinently be stressed: first, these items deserve attention because of their significance as mementoes of a great trading era, and because their extraordinary variety of form and decoration affords endless opportunity for studying the interplay of stylistic influences; second, granting their general inferiority to contemporary Chinese porcelains of the highest grade, they exhibit varying degrees of excellence, or of debasement, which permit their classification and relative appraisal on primarily æsthetic grounds. I might add, too, as an expression of purely personal opinion, that, while mulling over

Fig. 2 — Bowl and Saucer *(1723-1735)*
Period of Yung Chêng. Delicately executed European figures painted on fine eggshell porcelain by an accomplished artist. The man wears a rose coat; the woman, a blue over-dress with sea-green skirt. The handsome floral scroll, balancing the figures, is gilded. Diapering in red and gold. A rare and exceptionally choice example. *Diameter of saucer*, 6 in.; *of bowl*, 5 ½ in.

simon-pure Chinese ceramics is doubtless more edifying than consorting with their slightly vulgar relatives of the Lowestoft branch, the more cultured occupation is considerably the less exciting of the two.

Some of the reasons for this perhaps deplorable preference have been implied, if not categorically stated, in the chapters which, at irregular intervals, have preceded the present one. Aside from the general interest which Lowestoft commands as an exotic product of mixed antecedents, the decorative motives displayed by the ware are so numerous and so diverse that one can never tell when he may encounter a hitherto undiscovered subject. In many instances, the task of determining the precise meaning and perhaps the particular source of a pictorial composition on plate or bowl becomes a fascinating pursuit. Again, questions regarding the historical significance of a fresh find and of the latter's rarity in a given category must constantly arise.

Such concerns should suffice to keep both student and collector actively alert. Nevertheless from time to time, the iconographic enthusiast should close his mind against other demands and devote himself to pondering examples of Lowestoft solely in terms of their quality. In so doing he may be surprised to observe how wide is the spread between the best and the worst, and how many gradations lie between the two extremes.

Why such gradations occur is readily explained. When European traders first began to purchase porcelain in the Orient for transport to their home markets, they acquired the native wares as they found them — for the most part the familiar underglaze blue and white types. This porcelain was of prevailingly good quality — thin, quite clear in its whiteness, compact in body, yet in tableware inclined to brittleness. Its decoration consisted of "heathen designs": lissom female figures, pagodas, dragons, flower arrangements, and the like. At the outset, the western traders had no thought of ordering utensils of special shape or of furnishing their own decorative patterns for the Chinese enamelers to copy. But their benevolent acceptance of what the oriental merchants had to offer did not long endure. It is quite evident that, even as early as the decade of the 1690's, attempts to Europeanize oriental porcelain were under way. The well-known blue and white items picturing the Rotterdam riot afford testimony in point (ANTIQUES, June 1929, *p. 487*). So likewise does the blue and white armorial plate pictured on the Cover of ANTIQUES for June 1932. Others might be cited. In these pieces, however, we still encounter an excellent grade of white porcelain, carefully executed painting in the blue, and — characteristic of Chinese wares of the period — decorative devices penciled on the under side of the plate rim. When, during the beginning years of the 1700's, European customers of high estate placed orders for plates adorned with a monogram or a family crest, these elements frequently became but secondary additions to pieces otherwise predominantly oriental in design and quality. Several

such items are pictured in *Armorial Porcelain of the Eighteenth Century*, by Sir Algernon Tudor-Craig. Among them we find bowls and plates displaying characteristic K'ang Hsi and Yung Chêng decorative motives amid which English heraldic devices have been ingeniously planted. The latest of these may be ascribed to about the year 1730. Throughout the same period Chinese artists reproduced many a European portrayal in the finest of eggshell porcelain (*Figs. 2, 3, and 4*).

Meanwhile commercialism was marching on. The eighteenth century was no more than fifteen years old when the profit possibilities in made-to-order porcelain in forms adjusted to western usage and embellished with designs dictated by western taste dawned upon the thrifty merchants of the East India companies. The agents of the Chinese potteries in Ching-tê Chên were responsive to the idea and the masters of the decorating establishments in Canton were equally amenable. Thus the great productive era of occidentalized Chinese porcelains was launched. So large an undertaking implied intensive and extensive effort to enlarge the western market. And this, in turn, involved a constant battle on the part of rival traders to force down what we may properly term the manufacturer's price. In so far as concerns the money side of the transaction, the West apparently defeated the East; but we may well doubt that the goods delivered were worth more than was charged for them. Perhaps, indeed, the shrewd Chinese agents profited more from these bargain orders than from those placed by really particular customers.

If one examines enough run-of-mine Lowestoft he will find ample evidence that culls from the kilns — warped or sooted in the firing, sometimes with a badly pitted glaze — were expressly preserved for the foreign-devil chiselers. Otherwise such imperfect items would probably have been destroyed as unfit for use. On the other hand, there were customers, particularly those who sought armorial sets, who demanded the best obtainable and were untroubled regarding the expense incurred. Such persons seem to have been appropriately and honestly served.

I am inclined to believe, however, that little if any of the later eighteenth-century porcelain decorated in China primarily for the European market is so fine in body as that employed currently for oriental consumption, or as that which prior to 1730 had been embellished with western designs. A Rotterdam riot plate (*c. 1690*), if held against an electric globe in a dark room, will show almost white by the transmitted light, and will reveal in its fabric no moons due to imperfect mixing of the ingredients. On the contrary, a plate of the mid-eighteenth century or later, similarly tested, is likely to reveal a cloudy "duck-egg" hue and to be quite astonishingly moonstruck. The glaze of eighteenth-century European-market porcelain is often of quite definitely bluish cast, more noticeable on the underside than on the face of plates, where polychromy tends to confuse perception. The curdled "potato soup" glaze frequently occurring on the large platters brought home by seafaring ancestors in the late 1700's and early 1800's by no means signifies excellence, though it is frequently regarded with affection. It seems to be confined to large pieces, such as platters and urns, so heavily coated that the glaze crawled or bubbled in the firing.

Little more need be said regarding the substance of Chinese Lowestoft. The quality of potting and of glazing in one adequately decorated piece is likely to equal that in another. There are occasional distinguished exceptions to this rule; but they will be readily recognized when encountered. Pieces that are warped, or sootmarked, or seriously pitted or crazed, are usually uninteresting in other respects and should be passed by. Furthermore, enough undamaged articles survive and are purchasable at reasonable figures to remove any excuse for acquiring pieces that are perceptibly chipped or cracked or have suffered material repair.

It is chiefly in the domain of decoration that the student of Chinese Lowestoft will have opportunity to exercise his powers of discrimination. The decoration of Chinese porcelains occupied people of all ages, from infancy to

senility. Some of these artisans were extraordinarily able; some were of very commonplace calibre. The best of them could copy with impeccable fidelity almost any pattern that was placed before them. It has frequently been stated, and is quite generally believed, that, even when supplied with a model, a Chinaman could never achieve a rendering of the human form satisfactory to western eyes. This is not strictly true. The artisan or artisans who perpetrated the numerous rubbery delineations of the Judgment of Paris, and many another mythological or religious scene, were indeed short on anatomy; but we may find no fault with the Decatur profile previously mentioned, with the figure of a huntsman on the bowl pictured in Figure 5, and very little with the better copies of Picart's *Pilgrims of Cytherea* illustrated in ANTIQUES for June 1929 (*Cover and p. 488*). The figure drawing on the Cincinnati certificate bowls, previously referred to, compares favorably with that on the certificates

Fig. 5 — HUNTSMAN PLATE (*1740–1750*)
The huntsman wears a blue coat. His horn is gold. The handling of the figure is exceptionally vigorous and free from anatomical distortion, though the delineation of the hounds leaves something to be desired. The extension of the composition across the rim is unusual. No doubt the portrayal was taken from a European picture

Fig. 6 — REBECCA AT THE WELL (*1740–1750*)
Enameled in full color and more effective in the original than in photographic reproduction. The figure drawing is well above the average of Chinese delineations, but the work as a whole cannot compare with that of the earlier bowl and saucer, pictured in Figure 2

Fig. 7 — DISH IN CHINESE TASTE (*Ch'ien Lung*)
Entirely unrelated to foreign-market wares. Pictured to illustrate supposed Chinese preference in matters of both form and decoration. A rimless plate exhibiting charmingly disposed floral sprays upon a pure surface untroubled by elaborate bandings, or other distracting ornamentation. Some authorities on Chinese porcelain maintain that plates with broad flat rims, presumably for condiments, were first made for the European market. If so, the shape must very quickly have found favor among the Chinese, who appear likewise to have been frequently ready to accept floridly decorated porcelain in place of the chaste wares exemplified in the present picture

themselves. Decorators capable of achieving such work were quite naturally few, and their charges no doubt sufficiently above the usual level to prevent their employment save in exceptional instances.

Viewed from the purely qualitative standpoint, the finest Lowestoft wares will correspond in date closely with the finest products in the category of Yung Chêng and Ch'ien Lung porcelain, and they will exhibit much the same features of excellence — namely, a swift and dexterous linear quality in the drawing, clear and lively color, which means pinks that have not been fired to a blackish hue or even to a sullen blood color, clear luminous greens, delicate yellows untainted with a saffron tint, blues as liquid as the sky, and purples that might have been ravished direct from a lilac bush. The harsh, rusty iron reds of a later period will be notable for their absence.

Aside from a considerable measure of brilliance in drawing and exceptional purity of color, the fine pieces will reveal meticulous care in the execution of details. It is, of course, useless to attempt to describe such subtleties in words. As already suggested, not until the mind has been immunized against all sentimental or associational bias will any differences in quality be recognized

Fig. 8 — EWER (*probably Yung Chêng*)

A Chinese porcelain version of the French so-called helmet pitchers — of silver or pewter — dating about 1700 to 1740. The decoration of this ewer, which features barnyard fowl among peonies, appears to be quite Chinese in character. Hence the piece is interesting as illustrating a mingling of European form and purely oriental ornamentation. It may be that the rather decadent flat-lipped helmet pitchers which accompany so many late eighteenth- and early nineteenth-century so-called Lowestoft teasets stem from earlier and more elaborate forms like that here pictured. European potters occasionally employed the helmet form. See, for example, Hannover's *Pottery and Porcelain* (*Vol. III, Figs. 179 and 251*). A splendid French pewter *aiguière-en-casque*, or helmet ewer, is pictured in Figure 110 of the late H. H. Cotterell's *Pewter Down the Ages*; a Swiss example (*c. 1700*) in ANTIQUES for September 1927 (*p. 216*); German, ANTIQUES for November 1928 (*p. 430*) and for February 1929 (*p. 132*); French, ANTIQUES for February 1928 (*p. 134*). *From the Victoria and Albert Museum, London*

— or admitted — even when strongly contrasting examples are placed side by side for comparison. An attitude of unquestioning loyalty in such matters prevents that mental and spiritual detachment which is essential to unclouded vision and unhampered judgment. Most of us may consider ourselves fortunate that our friends accept and cherish us for obscure reasons with which objective scrutiny has very little to do. We may add the corollary that what is technically the most nearly perfect work either of man or of nature is by no means invariably the most interesting. Were this not so, the phrase "beautiful but dumb" would never have been coined. Be that as it may, the eye gains critical vigor by being subjected to occasional setting-up exercises, even if considerable anguish is experienced in the process. The purpose of these notes, but more particularly of the accompanying illustrations and their captions, is to impose just such a penitential burden upon the reader.

A Postscript to Lowestoft

IN DISCUSSING the Chinese foreign-market porcelains popularly called oriental Lowestoft, I have, on sundry occasions, indulged in surmises, which, though reasonable, could not at the time be substantiated by documentary evidence. One of these, to the effect that the bargain-hunting European or American buyer of porcelain usually received nothing better than he paid for, seems to be justified by an article contributed by Walter Muir Whitehill in the *Essex Institute Historical Collections* for October 1937. Mr. Whitehill quotes at length from the notebook kept by Thomas W. Ward, master of the ship *Minerva* of Salem, during a stay at Canton in the autumn of 1809. Probably for the information of his principals in New England and for the guidance of other shipmasters whom they might send to the Orient, Ward not only jotted down comments upon Chinese business methods, but sketched shrewd characterizations of the Chinese merchants with whom he came in contact. Thus he spoke highly of Eshing, who, he says, "deals chiefly in silks but also handles Nanking ware and tea." One Loonshong, a general dealer, "will do well with looking after." Four interesting mentions are of Yinqua, "lacquered ware," Cumshing, "silversmith," Tyshing, "ivory, combs, fans, etc.," Ashie, "cabinetmaker," all "head men at their business." Here are several more extended and illuminating observations:

Tom Birdman is one who buys & sells every thing, but most in the Ship Chandlery line, & whom we were frequently obliged to deal with some way or other. He is without doubt as great a villain as ever went unhung.

Tom Bull, a ships Comprador, is like all other Chinese you deal with, except in one particular: he is an honorable scoundrel, and will tell you how much, & why, & wherefore he cheats you. He is as good as any of them. I dealt with him considerably in selling my outward cargo, & had some trouble, but he was pretty punctual for a Comprador.

Old Synchong is head China Ware Merchant, is sometimes much dearer, often a little cheaper, generally better China & always best packed of any man in Canton. Is a close fisted old miser, gets drunk every day, but performs his contracts & whatever you can bind him to, he will fulfill. I prefer dealing with Synchong to any other.

Exching is next . . . has much business — some meanness about him — does not pack so well, and China ware not generally so good, great breakage — has considerable business.

Sonyeck you can make good bargains with, but he is rather slippery . . . rising in the world, active & industrious, get no cyphered China of him. [This probably refers to monogrammed pieces.]

Fouchong is a pretty good man, & well spoken of by the Philadelphians.

Among the names in this list that of Synchong is familiar; for Synchong was the entrepreneur who in 1812 had his name writ large on the punchbowl made under his auspices for presentation to the Corporation of the City of New York. (See ANTIQUES for April 1932, *p. 175*). Shipmaster Ward adds this sapient remark, "The only way of trading with safety is perhaps by dealing with those whose characters & standing are such as to secure their honesty by ties of interest."

LOWESTOFT CHINA

By MRS. JACQUES NOEL JACOBSEN

PROBABLY NO OTHER CERAMICS have stirred up so much dissension as the china that was made and the china that was not made at Lowestoft. Though the whole subject has frequently been explained, to the majority of collectors Lowestoft remains an enigma. They ask, "What is Lowestoft and how is it different from Oriental Lowestoft or Oriental export china?"

If that small English factory that never employed over seventy workers had made all the china attributed to it, it would have been the most prolific of all time. Most of the china that people insist on calling Lowestoft (they may even modify it to Oriental Lowestoft) was never within miles of the town of that name in England, but was made and decorated in China. It should be called Chinese export porcelain and not Lowestoft.

A china factory was located in the town of Lowestoft and it produced some fine pieces between the years 1756 and 1803. According to Gillingwater's *History of Lowestoft*, published in 1790, Hewlin Luson, squire of Gunton Hall near Lowestoft in Suffolk, found some white clay on his estate that he thought might be suitable for making porcelain. He sent samples of the clay to London (possibly to Bow or Chelsea) for testing and found that it could be used for this purpose. In 1756, encouraged by the results Luson erected a kiln and hired workers from London to begin manufacture. Unfortunately these workers had been bribed by their former masters to spoil intentionally the articles made at the new works. These tactics deterred the squire from production, but a group of men revived the interest a year later. This group included Philip Walker, Robert Browne, a chemist, Obed Aldred, a bricklayer, and John Richman, a merchant. This strangely assorted group of men thwarted the deliberate spoiling of the ware by an ingenious method. Browne, the chemist, beat the potters at their own game. Disguised as a workman, he obtained employment at either Bow or Chelsea and bribed the workmen to conceal him in an empty hogshead while the managers mixed the ingredients of the paste. Of course, this process was a guarded secret, but he returned to Lowestoft with this valuable informa-

tion. After his return, he assumed the management of the factory, which by 1770 was carried on under the name of Robert Browne and Co. He retained this post until his death when he was succeeded by his son, a second Robert Browne. The earliest date on any piece of Lowestoft is 1761. Although the company had serious setbacks at first, the china produced was satisfactory and the company set up a London agent whose advertisement appeared in a London paper March 17, 1770.

Lowestoft china is pleasing to the sight. It is usually a creamy white color and it is always of a soft-paste composition. When held to the light it has a yellowish tinge. The color of the glaze, which is usually slightly blue, may disguise the creamy whiteness of the paste. The glaze has a tendency to run thicker in such places as the inside edge of a rim or the joining of a handle, and it is frequently speckled with tiny black dots or bubbles. The lids of the teapots are always glazed all over the flange. The modeling is usually rough and crude and the bottoms are roughly finished, although the shapes are regular.

Chinese figures, or conventional flowers in sprays or ribbons with green leaves were the usual polychrome decoration. Roses, painted by the Frenchman, Thomas Rose, were painted in chocolate red, purple, and pink, and were invariably shown with a stem. Also popular were the diapers, especially a trellis pattern, that were used on cups, saucers, and bowls. Several pieces were decorated with views of local buildings. Perhaps the most famous is the view of Lowestoft Church. Generally speaking, the decoration was poor and usually in imitation of either Oriental or early Worcester porcelain. The early period was almost wholly one of underglaze blue. In most of the blue specimens the blue has run.

Marks on Lowestoft are not very conclusive. Although some pieces were marked *A Trifle from Lowestoft*, many outright copies of marks of other potteries were made, as was the custom of the day. The crossed-swords mark of Meissen was a popular one. Some of the pieces were marked with a crescent, thought to be an imitation of the Worcester crescent. Letters and numerals

ENGLISH LOWESTOFT, with underglaze blue decoration. All but one of the pieces are dated.

ENGLISH LOWESTOFT. *a, d, g,* local souvenirs decorated in blue, puce, sepia, and brighter colors. *b,* birth tablet with Oriental scene on reverse. *c,* part of a wedding service, decorated in gold and red. *e,* imitation of Chinese design with pink scale border, flower vase, and floral sprigs. *f,* blue transfer-printed mug.

that appear on the inside of the rim at the bottom are merely workmen's marks.

Not so long ago any piece of china that bore an armorial design or a blue trellis-work border and a floral medallion was called Lowestoft. Gradually collectors and connoisseurs realized that this all-inclusive label included a great deal of totally dissimilar material. They recognized that it was not all made and decorated in the little fishing village of Lowestoft, but that most of it was of Oriental origin, though some people maintained that Oriental china was brought to England and decorated at Lowestoft.

The confusion all dates back to the time about 1863 when William Chaffers was writing his monumental book on ceramics. He visited the town of Lowestoft in search of material, and there he found many specimens of porcelain that the old villagers swore had been manufactured at the local pottery. Actually they were of Chinese make, and had Chaffers considered that a small factory of seventy workers could not have possibly turned out the enormous quantity of ware he found, he would not have made statements that confounded collectors for a generation.

His information caused a storm of protest. What was the differ-

ence between Lowestoft and Oriental china? There were violent debates on the subject and Professor Church even went so far as to omit any mention of Lowestoft in his book on ceramics. Gradually china collectors realized the error but the damage had been done. They found that many pieces, bought as Lowestoft, were in reality Chinese pieces. The serious harm in this situation was the suspicion cast on the original Lowestoft. Rather than attribute too much to the Lowestoft factory, collectors went to the opposite extreme of refusing to believe that any porcelain had been made there. Confidence was restored only in 1902 when excavations took place on the site of the old Lowestoft factory, which revealed fragments of china, several molds, and other pieces of evidence that were of value for identification purposes.

In 1902 W. W. R. Spelman undertook the Herculean task of getting to the bottom of the mystery by a careful study of the *trouvaille* revealed under the old factory floor. By chemical analysis, Spelman found that specimens of clay found at the excavations were suitable for the manufacture of china. Several molds were found that immediately identified pieces that had been ascribed to other potters. In the famous Crisp collection of Lowestoft there is a teapot decorated with Chinese scenes. One-half of the mold (fortunately the dated half) in which this teapot was made was one of the pieces unearthed. Several pieces were found in the biscuit state ready for firing. The paint, not being fixed by a glaze, easily rubbed off. This proved that china was decorated at Lowestoft. Several nests of cups and saucers that had run together in the firing were found, which proved that firing was done at Lowestoft. Spelman's monograph leaves no doubt that china was made, decorated, and fired at this factory. He also found parts of figurines and assumed that they were also made at the factory. Perhaps the most interesting conclusion from the diggings was the fact that only articles of soft-paste porcelain were found. This is an important point in differentiating between ware made at Lowestoft

ENGLISH LOWESTOFT (*below*). *From the Philadelphia Museum of Art.*

ORIENTAL EXPORT PORCELAIN PUNCHBOWL (*below, right*). *Collection of Mrs. Lee Layton.*

and ware made in China, for Chinese porcelain is hard paste.

The Lowestoft proprietors closed their doors in 1803, owing partly to the competition of the Staffordshire potters who had clay and coal at their doors; and partly to the loss of their wares worth several thousand pounds sterling in Rotterdam when Napoleon seized Holland. For thirty years after the Lowestoft factory closed, Robert Allen, the manager, continued in business at a shop in Lowestoft where he fired china articles which he procured from Rockingham and other places in England, and from the Orient. He signed some of these articles *Robert Allen*, or *R. A.*, or *Robert Allen, Lowestoft*, or *A Present from Lowestoft*, and so forth. We know that he did at least some decoration of Oriental china from the teapot signed *Allen Lowestoft* in the Schreiber collection at the Victoria and Albert Museum, one of the articles that have confused collectors for years. W. B. Honey maintains that the major decoration of this pot is Chinese, but that Allen added his mark.

There is no proof, however, that the Lowestoft factory decorated Oriental porcelain during its period of operation. Lowestoft, geographically, is situated on the east coast of England ten miles south of Yarmouth. Just opposite in Holland is Rotterdam, a great port of entry for merchantmen from the East. There was a tax on undecorated china brought into England from the Orient between 1775 and 1880, but it could easily have been shipped in duty-free from Rotterdam where the embargo did not obtain. However, if quantities of undecorated Chinese porcelain had been imported, a certain amount would have been found in England; and it has not.

By the time all this confusion between Lowestoft and Oriental porcelain had been fairly straightened out by the investigators, the damage had been done. The name Lowestoft was being applied indiscriminately by museums, collectors, and dealers to a vast body of Oriental china in spite of the contrary evidence afforded by shape, paste, and glaze. Recently there has been considerable effort to call these pieces "Chinese export porcelain." It is not a fancy title but it is exactly what these pieces of hard paste are. Chinese export porcelain, the miscalled Oriental Lowestoft, or Sino-Lowestoft has no connection with the town of Lowestoft, England. This china was made in China exclusively for

Oriental Export Porcelain Plate (*below*). *Photograph courtesy Metropolitan Museum of Art.*

Oriental Export Porcelain (*below, right*). Belonged to Governor DeWitt Clinton (*1769–1828*), and his wife, Marie Franklin. Bears their initials. *Collection of Henry O. Tallmadge. Photograph courtesy Museum of the City of New York.*

export and usually in accordance with orders brought to China by the officers of the sailing ships. It was called "East India China" because it was shipped by the East India Companies.

Chinese export china was made in the town of Ching-te-chen for English, American, Continental, and Near Eastern families. Dinner services, punchbowls, and tea services were made, chiefly in Western shapes. The Chinese are adept at copying and would decorate pieces of china with monograms, coats of arms, patriotic or fraternal emblems, or pictures of ships. There is a story that one American matron sent a sketch of her coat of arms with explicit instructions about the colors to be used. To be sure there would be no mistake she labeled *This in red* and *This in blue* in appropriate spots. The painstaking Chinese thought the directions were all a part of the design and laboriously copied the words. Sometimes it took more than two years for the orders to be filled. The china pieces were potted in the town of Ching-te-chen. Glazed but undecorated they were brought overland more than five hundred miles to the town of Canton where the design was added. After this process, they would be fired a second time. After careful packing, they would be stowed in the hold of another vessel and used as ballast for the return trip to the States. Because this china was remarkably well made and considerably cheaper than a corresponding article of English manufacture, great quantities of it were shipped. The chances are that some of the china in your own cupboard was brought from the Orient in this way.

Punch bowl, 10¼ inches, decorated on two sides with a portrait of the U.S.S. *Franklin*. The 74-gun frigate was built in 1818 in Philadelphia, and designed by Samuel Humphries.

Fig. 1. Covered cup, possibly made for the English market, late seventeenth century. Height 5⁷/₁₆ inches. *Metropolitan Museum of Art.*

Fig. 2. Puzzle jug, made for the English or Dutch market, early eighteenth century. Height 8 inches. *Metropolitan Museum of Art.*

Crosscurrents in China Trade porcelain

BY CLARE LE CORBEILLER,
Associate curator,
Western European Arts,
Metropolitan Museum of Art

IT IS BECOMING increasingly apparent that many design sources for China Trade porcelain are to be sought outside the context of trade by the European East India companies. Subsumed in the official east-west traffic were a number of others, formal and informal: the dissemination of religious and secular prints in the East by missionaries; the presents of embroideries and "pretty newfangled toys" that smoothed the paths of ambassadors; the European trade goods that were shuttled along the coasts of India; the importation of Chinese lacquers and silks, as well as porcelains, and their interpretation by European craftsmen; the intra-European traffic in decorative arts (for example, the massive export of Dutch tiles to Portugal in the later seventeenth century); and the very existence of Canton as an international market place. Resulting from this was a complexity of interchange that is an essential characteristic of China Trade porcelain.

Conspicuous in the early period of the trade was an experimentation with forms, presumably motivated by the lack of Western shapes indigenous to hard-paste porcelain and a desire to exploit the potential of the material and evolve styles natural to it. The shape of a small covered cup (Fig. 1) is of mixed English and Chinese origin. In general outline it represents a transition from the squat silver cups of the 1680's and 1690's to the footed one of the Queen Anne period. The unusual design of the handles, however, is Chinese and is said to be characteristically provincial.[1] The tripartite tulip pattern is, again, English, borrowed from a delftware style of the late seventeenth century, while the borders simulate either the "blue-dash" ones of delftware or the gadrooned ones of silver.

Fig. 3. Teapot with design by Cornelis Pronk (1691-1759), made for the European market, c. 1740. Height 4¹⁵/₁₆ inches. *Collection of Mrs. Walker O. Cain.*

Of medieval English origin, the puzzle jug was a popular trick piece for several hundred years. Versions like the export one in Figure 2 are probably not based on English prototypes, however, but on Delft copies made at the turn of the seventeenth century, many of which were decorated in traditional Chinese manner. It is likely to have been these China Trade echoes of an Anglo-Dutch exchange that were imported into France and served as models for the Rouen faïence versions painted in K'ang Hsi style.

The introduction into Europe, modification, and repatriation of Chinese motifs underlie the decoration of many export porcelains. Several designs made for the Dutch East

Fig. 4. Pair of horses, made for the Continental market, second half of the eighteenth century. Lengths 10 and 10¼ inches. *Collection of Mrs. Franklin D. Roosevelt Jr.*

Fig. 5. Plate with the arms of Napier of Ballikinrany, made for the Scottish market, c. 1745. Diameter 9 inches. *Collection of Mr. and Mrs. Rafi Y. Mottahedeh.*

India Company by Cornelis Pronk include elements borrowed from blue-and-white wares imported by the company during the K'ang Hsi period (1662-1722). The plates of Pronk's so-called "Visit of the Doctors to the Emperor" pattern, which match the teapot shown in Figure 3, incorporate exotic fish clearly inspired by those found on early eighteenth-century cups painted with a subject known popularly in Holland as "The Cuckoo in the House." Another aspect of the Westerner's assimiliation of Chinese style is seen in a pair of white horses (Fig. 4) whose formalized grace evokes the style of the Jesuit painter Giuseppe Castiglione (1688-1766), who entered the court of Peking in 1717 and spent the rest of his life there.

An English traveler in the East sketched a design whose recurrence on English porcelain has been thought to have provided the source of China Trade versions. The opposite appears to be the case, however. The Valentine pattern has recently been attributed to the artist Peircy Brett, who accompanied Commodore George Lord Anson on his Pacific expedition from 1740 to 1744.[2] Brett's composition of an altar of love and other sentimental emblems in a landscape with a palm and garlanded breadfruit tree first appeared as the principal decoration of Anson's own armorial China Trade service made in 1743; elements of it recur as the border decoration on a number of export plates of about the same date (see Fig. 5); it appears only later on English pieces.

Engravings represent another aspect of stylistic interchange. Portable, topical, and above all, available, they were ideal as design sources. Sometimes, in cases of particular personal interest, they were copied faithfully onto export porcelains. Samuel Vaughan's bookplate was the model for the armorial on the cup shown in Figure 6; engraved views of Swedish castles compiled in the early eighteenth century were duplicated on a punch bowl and platter (Fig. 7, 8) presumably made for a Swedish buyer but believed to have been in America since before the Revolution.

Often, however, subjects that are obviously based on engravings have been lifted from larger compositions; or reinterpreted—as seems to have occurred on the punch bowl in Figure 11, where the buildings are suspended like stage props against a white backcloth; or combined with

Fig. 6. Cup with the arms of Vaughan impaling Hallowell, made for the Anglo-American market, 1745-1750. Height 2½ inches. *Metropolitan Museum of Art.*

Figs. 7, 8.   Covered (cover not shown) punch bowl and platter with views copied from engravings published early in the eighteenth century in *Suecia antiqua et moderna* and *Suecia antiqua et hodierna*, made for the Swedish market, 1745-1750. Diameter of platter, 21¾ inches. *Metropolitan Museum of Art, Pulitzer Fund*.

Fig. 9. Dish, made for the Continental market, 1750-1760. Diameter 15¾ inches. *Metropolitan Museum of Art, bequest of George D. Pratt.*

Fig. 10. Chamber candlestick, probably made for the English or American market, c. 1800. Height 3½ inches. *Collection of Mr. and Mrs. Peter H. B. Frelinghuysen.*

decorations from other sources, like the scheme of a large dish (Fig. 9) in which the central motif, certainly copied from an emblem-book engraving, has been enclosed in a flamelike cartouche similar to ones noted on Höchst faïence. Since the Chinese painters could be counted on to reproduce exactly the designs they were given, variations of this sort must be due to intermediate designs. We need to know much more, for example, about the export of the watches whose cases are enameled with allegorical subjects; about the nature of the prints presented to K'ang Hsi by the Jesuits in 1722; about the rapport (if any) between the imperial factories and the private kilns that produced the export wares; about the degree of control the Europeans could exercise from Canton over orders for porcelain to be made at Ching-tê-chên, six hundred miles away in Kiangsi province. These are only some of the factors to be considered in accounting for gaps between what seems to be the ultimate source of a design and its final version on Chinese porcelain. Certainly until 1774, when for the first time the English East India Company was required to place its orders a full season ahead, there

is evidence of considerable flexibility and spontaneity. The regulation imposed in 1774 led inevitably to a more impersonal, standardized selection of patterns and models. It is not coincidental that all the porcelains decorated with quartered sample borders—of which the chamber candlestick in Figure 10 is a hitherto unrecorded example—are datable to the last years of the active porcelain trade between China and Europe.

The objects illustrated in this article and others may be seen until January 27 at the China House Gallery in New York City in a show of China Trade porcelain organized by Mrs. Le Corbeiller.

[1]Soame Jenyns, *Ming Pottery and Porcelain*, New York, 1953, p. 76.

[2]David Sanctuary Howard, ''The Pearl River on Porcelain,'' *Country Life*, June 21, 1973, p. 1803.

Fig. 11. Punch bowl with a view said to be of Grey Monk's Square in Copenhagen, made for the Scandinavian market, c. 1775. Diameter 12½ inches. *Frelinghuysen collection.*

Maiolica (tin-enameled pottery) jar from Faenza, c. 1500-1510, reflects the concern of the Renaissance potter in simulating the effect of the superior Chinese medium. Here a freely sketched, open design has been achieved against the foil of a white ground.

Chinese porcelain

interchange

BY CARL C. DAUTERMAN

WHEN SPEAKING OF EUROPEAN CERAMICS it is customary to acknowledge that most of the significant developments from the sixteenth to the eighteenth century can be traced to Chinese origins. So great is our familiarity with the ways in which the Celestial Kingdom enriched the life and arts of the West that we are prone to regard this influence as occurring in a series of great waves flowing from the East, never to return. There was, however, a reverse current.

One has only to visit the pottery and porcelain collections of a large museum to gain a sweeping impression of the reciprocal transmission of techniques, forms and motifs. Great barriers of time and space can be easily crossed in this way. Shown here are objects currently on view in widely separated galleries of the Metropolitan Museum of Art. Each marks a milestone in the history of ceramics. Taken together, they recall the familiar story of the adulation and emulation of things Chinese—but with a counter-effect at the end. For China, with a five-hundred-year monopoly of porcelain, eventually had her own course deflected by her contacts with the West.

An early adjustment was the stepping up of production, which not only affected the coveted blue-and-white, but resulted in the creation of a distinct class of porcelain which in appearance was un-Chinese, being intended solely for the Western market. In these pages it would be superfluous to make more than this passing reference to the so-called China-Trade or Oriental Lowestoft

Delft plate with blue-and-white decoration. A late seventeenth-century example of a Far Eastern design interpreted in a Near Eastern medium (tin-enameled pottery) which was introduced into Europe by the Moors.

Meissen teapot, c. 1715-20. A typical example of Europe's first porcelain, which drew heavily upon the Chinese idiom for its forms and motifs. Here the decoration, by C. K. Hunger, is in raised gilding and enamel.

This Medici porcelain ewer (Florentine, c. 1580-1600) represents the earliest surviving Occidental porcelain. Four of the fifty or so pieces ever made are now at the Metropolitan. Its "soft-paste" composition was an important by-product of the quest for the true porcelain formula.

Another by-product of the attempt to produce true porcelain was milk-white glass. This South Staffordshire vase with chinoiserie decoration, c. 1760, is an instance of Western success in making glass that looked like porcelain.

porcelain, with its Occidental shapes, heraldic motifs, chinoiseries, and the like.

Another facet of the commerce with China, though less well known, had a more profound effect. This involved the adoption of a Dutch pigment which radically changed the palette of the porcelain decorator. Made from chloride of gold, this color was the creation of Andreas Cassius, a physician's assistant at Leyden, in the third quarter of the seventeenth century. Europeans called it the "purple of Cassius," and later, the *rouge d'or;* to the Chinese it was the "foreign color."

At the opening of the eighteenth century the characteristic color scheme for Chinese polychrome porcelains was that of the *famille verte*—a brilliant combination of green,

yellow, aubergine, blue, and iron red. During the 1720's, with surprising suddenness, this was abandoned. The clear apple green which had dominated these harmonious colors was rejected, as was the iron red which had given a masculine strength to the *famille verte*. In their stead appeared a variable rose pigment, often opaque and viscous-looking.

The effect can hardly be exaggerated. It was truly revolutionary to have a major division of porcelain production eclipsed by this pervasive pink. The feminine look of the new *famille rose* colors received official sanction among the palace porcelains of the emperor. The ascendancy was not only complete but permanent, extending to the present day.

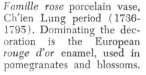

Painted enamel tray with cover, bearing the arms of Saldanha de Albuquerque. The service to which it belongs consists of both porcelain and enamel, and was painted at Canton about 1760-1770.

Famille rose porcelain vase, Ch'ien Lung period (1736-1795). Dominating the decoration is the European *rouge d'or* enamel, used in pomegranates and blossoms.

In addition to the blue and white, the Chinese *famille verte* profoundly influenced the decoration of European porcelain. The masculine color scheme and the fondness for pictorial reserves in a single-color or patterned ground can be seen in Meissen, Vincennes, and Chelsea of the early periods.

It would be fascinating to discover how the knowledge of this foreign color was first transmitted to the Orient. Soon after its discovery it appeared in the work of the German enamelers on copper. Within a few more years it was employed in the ruby glass of Potsdam. Next we find it bringing distinction to the early porcelains of Meissen, Vincennes, and their imitators.

There is the possibility of an even more direct transferral in China from the enameler's palette to that of the porcelain decorator. While it is true that the Chinese practiced the art of enameling on metal as early as the Yüan Dynasty (1280-1368), they were nevertheless fascinated by the European enamel work which was being imported about 1700. At Peking the Emperor K'ang Hsi opened a studio for enamelers, where French missionaries provided instruction in the technique as it was practiced at Limoges. In Canton, center for decorating export porcelain, shops were set up to produce enamel for foreign markets. And it is precisely here that we find the rose-pink color applied interchangeably to objects of enameled copper and to porcelain.

As evidence we illustrate an enamel dish and cover which form part of a huge service made for the Portuguese family of Saldanha de Albuquerque. Although principally of China-Trade porcelain, the service incorporates a number of covered dishes decorated to match, but executed in enameled copper. The uniformity of style and detail argues for the existence of a group of artisans working closely together, presumably in the same shop, and sharing the foreign pigment for decorating both porcelain and enamel. It may be that the transfer to porcelain was initially effected in this manner, possibly even at Canton.

Following the course of the purple of Cassius in the later eighteenth century, one is presented with the curious spectacle of two great cultures, half a world apart, sharing a Dutch invention out of which each creates something strongly nationalistic. In Europe, the *rouge d'or* led to the *rose Pompadour* and, in the porcelains of Sèvres as in the paintings of Boucher, breathed the very spirit of the courtly style of Louis XV. In China, as the core of the *famille rose*, it became the quintessence of Imperial Ch'ien Lung taste in porcelain.

The westward flow of ideas had created a counterflow.

Ch'ing dynasty 1644-1912

Shun Chih	1644-1661
K'ang Hsi	1662-1722
Yung Chêng	1723-1735
Ch'ien Lung	1736-1795
Chia Ch'ing	1796-1820
Tao Kuang	1821-1850
Hsien Fêng	1851-1861
T'ung Chih	1862-1873
Kuang Hsü	1874-1908
Hsüan T'ung	1909-1912

Oriental porcelain frivolities

BY PAMELA C. COPELAND

WHEN IT WAS suggested that I should write an article on my collection of porcelain figurines, I was immediately impressed by how little I knew about them. Upon reflection, I determined to write the article if for no better reason than that my collection appears to be the only one in the United States that is restricted to Oriental porcelain figurines.

The need to have some objects—almost any—to place in two architectural cupboards in our newly constructed house was what started me on the collection nearly thirty years ago. They were to be merely accessory to the eighteenth-century American surroundings in which they were to be placed.

Already in our possession were a pair of recumbent elephants and a mussel shell which had been in my grandmother's house, and which she referred to simply as Chinese. The former, given her as a wedding present in 1858, were probably made in the Tao Kuang period The shell I believe to have been made after the reconstruction of the Ching-tê Chên factories in 1864, following the Taiping rebellion. As I had always been amused by the elephants, the die was cast: why not use them in one cupboard and acquire other figures to go with them? In 1937, with just that much knowledge, I went shopping.

The dealer with whom I first spoke said that indeed there were various animal forms in Oriental china. Would I consider Chinese export porcelain? In that manner I was introduced to the fascinating art of the Chinese potter of animal, bird, and figure subjects which appeal to me on account of their spontaneity, imagination, and whimsical humor. Since then, I've learned that this individual and highly specialized art was at its best during the reign of the Emperor K'ang Hsi.

Even though I had no ceramic scholarship, it was not long before I was able to notice certain differences among the objects themselves. My eye became aware of variations in form and proportion; of the fact that the decoration was either free and bold, or conventional, tight, and hesitant, so that the figures lacked a certain spirit. Later, I was to sense a difference in the quality of the modeling of the figures.

These untutored observations led me to ask a recognized authority in the field of Far Eastern art to examine the pieces I had acquired, in which I had a growing interest. His survey revealed that the pieces covered a span of three hundred years, from the reign of K'ang Hsi through the reign of Tao Kuang and even later. The opinions of this expert were substantiated by the group of scholars who participated in the seminar on ceramics held at the Henry Francis du Pont Winterthur Museum in March 1964. At the seminar it was also demonstrated that some of the figures were Japanese.

There was a wide discrepancy between this dating and the casual identifications that I found in a recheck of the bills for the figures, such as "mid-eighteenth century," "early 19th century," "circa 1780," or even just "antique Chinese Lowestoft." Moreover, some of the items offered to me as Chinese porcelain, and bought by me as such, have turned out to be of European manufacture. I realized that further study was needed, and that some technical knowledge is essential to the collector of these figures.

Chinese porcelain contains two feldspathic ingredients: kaolin, a highly plastic substance which remains white when fired, and petuntse, which is fusible. Figure forms, in general, were made by pressing thin cakes of moist clay against molds of the desired shape. A figure was usually composed of several different molded parts which were fitted together while still moist, and attached (luted) with a little slip. This joining operation required an adept artisan, as the quality of the figure depends upon the skill with which the component parts were put together. The more elaborate the figure form, the greater was the number of molds needed. The smaller pieces—hands, hats, scrolls, fruits—were luted on separately and often indicate the individuality, imagination, and even lack of training of the luter. It is essentially these personal variations that are the charm of the figures to me.

Another method of forming figures known as slip casting was a European process adopted by the Chinese. It is said by some to have been invented by Staffordshire potters as late as the 1740's, while others believe it originated in Italy. The porcelain mixture is diluted to the consistency of batter and poured into a mold. Figures that are slip cast are much thinner and smoother on the interior than the pressed forms.

Some of the most notable pieces of Chinese porcelain take the form of figures, animals, divinities, birds, and occasionally of real personages. By the late sixteenth century direct contact was freely established between Europe and China, and porcelain was an important trade item. It has been said that the animal, bird, and figure forms are the outcome of this increased contact with the Western world. Certainly, European taste affected the Chinese potter; nevertheless, many of these forms had been used by the Chinese for ages to represent the supernatural and mystical.

Except as noted,
all illustrations are from the author's collection;
photographs by Willard Stewart.

I AM FORTUNATE in having two groups of the so-called Governor Duf and his wife, and single figures of Louis XIV and Madame de Maintenon. The former show a European couple frequently said to represent one Diederik Durven (mispronounced Duf or Durf by the Chinese) and his wife; Durven, a Dutchman, was sent by the East India Company to Batavia in 1705 and was governor general there from 1728 until dismissed from office in 1731. It is now believed that this identification is one of the myths that have grown up around Chinese "Lowestoft," and that these figures simply portray anonymous Europeans living in the Orient (see ANTIQUES, January 1962, p. 112).

Though the two groups illustrated here are very similar, it is clear that they were made from different molds. In one group they are holding hands, in the other they are not. The hats are different, as are the wigs on the gentlemen. In one he has a bow tie and in the other he wears gaiters. There are also noticeable differences in the women's dresses, and in all of the faces. One base is rectangular and painted in iron red and aquamarine, while the other is lower and flower-edged, with a peony painted in the conventional rose color. There is still a third version of this couple portraying them dancing. All are decorated in *famille rose* colors and are of the Ch'ien Lung period.

The pair of figures always known as Louis XIV and Madame de Maintenon is one of three such pairs that were in the Ionides collection. The models vary considerably. In one, Louis XIV wears gloves and carries a hat in his right hand; in another, he carries a baton in his outstretched left hand. In the example illustrated, he wears no gloves, carries no hat or baton; but his left hand is outstretched. Madame de Maintenon may have her right hand free of her body or hanging at her side, while her left hand may be at her waist or outstretched, as in the illustration. There are also many versions of their clothes, which were probably copied from European engravings, but no subject escapes the Chinese modeler's touch of derision when he portrays the foreign barbarian. These figures, brilliantly painted, are in the *famille verte* decoration used during the reign of the Emperor K'ang Hsi.

In early Chinese mythology, mandarin ducks were a symbol of married bliss and fidelity. The large duck tureen shown is one of a pair modeled after Meissen originals made in 1781 (see Carl Albiker, *Die Meissner Porzellaniere*, Pl. LVI, Fig. 235). The illustration is of the drake, with black wing tips and brownish feet; the duck, not shown, has white wings with coral-color feet. On both, the breasts and tails are incised below the glaze with feather markings. The interiors have small numerals on bodies and lids. They date from the Ch'ien Lung period.

The other little duck tureen, painted in poor-quality enamels of the *famille rose* palette, is undoubtedly modeled after one made at the Bow or Chelsea factories which the Chinese copied, even attempting the marks on the interior of the body. I seriously doubt that my example in Chinese porcelain is any earlier than late Chia Ch'ing. There are examples in other collections which may be of an earlier date.

Top left.
European couple,
Ch'ien Lung, 1736-1795.
Height 9 inches.

Bottom left.
European couple,
Ch'ien Lung, 1736-1795.
Height 10 inches.

Top right.
Louis XIV and Madame de Maintenon,
K'ang Hsi, 1662-1722.
Heights 10 and 8½ inches.
Ex coll. *The Honorable Mrs. Ionides.*

Center right.
Duck tureen, one of a pair,
Ch'ien Lung, 1736-1795.
Length 7 inches.
Ex coll. *Lady Baron.*

Bottom right.
Duck tureen,
late Chia Ch'ing, 1796-1820.
Length 3¼ inches.

THE WATER-BUFFALO VASES clearly show the evolution and, in the opinion of some, the deterioration of a design. The one illustrated on the left has been in the Victoria and Albert Museum since 1856. I took the vase on the right to London in order to compare the two. The molded details show a close similarity, but the pieces are not from an identical mold. The trunk of one is painted over with flower sprays and butterflies in *famille rose* colors, the other is painted in naturalistic brown. However, the coloring of the *ling chih* fungus, one of the Taoist symbols of long life, employs the same blue and turquoise enamels. Both vases are thought to date between about 1796 and 1820, but mine gives a strong impression of being the later. Two vases similar to mine were seen at a recent antiques show, one with a water buffalo and the other with a spotted deer, which is also a symbol of longevity associated with Taoism. Therefore, one can assume that these little pieces were probably intended for presentation and not for the export market.

It is said that the Portuguese, arriving in Macao in 1516, were responsible for bringing to China the first sleek, hound-type dog that the Chinese had ever seen, but I doubt it. The men of the Han dynasty (206 B. C.-220 A. D.) were great hunters, to judge from the number of hunting scenes they depicted which showed two breeds of dog: the fleet greyhound they used for deer hunting and a heavier dog of the mastiff type. I have also seen in a European private collection a seated hound made in the Han dynasty of a porcelaneous ware with a green glaze which is certainly the antecedent of the hounds illustrated here.

The large figure of a seated dog dates from the period of Ch'ien Lung. The hair is naturalistically colored in brown with white markings; from the sepia collar hangs a gilded bell of submission. An unusual detail is the cutout in the shape of a pomegranate in the back. The pomegranate came from Parthia to China in the second century B. C. It was portrayed in the Han dynasty and the Taoists adopted it as their symbol of longevity or quest for immortality.

The figure of the seated spaniel on the left is also naturalistically colored in brown but the painting is less good than on the large dog. Nor is the expression as well done about the eyes: the spaniel is definitely staring. These facts plus the use of pale aquamarine for the collar places this dog in the reign of Chia Ch'ing.

The hound on the right shows inferior molding and sloppy coloring done by stippling with a sponge rather than by painting with a brush. The eyes have no expression. These facts indicate that the dog was made after the re-opening of the kiln in 1864, when quality in workmanship was lacking. Even in the illustrations one can note the variations in modeling and painting of the eyes. The best are rounded—three dimensional—with the iris left in the biscuit. The pupil is always black or brown enamel. The seated figures of spaniels one finds enameled in coral red with the collar and bell in aquamarine are also of this late period.

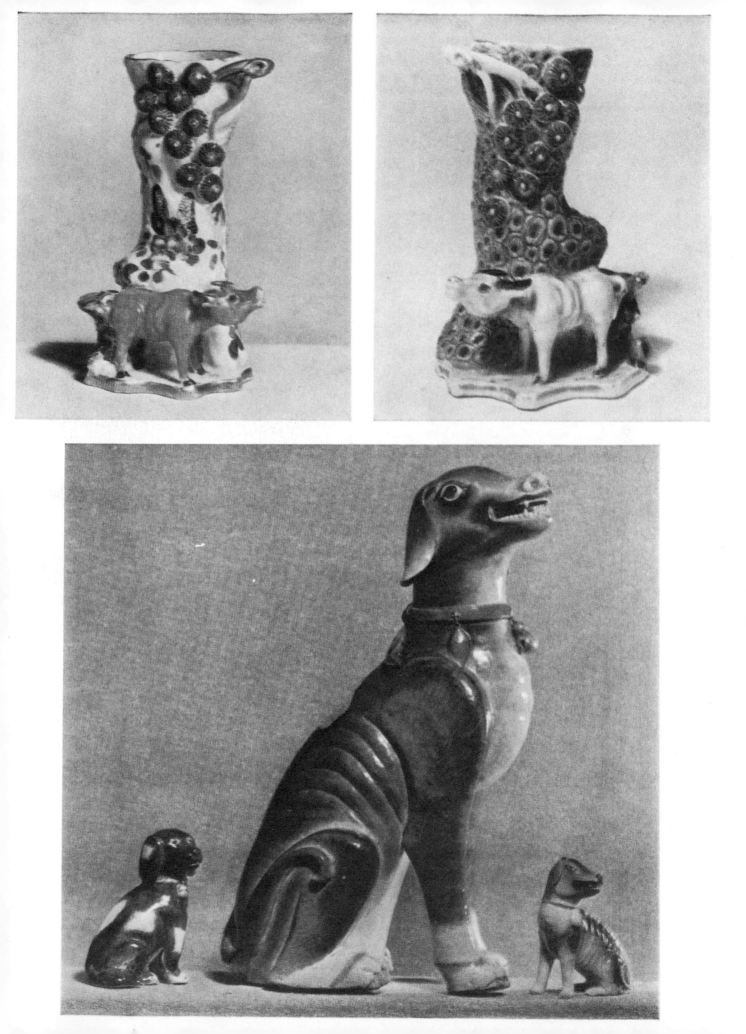

THE COCKEREL ON THE LEFT, one of a pair of the K'ang Hsi period, is superbly modeled with life and vigor in its body and its head turned to the front. The crest and wattles are in deep red on the biscuit, while the brilliant plumage is enameled in *rouge de fer* on the head and down the neck, with the wings in green, blue, and black. The long tail feathers are also black. He is standing on a pierced, dark-brown rockwork base with the other foot curled under him.

The cock is the bird of fame and when shown with a flower it must be the peony, the flower of riches and honor. The standing cockerel, one of a pair, in the center, has proven to be twentieth century, not only because of its clumsy, heavy modeling, with a useless leg unable to support the body, but also because of the use of the wrong flower. That is something a Chinese would never have done, unless for export when he felt that no one would know or care about the correct use of symbols. These cockerels are decorative ornaments but that is all that can be said in their favor from a collector's point of view.

The *famille rose* cock tureen on the right is an extremely rare item of the Ch'ien Lung period. The painting is of the finest quality in brilliant enamels, the long feathers touched with gilding. The painting of the combs of these three cocks has achieved very different effects. The *rouge de fer* applied to the biscuit of the standing cock is dull and dark. That of the modern cock is off-color and applied too thickly so that it lacks the translucency and unctuous richness which is the special quality of the Chinese enameler. This quality may be seen in all its glory on the cock tureen, where the fine color is applied over the glaze.

And now we come to the elephants. The naïve and fanciful portrayal of these animals has fostered the belief that they were unknown to the Chinese and were modeled from imagination only. But a mention of the elephant occurs in the *Book of Odes* compiled by Confucius, and elephant-shape bronze sacrificial vessels for wine were in use during the Chou dynasty (1122-255 B. C.) under which Confucius lived. It seems probable that the elephant came to China from India through the introduction of Buddhism; the elephant is associated with Buddha as the animal which carries the vase of sacred jewels. Why it is so often portrayed as a rather cozy figure, I've no idea.

The tureen in the form of a recumbent elephant, with a small spotted black and white dog on his back, is one of a pair which have matching saucers. They are of the Ch'ien Lung period. The large figure of the seated elephant has a creamy gray body and yellow tail and toes, while the ear is lined with pink. The end of the trunk is clearly formed in the *ju-i* head motif. An inscription inside the body states it was made in the time of Chia Ch'ing, coming from the Jade Palace. The elephants in blue and white have unusually fine painting depicting the Eight Immortals indulging in various pursuits, in a landscape with the gate of the city in the background. These date from the latter part of the K'ang Hsi period.

Top left.
Cockerel, one of a pair,
K'ang Hsi, 1662-1722.
Height 14 inches.
Formerly in a Scottish collection.

Top center.
Standing cockerel, one of a pair,
twentieth century.
Height 17 inches.

Top right.
Cock tureen,
Ch'ien Lung, 1736-1795.
Height 15½ inches.
Ex coll. *Lady Baron.*

Center left.
Elephant tureen with matching saucer, one of a pair,
Ch'ien Lung, c. 1760.
Length of tureen, 6¾ inches.

Center right.
Seated elephant,
Chia Ch'ing, 1796-1820.
Height 12 inches.

Bottom.
Pair of standing elephants,
late K'ang Hsi, 1662-1722.
Height 5½ inches.

THE FIGURE of the recumbent stag is painted in *rouge de fer* with white spots and black hooves. The antlers are carved of wood and are removable, a feature that can be seen also on a blue and white spotted deer of the sixteenth century with the figure of the god of longevity seated on his back, in the British Museum. I believe this stag to have been made at the end of the reign of Ch'ien Lung. (It appeared on the cover of ANTIQUES for December 1952.)

The large and important biscuit figure of a standing stag is naturalistically modeled and colored with manganese cloven hooves and yellow body, brown fur markings and white spots, and has antlers which have been partially restored. He has a very provocative and alert eye, and is evidently well aware that he is the object of much fervent admiration. He is of the K'ang Hsi period.

The remaining figures are Japanese porcelain. The tiger is an example of Arita ware of the late seventeenth century and is one of a pair. They are naturalistically modeled, seated, with their heads turned. The rockwork bases are decorated in bamboo and grass. The well-modeled lively fish is a tureen. The scales are picked out in gold. He cannot be dated any earlier than the very end of the eighteenth century. The little figure of a boy with a drum is one of a pair done in the school of Kakiemon.

I am hoping to acquire a fine human figure in Japanese porcelain for comparison with its Chinese counterpart, but my main interest will always remain in Chinese ceramics. I intend to search for the animal forms listed in the early bills of lading of the English East India Company, some of which appear to have been made in quantity though so far I have been unable to find an example.

In the meantime, I have learned not to purchase any more "unique" specimens. It is far wiser to buy a figure that bears some similarity to one in another collection or that has been recorded in a publication. Also, I have learned to resist figures, human or animal, with blue eyes! They are fatal.

My interest in this fascinating art of the Chinese potter grows with my increasing knowledge of this medium of expression.

Top left.
Recumbent stag,
Ch'ien Lung, 1736-1795.
Height 10½ inches.

Bottom left.
Standing stag,
K'ang Hsi, 1662-1722.
Height 22½ inches.
Ex coll. *The Honorable Mrs. Ionides.*

Top right.
Tiger, one of a pair,
Japanese, Arita, late seventeenth century.
Height 9½ inches.

Center right.
Fish tureen,
Japanese, late eighteenth century.
Length 6½ inches.

Bottom right.
Boy with a drum, one of a pair,
Japanese, school of Kakiemon, c. 1700.
Height 2½ inches.

Imitations of Chinese Lowestoft

By Homer Eaton Keyes

IMITATION is said to be the sincerest form of flattery: but it is likewise one of the insincerest means of commercial exploitation. The popularity of old porcelains and earthenwares and the comparative ease of approximating their appearance have led to their being both flattered and exploited to an almost unbelievable extent. The flattery may be credited chiefly to sundry enterprising manufacturers who know how to capitalize the "quest for the quaint" pursued by folk who have no concern for the actual age or authenticity of objects in which they find a sentimental or æsthetic appeal. Actual exploitation is mainly restricted to those shopkeepers who represent reasonably accurate copies and adaptations of early designs as genuine originals. There is, of course, no gainsaying that the makers of imitation porcelains, like makers of other imitations, often play into the hands of the retailer of spurious antiques. Nevertheless, so large a proportion of their output is sold legitimately and through legitimate channels for what it really is that they may be held guiltless of dishonest intentions. There is nothing improper in copying; but only in misrepresenting the copy as an original work. In the domain of porcelains, so-called Chinese Lowestoft has been so widely adapted, copied, and fraudulently improved, that no consideration of the general theme would be complete without reference to this sometimes perplexing blot on its 'scutcheon.

Fig. 1 — IMITATION OF CHINESE LOWESTOFT, BY SAMSON OF PARIS
Rose jar, whose profusion of decorative motives results in overloading the piece instead of achieving the balance and restraint characteristic of genuine Chinese items

At least one group of what we may term adaptations of Lowestoft is utterly free from any taint of disingenuousness. This group, sold under the trade name of *Spode's Lowestoft*, while it carefully reproduces a number of the old Chinese European-market decorative patterns, receives the latter in part by a process of printing instead of freehand enameling. The body of the ware is not porcelain, but a fine earthen material. Hence, if a piece is held against a strong light, no translucence will be observable. At its best in plates, Spode's Lowestoft may be recommended to persons who wish their dining-room fitments to be in correct eighteenth-century taste, even if not of true eighteenth-century vintage.

Far less readily distinguishable from original pieces, whose fabric they closely approximate and whose decoration they reproduce often with deceptive fidelity, are the Lowestoft reproductions made in Paris by the firms of Samson and of Vivinis. Concerning the former, ANTIQUES published, in May 1923, an adequate article by the late Frederick Litchfield. The founder of the establishment, M. Edmé Samson, a ceramic decorator, began business in 1845. His son Emile developed into a potter and manufacturer who has won world-wide repute for his imitations, not only of Oriental porcelains — both Chinese and Japanese — but of old faïences and enamels, and of the earthenware and porcelain products of various old European and English

Fig. 2a — ARMORIAL PLATE, CHINESE
Note delicacy and refinement of decoration.
Formerly in the collection of W. Quennell, Esq.

Fig. 2b — ARMORIAL PLATE, IMITATION BY SAMSON
Note difference between quality of design and character of technique in this and in Figure 2a

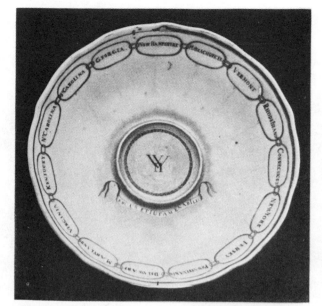

Fig. 3a — Saucer from the Martha
Washington Teaset, Chinese
From the Metropolitan Museum of Art

Fig. 3b — Imitation of Martha Washington Plate, French
With better lettering than usual, and a curious reduction of sunburst to a single group of rays.
From the collection of Mrs. Katharine Willis

factories. Many of the dainty figurines of eighteenth-century type to be found in glass and china stores, and in too many antique shops, emanate from the Paris ateliers of Samson; for, at last accounts, the business was still flourishing.

Samson's copies of Chinese vases and similar important pieces in the *famille verte* category are astonishingly accurate and none too readily reveal their lack of complete *bona fides*. His ventures into the later realm of the *famille rose* are less successful, probably because of the difficulty of capturing quite the facility of touch, and quite the exquisite refinement of enamel color that characterize the best Chinese work of this period. Of plates, vases, teapots, caddies, pitchers, and what not else, in the manner of the armorial Chinese Lowestoft, Samson has turned out tremendous quantities. After long experiment he has succeeded in evolving a porcelain body closely approximating that of the Chinese wares, and his workfolk have been well trained in following Chinese decorative forms.

So many owners of Samson pieces are firmly convinced that their possessions are choice examples of Oriental craftsmanship that we may not deny a fairly close resemblance between imitations and originals. Nevertheless, to the fairly practiced eye this resemblance is usually rather superficial. The body and glaze of Samson's porcelain are usually much whiter than those of the Chinese wares, and the pieces themselves do not show the evident traces of the potter's hand that are discoverable on most Chinese items. Lay a

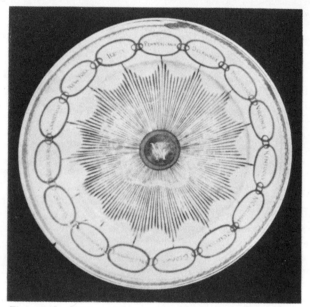

Fig. 3c — Imitation of Martha Washington Plate, by Samson
With poorer lettering than that of Figure 3b, and coarse sunburst

Fig. 4a — The Vivinis Mark (*enlarged*)

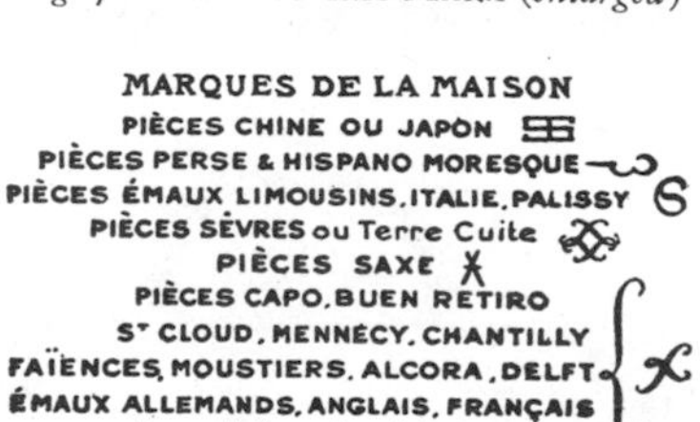

MARQUES DE LA MAISON
PIÈCES CHINE OU JAPON
PIÈCES PERSE & HISPANO MORESQUE
PIÈCES ÉMAUX LIMOUSINS, ITALIE, PALISSY
PIÈCES SÈVRES ou Terre Cuite
PIÈCES SAXE
PIÈCES CAPO, BUEN RETIRO
ST CLOUD, MENNECY, CHANTILLY
FAÏENCES, MOUSTIERS, ALCORA, DELFT,
ÉMAUX ALLEMANDS, ANGLAIS, FRANÇAIS
Porcelaines Anglaises, etc

Fig. 4b — Marks Used on Porcelain and Pottery by Samson
The first of the list is that employed on pseudo-Oriental goods

Samson armorial plate face down beside an apparently similar Chinese example. The one will be almost perfectly smooth and even of surface; the other will show innumerable slight irregularities and depressions that look like, and probably are, the finger marks of the workman impressed in the biscuit while the wet clay was being pressed down upon its mold.

Again, Samson inclines to overload his armorial pieces with a profusion of decorative motives in rather coarse scale, a practice against which the Chinese ceramic painter was safeguarded by an unerring sense of balance and restraint. This overloading occurs perhaps more frequently on the French jars, vases, and pots than upon the plates. It is, for example, all too obvious on the Samson rose jar of Figure 1, but less apparent on the Samson plate of Figure 2b. The latter, however, when brought into comparison with the fine Chinese piece shown beside it, reveals in the handling of its ornamental details a lack both of refinement and of creative *élan* that betrays its spuriousness.

In theory, all of the fabrications emanating from the house of Samson carry the maker's mark as an indication of their origin. Each class of goods has its own distinguishing symbol, and since these symbols are not so well known as they should be, the entire series is here reprinted from Mr. Litchfield's article, though only the first one of the tabulations is employed on pseudo-Oriental goods (*Fig. 4*).

Fig. 5a — WASHINGTON MEMORIAL PLATTER, CHINESE
From a set made in China as a token of mourning for Washington's death.
From the collection of Mrs. W. Murray Crane

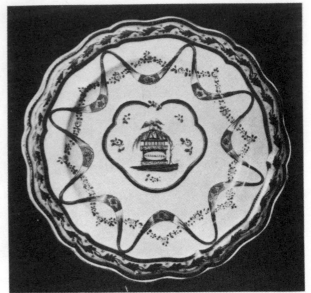

Fig. 5b — WASHINGTON MEMORIAL PLATE, IMITATION BY VIVINIS
Details of Figures 5a and 5b are shown below.
From the collection of C. E. Griffith

Of late, it would seem, these marks are not applied so consistently and conscientiously as was formerly the case.

Though less widely known than the house of Samson, that of Vivinis, likewise located in Paris, in our opinion produces better interpretations of Chinese armorial and *famille rose* porcelains. The firm's sign manual is a curious little square character, of somewhat Oriental flavor, inscribed in red on the bottom

of plates and other porcelain utensils (*Fig. 4*). It may be accompanied by a pattern number.

Vivinis's armorial and floral-sprigged designs in the Oriental manner are less liable to excessive profusion than are Samson's. One of his best imitations of Lowestoft is a rendering of the Chinese Washington memorial design cited in ANTIQUES for April 1932 (*p. 173*). Original and imitation are illustrated in Figure 5a and b. The latter is from a set of a dozen plates purchased as genuine Lowestoft for a wedding gift. From perhaps half of the dozen the vendor had laboriously scratched the Vivinis mark, and had then apparently given up the task. This mark, by the way, is far from well known even by connoisseurs of ceramics. We have seen more than one set of Vivinis "Lowestoft" catalogued by distinguished auction houses as "Worcester" or "Worcester type."

While the pseudo-Oriental products of Samson and Vivinis are probably the best of their kind, they are by no means the only ones in the field. Some European manufacturer, whose identity we have been unable to determine, has generously spread the market with imitations of the blue-with-gold-star border American armorial eagle design. He, or others, have

produced dinner sets of what appear to be purely imaginary armorial significance, but yet sufficiently beguiling in general aspect to impose upon innocence. The body of such of the latter imitations as we have examined is, however, not comparable to that achieved by Samson. It is heavy, and, though achieving a distinct curdling of surface glaze — too marked, in fact — is barely translucent. Apparently very few of these services have been brought to this country; for they are rather too coarse in texture and decoration to appeal to the particular person, no matter how inexpert.

The previously mentioned wares may none of them be considered in themselves fraudulent. Some are consistently carried in stock by dealers in modern glass and ceramics, and are sold as reproductions. There is no good reason why they should not be purchased and used precisely like any porcelain of historic implications. For lamp bases, furthermore, pseudo-Oriental urns and jars made in Europe are often desirable. Inevitably, however, such things lend themselves so readily to fraudulent purposes that it is well to be aware of their existence and to guard against being taken in by them. Likewise it frequently happens that,

Fig. 6 — EUROPEAN IMITATION OF AMERICAN-MARKET ARMORIAL EAGLE DESIGN
Blue-with-gold-star border. Rather coarsely executed

through sales of private effects, individual French pieces are released in the open market to the confusion of the inexpert dealer and the detriment of the casual collector.

European makers have produced comparatively little Lowestoft in imitation of American-market Chinese designs other than the blue-with-gold-star border types. The *Washington Memorial* plates are one notable exception to the rule. Another may be found in mugs and jugs adorned with floral festoons and sprigs and,

Fig. 7a — New York State Arms, Chinese
In the collections of the Rhode Island School of Design

Fig. 7b — New York State Arms, Fraudulent
Painted on real Chinese porcelain after removal of original decoration

by way of further ornament, portraying a ship surmounted by the motto *Success to the Fleet.* It is regrettable to note that a jug of this kind brought several hundred dollars at a New York auction not many years ago. At another auction, a pair of European vases showing the American armorial eagle sold for many times the price asked at a shop of imported reproductions whose show window on Third Avenue was, at the time, full of just such articles.

But the most dangerous imitations of Chinese Lowestoft are those achieved by removing the decoration from genuine old pieces of Oriental ware and substituting a rarer design that materially enhances their apparent value. This, obviously, is done with dishonest intent; and, because the porcelain itself is beyond criticism, the forgery is often hard to detect and almost impossible to prove — at least to the satisfaction of a jury. Readers of these notes will recall the sensation caused, not long since, by the controversy over a tea set bearing the New York State coat of arms. The set had been virtually sold, as a family heirloom, to a prominent collector, who, becoming suspicious of his purchase, submitted it to expert examination. The experts agreed that the porcelain itself was old Chinese; but that the coat of arms decoration was a recent forgery. Nevertheless, the ensuing row was not settled until Edward Crowninshield found the china painter who confessed to having perpetrated the work.

For reasons unknown, the arms of New York have been specially favored by the forger, though weird versions of the Cincinnati pattern occasionally turn up, and copies of still more ambitious patriotic embellishments have been attempted. A notable example of the latter is a plate from which the original flower sprigs have been removed to make way for a spread eagle perched on accoutrements of war in emulation of the device pictured on page 387 of Antiques for November 1930.

As we have already remarked, the obvious authenticity of the ware upon which these fraudulent designs are enameled carries with it a presumption of complete integrity that is not readily overcome even by the careful buyer. Seldom, however, can the modern imitator give a wholly convincing air to his handiwork. Something will be

wrong about his touch, or in the forms that he outlines. The swift, sure, calligraphic stroke of the Chinese artist will be wanting, and his amusing distortions of human and animal figures will be bunglingly translated. Such disqualifications will usually be felt, even if not fully recognized by the sensitive eye; but the subtlest admonition to consultation and comparison thus conveyed should never be ignored.

In some instances, examination of an item that seems too good to be true will reveal traces of a previous decoration. Since the eliminative process is usually accomplished either with the aid of abrasives or of acids, the porcelain glaze seldom escapes without acquiring dull spots or disfiguring scratches. While not always noticeable on first examination, some of these are likely to reveal themselves when the "improved" piece is held at different angles to the light. Whether or not the violet ray would enable the detection of new passages of enamel on old Chinese porcelain, we cannot say. Apparently, no experiments to that end have been made; at any rate, we have failed to encounter published record of them.

Unfortunately, it is quite impossible to give written directions or pictorial demonstrations that will be sufficiently clear to

Fig. 8 — Forged Decoration on Genuine Chinese Porcelain
Hybrid armorial eagle with pseudo-Cincinnati emblem

enable the neophyte easily to distinguish the false from the true either in Chinese porcelains or in any other domain of collecting. The most that words and illustrations may do is to direct attention. Reasonable expertness will come only by the actual seeing and handling of a good many specimens until vision is sharpened, and remembered comparisons become a part of instinctive critical equipment. To Ginsburg and Levy of New York, we have been indebted for opportunity to study a number of fine specimens of Chinese Lowestoft side by side with imitations and with out-and-out forgeries that the firm has been at pains to collect for its own instruction and that of its clients. A number of the illustrations accompanying these notes are from that helpful source.

Once the beginning collector has become fairly adept in distinguishing genuine Chinese Lowestoft from its imitations, he may well concern himself with the variations in quality that occur among specimens of unquestionable authenticity. On that topic far too little has been said or written.

The Yesterday and Today of Oriental Lowestoft

By J. A. Lloyd Hyde

IN THE *Providence Gazette* of May, 1804, appeared the following advertisement:

Yam Shinqua, Chinaware Merchant at Canton, begs leave respectfully to inform the American Merchants, Supercargoes, and Captains that he procures to be manufactured in the best manner, all sorts of Chinaware with Arms, Cyphers and other Decorations (if required) painted in a very superior style and on the most reasonable Terms. All orders carefully and promptly attended to. Canton (China) Jan. 8, 1804.

Note the phrase *procures to be manufactured*. The Chinese advertiser of more than a century and a quarter ago was neither a maker nor a decorator of porcelain. He was a middleman, who, no doubt, kept in his Canton shop a considerable stock of ware ready decorated with patterns known to be popular in the overseas trade, and, in addition, a considerable quantity of undecorated ware whose embellishment could be accomplished at reasonably short notice by local artists. To meet the requirements of particular customers, whose quantitative and qualitative demands were out of the ordinary, it would be necessary to take time — perhaps a full year — to "procure" the manufacture of specially designated forms and decorations. All this involved a somewhat complicated process. Orders for the blank ware had first to be placed with the potteries at Ching-tê Chên, four hundred miles to the north of Canton in the interior province of Kiang-si. Then as it came from the kilns, the porcelain must be packed for its long journey to

Fig. 1 — A Glimpse of Honam
The island opposite Canton where porcelain decorating has been carried on for centuries.
Photographs from the author's collection

Canton — a painful progress by river junk, horseback, and human portage. Arrived at its destination it was unpacked, examined, sorted, and transported to the shops of the decorators.

Porcelain painting in China has always been a village industry; and as most Chinese villages are made up of one large and ancient family, with complicated ramifications, it is really a family industry — each family, or village, jealous of its reputation for special skill in ceramic decoration. Most of the villages where the Canton artists worked were, and still are, situated on the island of Honam opposite the city, and today one may still find the families at work grinding their own colors and patiently applying them as of old — the little girls devoting themselves to one detail of the pattern, the little boys to another, while their elders handle the more difficult parts. Yam Shinqua, in common with the other porcelain merchants, of course knew the capabilities of the various artist families on the Island of Honam, and placed his orders accordingly, when necessary, supplying drawings which the decorator was instructed to follow to the letter.

The methods of 1804 were almost precisely those which had been in vogue from the very beginning of the trade in porcelain between China and the western world. Probably they even antedate the year 1627, when, as we learn from the records of the East India Company, the ship *Catharine* sailed from Macao for England with fifty-three tubs of chinaware. They had not

Fig. 2 — AMERICAN EAGLE PLATE: CHINESE LOWESTOFT (*c. 1800*)
Made for the Nichols family of Salem. A mug bearing much the same major design was illustrated in ANTIQUES for November, 1930, page 387

Fig. 3 — CHINESE PLATE
From a Chinese porcelain dessert service until recently in the possession of an English family. Rich gold border and delicately painted figures and landscape

altered in 1734 when five European vessels left Canton, their holds heavy with almost a million pieces of porcelain, for which the Chinese merchants had received some £12,000 sterling. They are, indeed, in force today.

In the old days, the porcelain was solidly packed in heavy wooden cases, which the ship captains stowed deep in the bottom of their vessels to serve both as ballast and as a "flooring" upon which other merchandise was placed. This practice was continued on English merchantmen until the year 1800, when the East India Company ceased to handle porcelain as a venture on its own account, and thus materially reduced the quantity of the ware carried in its vessels. Quite conceivably the growing popularity of English domestic wares and the increasing cost of handling the more commercial types of Chinese porcelain account for this move. Yet it was not until 1833, when the company lost the Chinese monopoly, that specially decorated porcelain — the so-called "Oriental Lowestoft" — was no longer manufactured. Twenty years later the destruction of the kilns at Ching-tê Chên, during the T'ai P'ing rebellion, put a quietus on Chinese enterprise in the field of porcelain. Later rebuilt, these kilns still supply the world market for Oriental porcelain, and still ship their product to Canton to be decorated.

It was, if possible, to weigh such historical information as I have above summarized against whatever evidence might be revealed to me on the spot, that, within the past three years, I have made three trips to China, and have visited Canton and such other centres as Macao, Hong Kong, and Shanghai. I hoped to discover here and there some relics of the old porcelain trade, some leftovers of eighteenth-century American and European-market wares among the shops, and at the same time to learn, at first hand, whether or not the Chinese porcelain-makers of today were as skilful as their ancestors of previous generations.

Part of my quest was unfruitful. Souvenirs of earlier trading days I found, but, as might be expected, they were articles of European and American manufacture that had been brought to the Orient to exchange for silks, tea, spices, and porcelain. It is interesting to note that the first foreign consulate of the newborn United States was established not in England or on the Continent, as one might suppose, but in Canton, as early as 1784, when the stars and stripes took their place among the flags of twelve other powers in front of the East India Company's warehouses. In the same year the American vessel *Empress of China*, having delivered a cargo of ginseng to the Chinese, sailed homeward for the port of New York with a cargo that included over six tons of porcelain. The articles of commerce subsequently sent eastward from American ports included things more durable than medicinal

herbs. I have, for example, found in the shops of Canton and Macao Sandwich glass lamps — vintage of the 1830's. Indeed, foreign glass, particularly in the form of lighting devices, seems to have been welcomed by the Orientals, who bought vast quantities of English and Irish glass hanging lights, hurricane shades, candlesticks and candle shades in a variety of styles.

Of eighteenth and early nineteenth-century porcelain, obviously designed for foreign markets, very little is discoverable on its native heath — and none at all that belongs to the armorial category, unless it be an occasional stray piece made for some foreigner long resident in China. As for the present status of porcelain-making and decorating, the case seems to be as follows. Ware continues to be made in Ching-tê Chên, where the old formulæ are still employed, and the old shapes closely approximated. The texture of the ware apparently differs little from that with which our ancestral Lowestoft has made us familiar. On smaller pieces the "lemon peel" glaze is like that of old. The richly curdled glaze characteristic of the large old-time shapes is seldom encountered in the modern items of similar size. The color of the old body and of

Fig. 4 — MODERN COPY OF EIGHTEENTH-CENTURY BOWL (*1930*)
Painted in Canton by way of testing the skill of the modern Chinese porcelain decorator. Not an unsuccessful piece of work

Fig. 5 — MODERN ARMORIAL PLATTER (*1930*)
Evidence of the deterioration in the art of porcelain painting in China

the new when examined by transmitted light appears to be the same; but the modern glazed surface as viewed externally by daylight is grayer, perhaps muddier, in tint, though the variation is so slight as to be noted only by careful direct comparison.

The fine art of decoration has, however, sadly deteriorated. It is still possible to order porcelain decorated in a special manner, but the carelessness with which commissions are executed and the exasperation induced by interminable delays are sufficient to discourage even the most ardent enthusiast. Wishing to try the experiment for myself, I proceeded according to immemorial custom and applied to one of the local porcelain merchants, Ng Cheung, who carries large stocks of export ware. The firm was not enthusiastic about undertaking my order. Eventually, however, they directed me to one of their decorators on the island of Honam. He was, they informed me, the last survivor of the old school. The results of his efforts are here reproduced — one a copy of an old Dutch-market design on a bowl that I supplied as a model, the other a coat of arms.

The first is reasonably successful — so much so that it might easily pass muster as antique. But the armorial product is rather dismal, with its coarsely handled borders, ghostly bird, and scroll that is both badly drawn and incorrectly spelled.

III European Market

In addition to the three largest importers of Chinese export ware, namely Portugal, the Netherlands, and Great Britain, a number of other European countries received large quantities of porcelain. Such imported pieces were often decorated with designs especially created for home consumption. Among these are the service made for Catherine the Great with the Russian double eagle; the services commemorating Louis XVI and Marie Antoinette for the French market; pieces with Meissen decorations for the German market; the service with the arms of Charles VI, Emperor of Austria; and numerous services made for the Scandanavian countries, all with appropriate decorative ornament.

The first article in this series, "Design Sources of Early China Trade Porcelain," is important for several reasons. The author, Clare LeCorbeiller, shows that the first pieces of export ware ordered decorated with Western designs were made for King Manuel I of Portugal in the period 1517–1521. These were painted with the King's coat-of-arms and were followed by pieces with the arms of other Portuguese families. Previously, it was thought that the first armorial pieces dated from the end of the sixteenth century.

Among the excellent illustrations included in this article are two of special interest. Plate II (p. 81) is an illustration of a profusely decorated floral plate with the arms of Robert French on the back. Armorial pieces with arms painted on the *back* are very rarely found. The tea service illustrated in Plate IV (p. 85) is of a distinct color design of yellow and violet; while it contains no rose or red colors, the set is still classified as belonging to the *famille rose* variety.

John Goldsmith Phillips, author of the well-known book on the McCann collection at the Metropolitan Museum of Art, *China Trade Porcelain,* presents his views that Western ceramic wares were used more often as models for the Chinese than were silver pieces in the eighteenth century. The similarities between contemporary European and Chinese pieces are strikingly illustrated. As Phillips notes, however, "none of these China-Trade porcelains are identical copies, although some of them were evidently made with just that idea in mind."

"Chinese Porcelain Figures of Westerners" by Joseph T. Butler illustrates a number of figurines of Westerners and highlights the fact that all-white pieces were made at Têhua in Fukien province. This is a fact often overlooked because of the dominance of Ching-tê Chên as the center of export porcelain production, particularly of polychrome figurine work in addition to the more familiar armorial services. Butler states that, with a few very rare exceptions, all the figures decorated in *famille rose* colors were made at Ching-tê Chên, while the all-white glaze, or *blanc-de-Chine,* figures came from Têhua.

The next article, "Porcelain as Room Decoration in Eighteenth-Century England," by Robert J. Charleston of the Victoria and Albert Museum, contains some interesting information as to the dates of manufacture of various forms. It also explains the shifts of fashion during the late seventeenth century and throughout the eighteenth century in England and the continent which resulted in a demand for particular porcelain forms. He points out that by the middle of the seventeenth century, tea and coffee were coming into use as beverages and this resulted in a large demand for the component pieces of services.

Charleston also traces the use of china for room decoration. Popular first on the continent for purely decorative purposes, the passion for Chinoiserie was introduced in England by Queen Mary II who had amassed a great collection while still in Holland. Daniel Defoe, describing Hampton Court in the 1720s after it had been thoroughly stuffed with jars, beakers, and vases by Queen Mary II, commented, 'The Queen brought in the Custom or Humour, as I may call it, of furnishing Houses with China-ware, which increased to a strange degree afterwards, piling their China upon the Tops of Cabinets, Scrutores, and every Chimney-piece, to the Tops of the Ceilings, and even setting up Shelves for their China-ware, where they wanted such places." Visitors to such a continental palace as the Schönbrunn in Vienna will also recognize this description of the "chinamania" which pleasantly afflicted the royal families of Europe.

The two final articles, "Dutch Decorators of Chinese Porcelain" and "German and English Decorators of Chinese Porcelain" are by one of the great authorities on early Chinese porcelain, W. B. Honey. The introductory note by Homer Keyes to the first article is very informative in itself on the subject of Western decorations. In it Keyes states that he had specifically requested Honey to write on this knotty and controversial subject for the magazine.

In both articles Honey's subject is the decorative work produced by painters in the late 1600s and throughout the eighteenth century, and not the "clobbered" pieces. This term, he states "is better reserved for the crude over-painting of blue-and-white, best exemplified by some nineteenth-century English work. . . ." The artists of which Honey writes are considerably more accomplished. The Dutch, as early importers, led the way in the decoration of a considerable amount of porcelain beginning around 1700. Germans, more accomplished in the art, produced relatively successful enameled designs throughout the mid-1700s. The English were last, but among the painters working with Chinese porcelains were the father of the well-known Thomas Baxter, also known as Thomas, and John Giles.

Despite the skill exhibited by the early European decorators, the designs themselves usually stand apart from those executed in China. According to Honey, there are several ways to detect the European origin. Some of these pieces have an overglaze decoration in bright colors laid over an underglaze blue decoration. Sometimes the applied color decoration will attempt to follow the outline of the blue and white design, but often it will not. Any geometric gold design or gold border that is laid on top of a blue and white design should be suspect. A gold design border that augments a *famille rose* design but seems too elaborate for the piece is also suspect. The gold used by Western painters has a bright, brassy look compared with the rich color used by the Chinese.

In the case of Western decoration on plain white poreclain or *blanc-de-Chine* made at Têhua in Fukien, Honey points out that the Chinese achieved a meticulousness in their decoration which seems to surpass that of the Westerners. This is especially true in comparing the Chinese execution of a coat-of-arms with a European example.

As to "clobbered" or fake decoration, the detective work is a great deal easier. Such added touches were given, in Honey's words, "in London to a great deal of usually indifferent Chinese blue-and-white during the second quarter of the nineteenth century." "Spots and rough foliage," he explains, "of crude pink, yellow, red, and yellowish green were added in almost complete disregard of the blue designs which were often entirely covered up."

Design sources of
early China Trade porcelain

BY CLARE LE CORBEILLER,

Assistant curator, Western European arts, Metropolitan Museum of Art

China Trade porcelain began appearing in ANTIQUES nearly fifty years ago, when the Oriental ware made for the Occidental market was so little understood that it was thought by some to have been made in England and usually went by the erroneous name of Chinese Lowestoft. A series of articles by Homer Eaton Keyes, of which the first appeared in March 1928, went far toward correcting popular misconceptions about the ware and indeed laid the groundwork for all that has been written about it since. Now Mrs. Le Corbeiller presents recent discoveries concerning the design sources of both forms and decorations for some of the earliest China Trade porcelain.

Fig. 1. Jug with the arms (upside down) of Manoel I, made for the Portuguese market, probably 1517-1521. Height 7⅜ inches.

Except as noted, all porcelains illustrated are recent additions to the Helena Woolworth McCann Collection at the Metropolitan Museum of Art, purchased through gifts of the Winfield Foundation.

Pl. I. Cup and saucer, one of a pair,
made for the European market, 1740-1750.
Marked in underglaze blue with a copy of the Meissen *AR*.
Height of cup, 3¼ inches.

Pl. II.   Plate with decoration after J. B. Monnoyer,
made for the Scottish market, 1740-1750.
The coat of arms of Robert French
is painted in colors on the back.
Diameter 15 inches.

ON BOARD A PORTUGUESE ship that sailed for Canton in 1516 was the Jesuit Father Tomé Pires, whose embassy to Peking was the ostensible reason for the expedition. His own mission ultimately failed, but that of his shipmates—to establish the first direct commercial contact between China and the West—did not: out of Portugal's first foray into China, from 1517 to 1521, developed the China Trade. And from the beginning porcelain, hitherto the much-prized luxury of rulers, was a constituent of that trade.

Until 1517 porcelain could be obtained commercially only indirectly. When Manoel I of Portugal (r. 1495-1521) wanted Chinese porcelain in 1509 he had to write to his viceroy in India to purchase it for him. It could also be bought at Malacca, whose Portuguese governor wrote the king in 1514 of "all kinds of satins and damasks and porcelains . . . The rulers of China are tyrants, and they sell in great quantities." This was indigenous porcelain, however, conforming in all essentials to Chinese (or at least Eastern) tastes.

What distinguishes the porcelains made after Portugal's landfall of 1517 can be seen in a jug in the Metropolitan Museum (Fig. 1), one of a small group of blue-and-white pieces that comprise the first true China Trade porcelains. Each piece is linked to the others by the inclusion in its decoration of one or all of three devices emblematic of Portugal's presence in China during Manoel's reign: the royal arms (always painted upside down), the Sacred Monogram, and an armillary sphere. Of the three the armillary, being his personal device, is specifically associated with Manoel and is a logical basis for assigning at least some of the eleven recorded pieces to the period 1517-1521. The Metropolitan's jug, two ewers, and a bowl are the simplest of the Manueline porcelains; and

the first three, being traditionally Asian in profile, may be taken as representative of the initial trade when the most the Portuguese might expect was to have their patterns painted on ready-made wares, whatever their shape. The decoration itself must have been at hand, perhaps in the form of insignia ornamenting bindings and title pages of prayer books or copies of the New Testament the Portuguese would have taken with them.

Throughout the sixteenth century, the decoration of export wares was limited to copies of two-dimensional patterns on porcelains essentially Chinese in form and character. This practice was radically altered in the seventeenth century by the Dutch, who converted the porcelain trade from an occasional, somewhat impromptu affair to a steady industrial market geared to European customs. At first the Vereenigde Ostindische Compagnie (which can more manageably be referred to as the V. O. C.), like the Portuguese, accepted what it could get. But as early as 1635 the company began to take a more assertive line. In that year the Dutch governor of Formosa reported to company officials in Amsterdam that he had supplied Chinese merchants with models of a wide assortment of shapes including salt cellars, flat broad-rimmed plates, mustard pots, ewers, and basins, "all made of wood, mostly turned." From later passages in the V. O. C. records published by T. Volker in 1954 it appears that some of the wooden models, which were to become a regular pattern source, were made in Holland, while others—including, in Volker's opinion, these first ones—were made by the Chinese themselves on Formosa. Why they should have been made at all is puzzling: fragility of the originals—which to judge from their description were probably pewter—cannot have been the reason, for in the same year the V. O. C. was importing Rhenish stoneware into China and Japan for copying. Neither, evidently, was visual comprehension an issue: in 1639 company officials on Formosa ordered porcelains to be copied from wooden samples sent from Holland, at the same time specifying that the flowerpots have "two handles like the drawing on the paper No. 11" and that the wine jugs be "ribbed like the drawing on the paper No. 12." From this time the traffic in patterns and models became at once more extensive and more reciprocal, each country giving to and taking from the other. While Chinese porcelain was exported to be copied at Delft or in Germany, Siegburg stoneware tankards, Dutch silver mustard pots, and glass or silver rummers were sent to China for the same purpose.

From the web of these exchanges and multiplications it is almost impossible to isolate a single source. In the case of the taperstick illustrated in Figure 2 the working model may well have been several steps removed from the original. Essentially a metal form, it is particularly close to examples in English silver of the 1690's when the square columnar style began to be relaxed. But variants can be found in brass and pewter, and there is no reason to doubt their existence in earthenware as well. From what we know of the communalization of styles and materials, this China Trade taperstick may have

Fig. 2. Taperstick made for the Dutch or English market, 1690-1700. Height 5¼ inches.

been copied from a wooden model—either Chinese or Dutch—itself duplicating a Delft version of an English metalwork original.

Three-dimensional models continued to be supplied throughout the eighteenth century. Few of the China Trade versions, however, bear so literal a resemblance to their prototypes as do a pair of cups and saucers in the Metropolitan (Pl. I). Except for the absence of handles on the cups, they conform precisely to a style current at Meissen about 1735 (an analogous cup and saucer in the Metropolitan, with the arms of Charles IV, King of the Two Sicilies, can be dated 1738-1740), and although an original model has not been discovered, there is further evidence of their being direct copies: on the bottom of each piece is the Augustan monogram *AR* painted, as it always was at Meissen, in underglaze blue.

With the success of the Dutch in establishing a repertoire of porcelain shapes acceptable to the Europeans, emphasis shifted once again to the decoration of export wares, and for this engravings were ideal. Neither bulky nor fragile, they could be copied with little fear of mistake and they tended to have wide currency, making them suitable for a variety of Western markets. It is just this availability of engraved subjects that often obscures their provenance. With casual—often unacknowledged—borrowing the rule rather than the exception, pictures passed freely from one artist and country to another, each draftsman taking his own liberties with "his" original. For all practical purposes the subjects of a pair of large plates in the Metropolitan (Pl. II) are copied from engravings by Jean Baptiste Monnoyer who, although successful in Paris, emigrated to England about 1679 and remained there for the rest of his life. Among his hundreds of engravings of flowers was the series *Livres de Plusieurs Paniers de Fleurs,* originally published in Paris under his *nom de burin,* Jean Baptiste. However, a comparison of the flower baskets on the Metropolitan's plates with Monnoyer's engravings offers some surprises. At first glance the compositions seem merely to have been reversed, but on closer inspection they are seen to be new arrangements altogether. That in Plate II is a combination of two engravings in the series (Figs. 3, 4). Most of the flowers on the companion plate are copied from a third engraving, but the remainder are not to be found in any other print in the series; thoroughly in style with Monnoyer's, they were probably borrowed from others of his designs. What must have happened was that Monnoyer's original prints were recomposed, redrawn, and re-engraved so as to appear in these altered and reversed versions. The unidentified artist responsible for this sleight of hand seems to have been English, as each plate is painted on the reverse (this is unusual for China Trade porcelain) with a coat of arms identified as that of Robert French (1705-1758) of Berwickshire, Scotland.

In spite of the ease with which they could obtain and circulate engraved material, at least two East India companies experimented with hiring staff artists. One of these was Christian Precht, whose single recorded sheet of sketches for the Swedish company is endorsed 1736; the

Figs. 3, 4. Two engravings from *Livres de Plusieurs Paniers de Fleurs,* by Jean Baptiste Monnoyer (1636-1699), Paris, n. d., from which the design on Pl. II derives. *Metropolitan Museum of Art, Rogers Fund.*

other was Cornelis Pronk, an Amsterdam drawing master hired by the V. O. C. in 1734. In his contract with the Dutch company Pronk agreed "to make and order all designs and models to our satisfaction, of all such porcelains as will be ordered from time to time in The Indies, with their colors properly put in, blue as well as gilt and other colors, and in various fashions." Two years later, the company at Batavia reported the receipt of "drawn samples recently received out of Holland for China," and although their identity is conjectural, they were fairly certainly Pronk's and probably included the so-called Parasol pattern—a composition in which a lady with an attendant holding a parasol stands at the edge of a marsh admiring the water birds. An unsigned drawing attributed

Pl. III. Dish in the Parasol pattern,
made for the Dutch market, c. 1737.
Diameter 19½ inches.

Pl. IV. Part of a tea service
made for the Continental market, 1735-1740.
Diameter of plate, 8 inches;
height of creamer, 5¼ inches.

Fig. 5. Design for the Parasol pattern, attributed to Cornelis Pronk (1691-1759). *Rijksmuseum, Amsterdam.*

Fig. 6. Plate painted in the Parasol pattern after a China Trade version of Pronk's design. Italian, Venice (Cozzi factory), c. 1740. *Privately owned; photograph by courtesy of U. Mursia & C. Editore.*

to Pronk in the Rijksmuseum (Fig. 5) shows the pattern adapted to a deep dish like one in the Metropolitan (Pl. III). The pattern is also known on a tureen, a lighthouse coffeepot, and a candlestick, but it turns up most frequently on nine-inch plates (it may be relevant that 432 of these were ordered in the newly received pattern early in 1737).

The chief interest of the Parasol pattern lies not so much in the design itself—which is a somewhat undigested combination of baroque formality and chinoiserie—as in its many variations in treatment and composition. Once a design was made available to Oriental porcelain painters there was practically no limit to the length of shadow it cast, but no subject seems to have been so variously reproduced as Pronk's Parasol pattern. In addition to the large blue-and-white dish (the only recorded example of its size) the Metropolitan owns a nine-inch plate painted in iron red, underglaze blue, and gilt. The palette of another small plate, in the Gemeentemuseum, The Hague, is primarily rose, blue, and green. Still other versions occur on Japanese export porcelain. Pronk's design was even recopied in Europe, as may be seen in a plate from the Cozzi factory (Fig. 6).

There is no indication that the Dutch or any other company retained staff artists after 1736-1737. The nature of the China Trade was against individual design: it was a mass-market operation intended (armorial services excepted) to reflect collective customs and appeal to collective tastes. For this reason a small incomplete tea service in the Metropolitan (Pl. IV) is of particular interest: it was so unmistakably *designed*. Both the decorative scheme of the panache and tasseled lappets and the palette of violet and opaque yellow are deliberate, and both are thoroughly European in conception. The motifs abound in the ornament engravings of Daniel Marot and his followers, while the two colors (the violet is a high-temperature hue in the *famille rose*) were introduced into China from the West during the reign of Yung Chêng (1723-1735). It is in the contemporary work of Claud du Paquier at Vienna that we find the regular combination of these distinctive features. Although overshadowed in Europe by Meissen, Du Paquier's style had considerable influence on China Trade porcelain, an influence which is remarkable for having been oblique: Austria had no direct trade with China. Transmission of the style will have been due in part to a handful of Jesuit missionaries, but the design and coloring of the Metropolitan's tea service goes beyond the mere copying of a pattern or technique: it reflects the full development of China Trade porcelain. Commercial and stylistic interchange between Europe and the Far East was at its peak in the 1730's. The early haphazard re-renderings of Western iconography had been replaced by a sure-handed technique, and experiments in color in the West were being assimilated on the other side of the world. In technique, versatility, and responsiveness to the fashions of a changing world, the style represented by the tea service is an achievement in intercultural exchange at the apogee of its development.

BY JOHN GOLDSMITH PHILLIPS

Western ceramic models for China-Trade porcelain

CHINA-TRADE PORCELAIN—known also as Oriental Lowestoft, Chinese export porcelain, and so on—represents one of the more fascinating aspects of the ceramic arts of the eighteenth and early nineteenth centuries. Aside from the undeniable charm of the porcelain in its own right, the story of its cultural and political background, its production in Ching-te-chen and Canton, and its distribution to the West via East India Company ships is full of vivid contrasts and surprises. This story continues to unfold in the light of contemporary research.

Take, for instance, the matter of the origins of the ware's forms, a small but significant aspect of the story. Although China-Trade porcelain is a true Oriental porcelain, its forms are often markedly Western. To account for this it must be assumed that the Chinese made use of Western models. Really to grasp the nature of the material, it is obviously important to know just what these models were.

It has been generally believed that the models used were specimens of Western silverware dispatched to the Orient to be copied. In my recent study of the McCann collection, however, it was not possible to iden-

A tureen (left) from a service made for the Danish market is completely European in form. More than that, it is a copy after a pottery tureen (right) made between 1747 and 1751 at the Höchst factory in Germany by Ignatz Hess. The China-Trade tureen was made between 1760 and 1770.

A China-Trade jardinière (left) modeled and painted in the rococo style follows closely, in both form and decoration, a jardinière (right) made between 1758 and 1766 at the Marieberg factory near Stockholm.

The Swedish pottery model (right) for a China-Trade urn decorated in blue and white with details in gold (left) was made at Marieberg in 1773. The Oriental version, directed toward the Swedish market, is dated 1775-1785.

A Marieberg flint porcelain urn (right) decorated with a portrait of Gustavus III served as the model for a pistol-handled urn in the McCann collection (left). The Marieberg piece, a characteristic example of Gustavian style, was made about 1775; the China-Trade urn, probably made for the Swedish market, dates from 1775-1785.

tify any of the many shapes of China-Trade porcelain as having originated directly from a Western silver model. So it seemed evident to me that the use of silver models was insignificant, if, indeed, it was practiced at all.

Search for the presumed models had therefore to be directed to some other Western material. A likely source seemed to be in the field of ceramics, for the China-Trade wares and the porcelains and potteries of the West have much in common. They are closely related with respect to use, and the commerce in China-Trade porcelain flourished to the degree that this export ware was a cheap and well-produced substitute for Western ceramics. Indeed, in my book *China-Trade Porcelain* I go so far as to describe China's export product as "a collateral phase" of Western ceramic art.

It is not surprising, then, once attention is turned toward such a possibility, to discover that a considerable number of China-Trade porcelains were in fact based on Western ceramic models. In this brief account, I do no more than illustrate a few instances observed in the McCann collection, which seem to establish beyond any reasonable doubt the use by the Chinese of such models. A further study of other collections along these lines would, I am sure, reveal even more fully the extent of this procedure, which seems to have been standard.

As will be observed, none of these China-Trade porcelains are identical copies, although some of them were evidently made with just that idea in mind. It is this marvelous degree of difference between the works of East and West—a difference based on the nature of the raw materials and manufacturing techniques and on the age-old traditions of artisans which tend to negate to some extent even the most painstaking attempt to achieve the perfect copy—that gives China-Trade porcelain its unique character.

Mr. Phillips is curator of Renaissance art at the Metropolitan Museum of Art and author of *China-Trade Porcelain*, published this month by the Harvard University Press. Like this article, the book is based on Mr. Phillips' study of the Helena Woolworth McCann collection, which is distributed among museums throughout the country. All illustrations are from *China-Trade Porcelain*.

 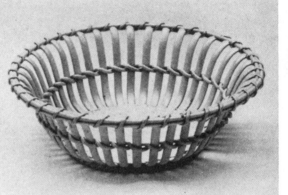

A cress basket made for the English market (left) is a faithful copy of a pearlware basket (right) made in Josiah Wedgwood's factory and dated about 1780. The China-Trade version differs from the Wedgwood model only in the addition of a copy of Bartolozzi's stipple engraving of *Autumn* (below), published in London in 1782.

The same Bartolozzi subject appears on a covered chestnut dish also made for the English market and dated 1785. The foliate decoration is taken from the print's surrounding ornament, the work of Pergolesi.

Chinese porcelain figures of Westerners

BY JOSEPH T. BUTLER, *Curator, Sleepy Hollow Restorations*

Fig. 1. Madonna and child. Tê-hua blanc de chine; height 7⅛ inches. An adaptation of the classic Chinese figure of Kuan Yin, Buddhist goddess of mercy (ANTIQUES, November 1928, p. 410; and May 1937, p. 243). Ex coll. *Homer Eaton Keyes; present whereabouts unknown.*

AMONG THE MOST CURIOUS and interesting objects to be found in Chinese export porcelain are some amusingly naïve figures depicting Europeans in costumes of the late seventeenth and the eighteenth centuries. Since the Dutch were the largest importers of porcelains from the Orient at the beginning of the eighteenth century, it seems reasonable to assume that these figure groups were intended to represent Dutch merchants and their families, living in China and engaging in their normal daily pursuits. A popular legend, apparently based on an account in G. C. Williamson's *Book of Famille Rose* (London, 1927), has it that the men in these groups portray a Dutch governor of Batavia named Diederik Durven and called by the Chinese Duf, or Durf; but there seems to be little substantiation for this theory.

In general, the figures can be divided into two categories. One is the series, predominantly in blanc de chine, produced at Tê-hua in Fukien province from the late K'ang Hsi period (1662-1723) through the Yung-chêng (1723-1736) and into the Ch'ien Lung (1736-1796). The other is a group decorated in polychrome enamels, many in the *famille rose* palette, made at Ching-tê Chên in Kiangsi. The latter are more difficult to date as they were produced over a longer period—probably from the late Ming dynasty (it ended in 1644) through the Ch'ien Lung.

As early as the Ming dynasty, when the Tê-hua kiln was probably founded, figural groups depicting immortals or Taoist genii were being executed in blanc de chine in this region; these often contained as many as eight figures, crowded together much as were the figures of Europeans in some of the groups made later for export. The kiln was noted for its representation of Kuan Yin, the Buddhist goddess of mercy—modified during the eighteenth century to represent the Christian Madonna (Fig. 1).

Made of a fine and highly kaolinic clay, the Tê-hua product is white and translucent to a degree, and it has sonorous qualities when struck. Its glaze is rich, thick, and translucent, varying in color from snow white to ivory with an occasional yellowish or pinkish tinge.

In some cases vitrification is so complete that the piece resembles glass.

Not all the Tê-hua export porcelain was in blanc de chine, though there is some difference of opinion as to where the polychrome examples were decorated. W. B. Honey (*Ceramic Art of China and Other Countries of the Far East*) seems to agree with the early eighteenth-century Jesuit priest Père d'Entrecolles, who wrote that all the decoration was executed in Europe. R. Soame Jenyns, in his *Later Chinese Porcelain*, disagrees with this theory on the basis of some objects in the British

90

Fig. 2. Family group. Tê-hua blanc de chine with snow-white glaze; height 6 inches. *Sleepy Hollow Restorations.*

Fig. 3. Family group. Tê-hua blanc de chine; height 6 inches. *Collection of the Honorable Mrs. Ionides.*

Museum which he believes were both produced and decorated in Tê-hua. The figural groups depicting Westerners were not the only European forms produced here —porringers and mugs in silver shapes were also made— but they do constitute the largest series.

The Tê-hua model most often seen represents a family grouped around a table and apparently taking tea; this is especially interesting because of its variations (Figs. 2, 3, 4). It is these groups, with their crowded figures, which most closely resemble the Ming dynasty portrayals of deities and other immortals. In each the two male figures are dressed in Dutch costume of the late seventeenth century, with tricorn hats; the females wear Chinese clothing and in stance and expression somewhat resemble the classic Kuan Yin figure. The central object is always a piece of Chinese furniture with a flowerpot in front of it. A dog stands before the male figures, and a monkey in front of the females. A group composed of similar elements but with only two human figures, illustrated in Figure 5, is representative of the much less common Tê-hua product decorated in enamel colors.

Another type of group shows two Europeans seated on the back of a Dog of Fo, with another human figure and two small dogs at the base. One of the largest and most imposing of the Tê-hua figures, the example illustrated on the frontispiece of this issue and discussed on the editorial page is of great interest also because it has a documented history of ownership in America. A com-

Fig. 4. Family group. Tê-hua blanc de chine with cream-color glaze; height 6 7/16 inches. *Sleepy Hollow Restorations.*

Fig. 5. Couple. Tê-hua porcelain decorated in enamel colors; height 6½ inches. A second small animal has evidently been broken off at the left of the flowerpot. *Victoria and Albert Museum, crown copyright.*

Fig. 6. Musician and boy. Tê-hua blanc de chine; height 6¼ inches. A companion piece, with the figures reversed, was shown in ANTIQUES, September 1928 (p. 214) and May 1937 (p. 243). *Ionides collection.*

Fig. 7. Torchbearer. Tê-hua blanc de chine; height 6 inches. This figure is found both with and without a base. *Ionides collection.*

panion group, recently acquired by Sleepy Hollow Restorations from the Honorable Mrs. Ionides, shows the same figures in reverse.

The musician and boy group shown in Figure 6 is known in several slightly varying versions which bear some stylistic resemblance to the larger tea-drinking groups. A companion piece, in reverse, was illustrated in ANTIQUES for September 1928 (p. 214) and May 1937 (p. 243).

Miniatures make up another interesting category. These are usually about two and a half inches high, and they too depict Europeans in various pursuits. A pair from the Ionides collection shows riders mounted on Dogs of Fo (Fig. 8), and another pair (these are actually whistles) from the same collection are riding a horse and a camel (Fig. 9).

The rider on a Dog of Fo shown in Figure 10, an English salt-glaze pottery piece, is shown here because it offers a remarkable comparison to the Tê-hua porcelain figures. The rider wears a hat very similar to those found in some of the Chinese groups (*cf.* ANTIQUES, September 1928, cover; and May 1937, p. 243). His Oriental features, his preoccupation with an Oriental game, and the position of the Dog of Fo, all indicate the potter's familiarity with the Fukien wares.

The porcelain of Ching-tê Chên is more familiar to Western collectors than the Tê-hua wares, for the great armorial table services were made here. It is said that porcelain was produced in this town (then called Ch'ang-nan) as early as the Han dynasty (206 B.C.-220 A.D.). Ching-tê Chên had its most brilliant period during the

Ming dynasty, but most of the porcelains made here for export were produced during the eighteenth century.

The area around Ching-tê Chên was especially rich in those most important ingredients of true porcelain, kaolin and petuntse, and the hard glassy glaze of the local ware was largely made of the latter. The well-known "orange peel" surface was a result of its vitrification.

Most of the porcelain produced at Ching-tê Chên for export was taken to Canton to be decorated in enamel colors. The figures of Europeans produced here are more sophisticated than those of Tê-hua, and they show a familiarity with European porcelains. Some Ching-tê Chên figures dating from the second half of the eighteenth century are copies of Bow and Chelsea models.

Probably the most familiar of the Ching-tê Chên groups are those which show a couple in various poses of the dance (Figs. 11, 12, and top of Contents page); these all have *famille rose* decoration. It is interesting to note that these figures, which are quite European in conception, are on typically Chinese bases.

Chinese figures of Europeans were apparently not so popular during the eighteenth century as were Chinese tablewares and figures in animal or bird form. They are consequently quite scarce today in both Europe and America—and to be cherished accordingly wherever they are found.

For help given me in connection with this study, special thanks are due to the Honorable Mrs. Ionides, Sussex; Benjamin Ginsburg, New York; and R. Soame Jenyns of the British Museum.   J. T. B.

Eighteenth-century Tê-hua porcelain figure group representing
a European couple seated on a Dog of Fo, with smaller figures. Height 11½ inches.
Collection of Miss Charlotte Van Cortlandt.

Fig. 8. Pair of riders on Dogs of Fo. Miniatures, Tê-hua blanc de chine; height 2¾ inches. *Ionides collection.*

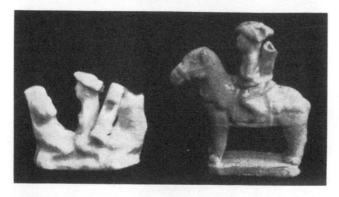

Fig. 9. Equestrian whistles. Miniatures; Tê-hua blanc de chine and polychrome. Height of figure at right (mounted on a camel), 2¼ inches. *Ionides collection.*

Fig. 10. Rider on Dog of Fo. English salt-glaze pottery; height 11 inches. *Cf.* ANTIQUES, September 28, cover; and May 1937, p. 243. *Collection of Miss Ima Hogg.*

Fig. 11. Dancing couple. Ching-tê Chên, polychrome; height 10 inches. *Ionides collection.*

Fig. 12. Dancing couple. Ching-tê Chên polychrome; height 8½ inches. *Ionides collection.*

Porcelain as room decoration in eighteenth-century England

BY ROBERT J. CHARLESTON, *Keeper, department of ceramics, Victoria and Albert Museum*

ALTHOUGH FRAGMENTS OF Sung porcelain have been excavated in Italy, the first Oriental porcelain to reach Northern Europe appears to have percolated through in the fourteenth century. In 1370 the Queen of Charles le Bel is recorded as having a porcelain pot among her treasures, and the famous Gaignières-Fonthill vase had reached Hungary by 1380. These isolated examples were probably brought as diplomatic gifts, and it was only with the direct contact of Portuguese ships with China in 1514 that porcelain began to come to Europe in more than individual examples. Even so the quantity was very small, and to these objects was accorded a degree of awe and respect consonant with their physical character and exotic decoration. To the Northern European, for whom pottery normally meant lead-glazed earthenware or, at best, tin-glazed majolica, this close-grained, white, resonant, shining substance must have seemed of a different order of things. Indeed, as late as 1646 Sir Thomas Browne could write: "We are not thoroughly resolved concerning Porcellane or China dishes, that according to common belief they are made of Earth," and well into the eighteenth century there were serious misconceptions as to the exact nature of the porcelain material.

About the end of the sixteenth century the foundation of the Dutch and English East India companies at last ensured to the countries of Northern Europe direct contact with the Far East. The importation of porcelain rose steadily in volume throughout the seventeenth century so that conditions of glut and consequent sharp price declines had to be carefully guarded against. An idea of the quantities involved is given by the *Journals* of the sailor Edward Barlow:

And having all things ready, on Monday the first day of February 1702/3, we set sail from a place called "Whampow" in the river of Canton in China, praying to God for a good passage to England, being a full ship and laden with goods, namely: 205 chests of China and Japan ware, porcelain . . . and a great deal more loose China and Japan earthenware, which was packed up on board.

By the middle of the eighteenth century the trade had grown to enormous proportions. In 1755, for instance, the *Prince George* was laden with 120 chests of porcelain, of which a single Chinese merchant accounted for 26 chests, containing 10,236 single plates, 200 table sets, 4,188 half-pint basins, and 742 coffee cups, the whole consignment being blue and white porcelain.

In the early 1600's most of the porcelain pieces which reached England appear to have been bowls and dishes. Thus in 1618, when some "East India" commodities were "put to the sale by the candle for readie money," the porcelain items were three "greate deepe basons"; and when in 1635 the Dutch wished to make a present to Charles I, they gave him "two large basins of China

earth." By 1660, however, tea and coffee were established beverages in England, and as porcelain was particularly appropriate for their drinking, orders to Canton were quickly modified to include the necessary pieces. In 1681 the London directors of the East India Company instructed their factors in China: "In Chinawares ye are to observe that great Beakers and Jars are much out of esteem, Basons of all sorts are in indifferent request, but that which will turn us best to accompt are Cupps of all kinds, sizes and colours and all sorts of toys of several figures and fashions, the more strange and novill the better. . ." Owing to the delays in communications and to the hazards of the trade, however, these demands probably fluctuated considerably, and the despised items of this list were never really permanently "out of esteem." The first mention of vases in the Dutch East India Company's records appears to be in 1636, when shipments from Formosa included "18 very large fine covered pots, . . . 23 half-sized ditto . . ., 66 ditto, somewhat smaller . . .," although various "flasks," "pots," and "flower-pots" are mentioned at even earlier dates in the archives. Supplies of porcelain were probably not so abundant in England at this date, but in Act IV of Wycherley's *The Country Wife* (first staged in 1672 or 1673), satirizing the chinamania of the time, Lady Fidget exclaims: "We women of quality never think we have china enough." To this Horner replies: "Do not take it ill, I cannot make china for you all, but I will have a roll-waggon for you too, another time." A roll-waggon was a cylindrical-bodied vase with a narrower short neck, current in porcelain of the mid-seventeenth century and of the reign of the Emperor K'ang Hsi (1662-1722).

In 1682 the future Queen Mary II, then in Holland, entered in her account book "March the 6 paid for a porcelane Jar . . . 63 [guilders]," and in the succeeding seven years until her accession to the English throne she was steadily buying porcelain, including "beakers and jars." It is to Mary, indeed, that we owe credit for the first really systematic attempt in England to amass porcelain and use it for the decoration of interiors as was being done on the Continent, notably by the Elector of Brandenburg. While still in Holland Mary had begun to decorate her apartments with porcelain in quantity. In 1687 Nicodemus Tessin, the famous Swedish architect, visited Hunsslardiek, the then Princess Mary's country house near The Hague, and described her audience chamber as "very richly furnished with Chinese work and pictures. The ceiling was covered with mirrors, which showed the room afresh, so that, with the most beautiful effect imaginable, the more one gazed into the reflections, the more endlessly extended the perspectives. The chimney-piece was full of precious porcelain, part standing half inside it, and so fitted together that one

Fig. 1. Design for a porcelain room, possibly at Hunsslardiek, the then Princess Mary's country house in Holland, by Daniel Marot (c. 1663-1752), late seventeenth century.

Fig. 2. Design for a porcelain room by Marot, late seventeenth century.

Editor's note: The color illustration appearing on this page and plates I through IX on the succeeding two pages appeared originally in an article entitled "The Reeves Collection of China Trade Porcelain at Washington and Lee University" by Callie Huger Efird and Katharine Gross Farnham (The Magazine Antiques, October, 1973, 674–677). These objects are among nearly three hundred pieces of eighteenth and nineteenth-century Chinese export porcelain bequeathed to Washington and Lee University in 1967 by Mr. and Mrs. Euchlin D. Reeves. *Courtesy, Reeves Collection, Washington and Lee University.*

China Trade covered jug made for the American market, c. 1800, inscribed *E Puilb Pupu,* a misspelling for the national motto, *E Pluribus Unum.* *Reeves collection at Washington and Lee University.*

Pl. I. Mug made for the American market, c. 1795. Inscribed *Saturday Night*.

Pl. II. One of a pair of double-handled cups made for the American market, 1795-1810. The medallion is a finely painted, close imitation of the great seal of the United States.

Pl. III. Large reticulated chestnut basket and stand made for the Western market, 1785-1820. The design is a good illustration of the Chinese distortion of what was probably a relatively small classical design.

Pl. IV. Wall vase with a narrow neck and fluted pouches made for the European market, 1780-1790. The unusual form is decorated with chinoiserie designs in *famille rose* colors.

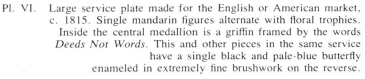

Pl. V. Coffee cup made for the Manigault family
of Charleston, South Carolina, c. 1810.
The initials *GHM* appear where the Fitzhugh medallion
would normally be. Surrounding them
is the inscription *Prospicere Quam Ulcisci*.

Pl. VI. Large service plate made for the English or American market,
c. 1815. Single mandarin figures alternate with floral trophies.
Inside the central medallion is a griffin framed by the words
Deeds Not Words. This and other pieces in the same service
have a single black and pale-blue butterfly
enameled in extremely fine brushwork on the reverse.

Pl. VII. One of a pair of teacups with shaped rims
made for the Western market, c. 1800.
The initials *M* and *A* flank the unusual pattern of hearts.

Pl. VIII. Dinner plate finely enameled in the
Black Butterfly pattern, probably made for
the American market, 1825-1850.

Pl. IX. Detail from a mug, made for the Western market c. 1790,
inscribed with the initials *WMP*.

Pl. X. Tea set decorated in gilt border, each piece with a different central motif, c. 1780.

Pl. XI. Hot water plate with memorial to George Washington. Monogram JRL for Judith and Robert Lewis (nephew of George Washington), c. 1800. Teapot stand, from set owned by Colonel Ephraim Williams, founder of Williams College, c. 1790.

Pl. XII. Lotus bowl, c. 1760. Diameter, 15½ inches.

Pl. XIII. Tureen and tureen stand with double coat of arms of Van Goudreian, 1769, Governor of the Honorable Dutch East India Company.

Pl. XIV. American trade bowl decorated in extremely rare eagle
design, c. 1790. Diameter, 11 inches.

Fig. 3. Garniture of three covered porcelain vases and two beakers painted in enamel colors and gilt. Plymouth factory, c. 1770. Height of tallest vase, 11½ inches. *Victoria and Albert Museum.*

Fig. 4. *The Lady's Last Stake,* by William Hogarth (1697-1764), 1759. *Albright-Knox Art Gallery.*

piece supported another." A surviving engraving by the French-Dutch artist Daniel Marot (Fig. 1), who became virtually court designer to William and Mary, may show this room.

After their accession to the English throne, William and Mary visited Hampton Court in February 1689, and decided to renovate the palace completely. In the meantime, apartments were to be furnished in the old Tudor Water Gallery, and these were elaborately remodeled under the supervision of Christopher Wren (1632-1723), probably in collaboration with Marot. Of this building Celia Fiennes records in her *Travels* (1694): "There was

the Water Gallery that opened into a balcony to the water and was decked with China and fine pictures of the Court Ladyes drawn by Nellor [Kneller] . . ." In his *Tour thro' the Whole Island of Great Britain* (1724-1727) Daniel Defoe comments, in writing of Hampton Court, on the "vast stock of fine *China* Ware, the like whereof was not then to be seen in England; the long Gallery, as above, was filled with this *China,* and every other Place, where it could be plac'd, with Advantage." Elsewhere in the same work he writes: "The Queen brought in the Custom or Humour, as I may call it, of furnishing Houses with *China*-ware, which increased to a strange degree afterwards, piling their *China* upon the tops of Cabinets, Scrutores, and every Chimney-Piece, to the Tops of the Ceilings, and even setting up Shelves for their *China*-ware, where they wanted such Places." All these forms of display were in evidence in eighteenth-century England, and another engraving by Marot (Fig. 2), although not certainly of Hampton Court, shows the sort of interior that Defoe described. The corner fireplaces with stepped shelves above for porcelain vases and figures may still be seen at Hampton Court. Many of the pieces survive from Queen Mary's collection.

The chimneypiece indeed was an obvious place for the display of porcelain and its use in that way became in the eighteenth century a fashion which is satirized in the breakfast scene in William Hogarth's *Marriage à la Mode* series (1749), and which may be seen recorded in more sober terms in some of Arthur Devis' pictures. Vases had long been produced in sets expressly for the mantelshelf. These *garnitures de cheminée* (Fig. 3) were normally made in odd numbers, an ovoid vase, usually covered, alternating with a slender cylindrical or concave-sided "beaker." This disposition is reflected in the advertisements of the English porcelain factories. The Chelsea sale catalogue for 1756 lists in alternate lots "One fine large jar enamel'd in flowers" and "Two large beakers ditto." Five was a more usual number than three, and the 1755 Chelsea catalogue even mentions "A set for a chimney piece or a cabinet, consisting of seven JARS and BEAKERS, *beautifully enamelled with flowers,* and the beakers filled with flowers *after nature.*" It is tempting to wonder whether the beaker-vases on the mantel in Hogarth's *The Lady's Last Stake* (Fig. 4) were filled with porcelain flowers rather than natural ones.

Tessin's description of the Hunsslardiek palace and Marot's engravings suggest that in Holland porcelain vases were often displayed in the fireplace itself, and this was true in England as well. Many of Hogarth's and Devis' pictures (Fig. 5) show a single large vase standing in the fireplace (presumably in summer only), and the 1710 inventory of "Mr. Blaythwayt's House at Dirham" (Dyrham Park, Gloucestershire) records a "Delf Flower pot in ye Chimney" in virtually every room. Large china jars might stand in any corner of a room. In a letter from Padua sent in 1758 to her daughter in England Lady Mary Wortley Montagu wrote: "Though china is in such estimation here, I have sometimes an inclination to desire your father to send me the two large jars that stood in the windows in Cavendish-Square . . ."

Such obvious places for the display of porcelain, however, by no means satisfied the chinamania of the late seventeenth and the eighteenth centuries. As early as 1708 Squire Blundell, a man of modest fortune in one of the more remote parts of Lancashire, recorded that he "placed my wives Chinea on her Screwtore," and ten years earlier the famous Anglo-Dutch cabinetmaker Gerreit Jensen (fl. c. 1680-1715) had supplied Lord Albemarle at Kensington with "a walnuttree scrutore with a step of walnuttree for Cheny on ye Top." The "step" was undoubtedly a series of receding ledges of the same kind as those over the corner mantelpieces in Hampton Court. The character of the porcelain thus displayed is illuminated by an advertisement of Queen Anne's reign:

Whereas the New East India Company did lately sell all their Chinaware, These are to Advertise that a very large parcel thereof (as Broken & Damag'd) is now to be sold by Wholesale or Retail, extreamly Cheap . . . It's very fit to furnish escrutores, Cabinets, Corner Cupboards . . ., where it usually stands for ornament only.

Even in faraway America this craze found expression

Fig. 5. *Mr. and Mrs. William Atherton,* by Arthur Devis (1763-1822), 1740-1745. *Walker Art Gallery, Liverpool.*

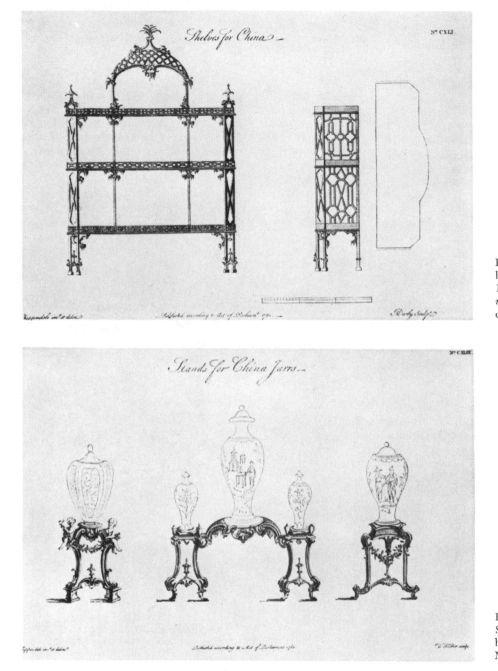

Fig. 6. Design for *Shelves for China* by Thomas Chippendale (c. 1718-1779). No. CXLI from *The Gentleman & Cabinet-Maker's Director* (3rd ed., 1762).

Fig. 7. Designs for three *Stands for China Jarrs* by Chippendale. No. CXLIX in *Director*.

(see ANTIQUES for October 1957, p. 332). A Boston inventory of as early as 1733 mentions "steps" for the top of a cabinet, and the inventory of one John Procter, taken in 1756, refers to "The steps and some small China . . ."

These modest contrivances, however, whether at Hampton Court or in the American Colonies, bear no comparison with the elaborate arrangements made at such palaces as Oranienburg, rebuilt between 1688 and 1695 by Friedrich III of Brandenburg. In the Porcelain Room (*Porzellankammer*) not only was every ledge and cornice occupied by rank upon rank of porcelain cups, saucers, and vases, but specially carved and gilded tiers of shelves rose like pyramids against the walls, laden with beakers and vases of appropriate scale in rigid symmetry and diminishing size from bottom to top. Although no traces of such arrangements appear to have

survived at Hampton Court, where they might most have been expected, they do seem to have existed in England, as the above passage from Defoe seems to suggest. Joseph Addison (1672-1719) wrote in the *Spectator* for May 1711, "Our rooms are filled with pyramids of china and adorned with the workmanship of Japan," and in his *Journal* for 1775 Samuel Curwen recorded of Windsor: "In Queen Anne's China-closet were wooden sconces gilt, on which are set china porcelain jars of various shapes up to the ceiling." The exact form of these sconces is not quite clear, and they may simply have been brackets disposed over the wall space. Between 1734 and 1740 Benjamin Goodison provided for St. James's "4 carved and gilt ornaments over the chimney with branches to do. to hold china—£30. For 2 carved and gilt do. for the corners of the closet £54." About the middle of the eighteenth century in the great dining room at Howth were "two large china lions on brackets. . ." Surviving designs by Thomas Chippendale and other furniture designers show how they conceived of furniture specifically with porcelain in mind (Figs. 6-9).

Some houses boasted a true "china room." Lord Oxford recorded in 1732 that in Sir Andrew Fountaine's house at Narford "His china room is a most wretched place, set out upon shelves like a shop, no red china, a mere baby room" (this last phrase possibly referring to a display of porcelain figures). Yet Sarah, Duchess of Marlborough, herself no mean china fancier, wrote two years later: "I have met with a china dish which is counted such a curiosity that it would please as great a virtuoso as Sir Andrew Fountaine. . ." Mrs. Lybbe Powys gives in her *Diary* for August 1778 a more circumstantial account of another such room:

The next day we were to pay a visit to Sir James Dashwood's, Kirtlington Park, two miles from Bletchingdon . . . Lady Dashwood's china-room, the most elegant I ever saw. 'Tis under the flight of stairs going into the garden; it's ornamented with the finest pieces of the oldest china, and the recesses and shelves painted pea-green and white, the edges being green in a mosaic pattern. Her Ladyship said she must try my judgment in china, as she ever did all the visitors of that closet, as there was one piece there so much superior to the others. I thought myself fortunate that a prodigious fine old Japan dish at once struck my eye.

By this date, however, the days of porcelain as a fashionable room decoration were numbered. The neoclassical wares of Josiah Wedgwood (1730-1795) and his rivals in pottery, and the ormolu and blue john (Derbyshire spar) ornaments of Matthew Boulton (1728-1809), were rapidly gaining favor. The change in fashion is dramatically illuminated from the highest quarter. Boulton himself wrote in a letter: "Then the queen sent for me into her boudoir showed me her chimney piece and asked me how many vases it would take to furnish it. 'For,' said she, 'all that china shall be taken away. . .'"

Fig. 8. Design for *A bracket with shelves for china*, by Thomas Johnson (fl. c. 1755-1766), 1756. *Victoria and Albert Museum.*

Fig. 9. Designs for shelves for porcelain by Matthew Darly (fl. c. 1750-1778) and George Edwards, from *A New Book of Chinese Designs*, 1754. *Victoria and Albert Museum.*

Dutch Decorators of Chinese Porcelain

By W. B. HONEY

Introductory Note

MANY studious and well-informed collectors still find themselves troubled by doubts as to the locality in which Chinese porcelains destined for the European market received their decoration. In view of the curious legends that have been disseminated in print and by word of mouth, this situation is by no means surprising. It has, for example, been variously contended (*1*) that it was customary for Chinese porcelain makers to export their wares in blank for decoration in England, or on the Continent, in accordance with Occidental taste; (*2*) that English and European porcelain manufacturers were in the habit of shipping their own wares to China to be decorated by Oriental artists and then returned to the home market; (*3*) that all, or nearly all, hard paste porcelain ornamented with patterns showing a mixture of European and Oriental conceptions and technique were both made and decorated in Lowestoft, England.

Fig. 1 — BOWL AND SPRINKLER (*late seventeenth or early eighteenth century*)
Chinese (K'ang Hsi) porcelain, painted in underglaze blue, with added Dutch decoration in black and gold lacquer.
From the collection of Mrs. R. H. I. Goddard

Now it so happens that not one of these broad and easy generalizations accords with the facts. The last of them is so utterly absurd as to have been long since laughed out of court. The second is, on the face of it, nearly as ridiculous. It is, of course, far from impossible that an occasional stray item of blank English or Continental porcelain should have found its way to China and there received an enamel garnishment. Indeed, some few specimens bearing evidence of such an adventure are said to survive, though I have never had opportunity to examine any of them. They would, however, represent the rarest of rare exceptions to common practice; for the cost in time, money, and breakage involved in juggling large quantities of brittle merchandise back and forth between two continents would have prohibited any considerable effort in that direction.

On the other hand, it is easy to realize the eagerness with which European enamelers would have welcomed the fair surfaces of Oriental ware as a field upon which to display their prowess. Two conflicting interests, one inimical to such practice, the other almost compelling its adoption, are to be noted. The first was exerted by the great East India companies, whose chief object was to make the utmost possible profit for themselves, without suffering compunctions as to the resultant effect upon home industries. For them it was far easier as well as cheaper to buy porcelain in China for decoration on the spot, according to specifications, than to transport the ware in blank to Europe, to be unpacked, distributed among the decorators, and thereafter repacked and shipped to its ultimate markets. A contrary urge would actuate those English and European potters and decorators who alike were struggling to sustain themselves amid the flood of finished Chinese wares imported by the powerful trading companies.

The devices employed by the potters to meet this terrifying Oriental competition may not here be discussed. For the decorators, aside from such direct coöperation as they might afford their local potters, two means of salvation were open. They could acquire and embellish perfectly blank pieces of Chinese porcelain; and they could, also, much more readily, add colorful glorification to modest blue-and-white Chinese items that were lagging in a market whose taste had succumbed to the lure of polychromatic designs. Patronage for the latter process would not have been hard to secure among those porcelain merchants who found themselves heavily overstocked with unsalable blue-and-white. Further patronage may well have come from persons who, while admiring the texture of Oriental porcelains, harbored a dislike for the Chinese ornamental modes.

So it has come to pass that, not infrequently, the collector will encounter articles of eighteenth-century Oriental porcelain in whose decoration, if his eye is sufficiently keen, he will discover definite traces of a European hand. Sometimes the western touch will be as unmistakable as the western subject. Sometimes the Oriental manner will have been so skilfully imitated by the Occidental decorator as to deceive any but the shrewdest of experts.

In brief, it appears that, while the vastly greater part of the importations of Oriental porcelains with which eighteenth-century Europe was deluged received its full quota of decoration in China — and to some extent in Japan — a very considerable quantity acquired some portion, or all, of its enamel embellishment in England and on the Continent.

Many books on Sino-European porcelain allude casually to this circumstance. None of them, in so far as I know, expatiates upon it,

Fig. 2 — DISH (*dated 1700*)
Chinese (K'ang Hsi) porcelain, painted in colors at Delft.
From the British Museum

European faïence on which an unfired color was added in default of a suitable pottery pigment. Red, in particular, was always a difficult color, and on some faïence of Delft, Ansbach, Dorotheenthal, and elsewhere, a lacquer red was sometimes used in combination with the fired blue. But since this lacquer has rarely survived in good condition, an almost meaningless blue design is, in many cases, all that remains. Unfired colors also were often employed on English porcelain figures, a circumstance that probably accounts for the numerous plain white specimens surviving. These latter are, of course, of eighteenth-century date.

True fired enameling, that is to say, overglaze painting in vitreous colors, was applied to pottery by the ancient Egyptians, to glass by the Romans and Byzantines and by the mediæval Islamic craftsmen, with whom the Rhages potters shared the process. In China it was in use during the Sung period (a specimen is known with red and green enamel datable to 1201). *But in modern Europe such overglaze colors were not applied to pottery until about 1625,* when the South German glass-enamelers began to decorate the Kreussen stoneware.

Later in the century, the Nuremberg craftsman Johann Schaper adapted his *Schwarzlot* (black monochrome painting) from window- and table-glass to faïence jugs. Towards the end of the same century, Abraham Helmhack and others, also of Nuremberg, began to use a full polychrome including a pink (which was still unknown in China) for the decoration of these same jugs in a technique partly derived from enameling on metal — a technique that had, of course, been practiced in France and Italy as well as in South Germany for two

despite its importance to the often confused collector. A single magazine article, cited below, has hitherto given it exclusive consideration. Hence it is gratifying that the English authority W. B. Honey, at the suggestion of ANTIQUES, has now undertaken to treat the subject fully and systematically, and to illuminate his discussion with copious and significant illustrations. Mr. Honey, whose *Guide to the Later Chinese Porcelain* in the Victoria and Albert Museum and more recent *Old English Porcelain* are books admittedly indispensable to the ceramic library, needs no introduction to students of porcelain. In the present instance, he offers the results of original research in a field hitherto virtually untouched, and correspondingly unyielding save to arduous spade work. — H. E. K.

THE seventeenth century stands out in the history of European ceramic art as a period of far-reaching revolution in taste. The vast Dutch importations of Chinese blue-and-white started such a rage that the potters everywhere turned from their gay polychrome majolica and began to make imitations of the Oriental wares. These imitations were, at first, in white tin-glazed faïence (which the potters nevertheless called *porcelein*). Eventually materials sharing more or less the essential character of the Chinese wonder-stuff were evolved. To have added any decoration to the veritable Oriental ware would, in the first flush of its vogue, have been unthink-

able — that is with the exception, needless to say, of mounting in precious metal.

This holds true for a large part of the seventeenth century. Even had the wish to apply such added decoration arisen, technical difficulty would still have prevented it. No fired decoration that could be applied to glazed porcelain was in use by the European potter at the beginning of the seventeenth century, though enameling had already had a long history in other crafts. Lacquering and painting in unfired oil colors were, of course, possible, and, as the latter part of the century saw a considerable importation of Chinese lacquer and an almost equal activity in imitating it, especially in Holland, it is not surprising to find examples (such as those in Figure 1) in which the Dutch lacquerer has embellished K'ang Hsi blue-and-white porcelain with his favorite *chinoiseries*.

Such decoration was naturally subject to injury, and once damaged would be liable to be "cleaned away," deliberately or otherwise. The same fate has befallen much

centuries or more before this time. These *Hausmaler* (or independent decorators) thus virtually rank as the inventors of the now familiar European enameling on pottery and porcelain; and it is to be remarked that, though the white-surfaced ware used for their painting was called *porcelain* — following the vogue of the Chinese — their subjects were purely German in style.

That they did not use veritable Chinese porcelain is doubtless to be explained by the difficulty of obtaining suitable plain white pieces. However, after the stabilization of China under K'ang Hsi, in the latter part of the seventeenth century, a vogue for enameled as well as blue-and-white porcelain developed. The consequent fresh wave of importation made available a supply of plain white ware, and thus cleared the way for the production of the interesting specimens that form the subject of this article and that to follow next month.

Three types of Oriental white porcelain predominate amongst the materials used by the European decorator, who was, on occasion, not averse to painting an already slightly decorated piece. Perhaps the most abundant was a type with rather bluish glaze and a decoration of lines incised in the paste, with now and then a narrow formal border or double line painted in underglaze blue. Next in quantity was the well-known *blanc de Chine*, the Fukien porcelains from Te-hua, particularly the small jugs of German form made especially for export. Finally, a great many undecorated *Japanese* pear-shaped bottles, usually of very inferior grayish-white porcelain, seem

Fig. 6 (above) — Plate (*c. 1720*)
  Chinese (K'ang Hsi) porcelain with an underglaze blue border, painted in colors at Delft. The painting shows the stork of the arms of The Hague holding a money-bag in its bill; the inscription may be translated: "The people of The Hague are wise: they want their money back!"
  From the H. W. Henderson collection, West Woodhay, Berkshire

Fig. 7 (left) — Bottle (*c. 1725*)
  Chinese (K'ang Hsi) porcelain with underglaze copper-red monsters. Additions painted in enamel colors at Delft.
  From the British Museum

Fig. 8 (below) — Mug (*early eighteenth century*)
  Fukien porcelain painted — chiefly in red and green — at Delft.
  From the Victoria and Albert Museum

to have found their way into the hands of the Dutch decorators. It is not unreasonable to surmise that Dutch traders imported these to the order of the decorators.

At times fine white pieces of other types are found. Little, if any, of this porcelain or the European painting on it can, in my opinion, date from before 1700, and much is as late as the 1740's. Somewhat later still, the English enamelers, to be discussed in my second article, used imported Oriental porcelains of yet different types.

Since the Dutch were the greatest importers at this time, it is natural that the first considerable body of European-decorated pieces should have come from Holland. Havard, in his history of the Delft potteries, states that, in 1705, one Gerrit van der Kaade opened a shop exclusively for the sale of Dutch-enameled Oriental porcelain, and Edme Gersaint in his catalogue of the Fonspertuis collection (1747) mentions work of this kind as done in Holland in his time, "often very *mal à propos*"; but beyond this nothing is known of the names or workshops of the Dutch painters. The most that is possible by way of identification is a division into classes.

To date, the only serious study of such wares has been made by W. W. Winkworth, who has discussed them in a delightful article in *The Burlington Magazine* (June, 1928, page 296). It is important to note that not only Oriental porcelain, but delftware (of the type often known as "delft *dorée*," erroneously supposed to have been the exclusive product of the Dextra and Pijnacker factories), Meissen porcelain, and even English salt-glazed stoneware were also decorated in these same Dutch workshops. The opprobrious name "clobber" is often applied to this work in general; but is better reserved for the

Fig. 9 — DISH (c. 1725)
Chinese (K'ang Hsi) porcelain, painted in colors at Delft. *From the British Museum, formerly in the Royal Saxon collection in Dresden*

Fig. 10 — DISH (c. 1725)
Chinese (K'ang Hsi) porcelain, painted in colors at Delft.
From the Victoria and Albert Museum

crude over-painting of blue-and-white, best exemplified by some nineteenth-century English work to be mentioned later. The eighteenth-century Dutch did, occasionally, smother blue-painted pieces in this way (sometimes using red only), but their better work is charming, and not without accomplishment.

Some of the earliest pieces, appropriately enough, are painted with ships flying the Dutch flag. That pictured in Figure 2 bears the arms of Zeeland on the stern and is dated *1700*. Similar decoration is found on delftware and Chinese-painted porcelain. The baroque scrollwork of the enameled delft is common also on the Dutch-decorated Chinese porcelain, often oddly mixed, as on the faïence itself, with Oriental birds and flowers. The little Fukien cups in Figure 3 show some crude baroque motives alone. The Japanese bottle in Figure 4 derives a double interest from the initials *B S* (perhaps the owner's), placed under the flowers in the medallion on the right, which were *painted in underglaze blue in Japan to Dutch order*, while the enameling of birds and plants, chiefly in red and turquoise, *is actually Dutch work*. The hot but slightly brownish tone of the red is characteristic of this class of painting, and helps to distinguish work that could easily be mistaken for Japanese.

Color as much as handling distinguishes the Dutch painting on many of the Fukien cups and mugs (*Figs. 5 and 8*). The flowers closely resemble the Oriental, but show an unmistakably European touch. Specimens of the kind have, however,

often been taken for the enameled Fukien mentioned in the Chinese records. Among other early types are some with topical subjects, particularly the wild financial ventures of the time. A set of plates in an English private collection is painted with satirical figures and inscriptions, which Doctor H. E. Van Gelder of the Gemeente Museum at The Hague informs me relate to the failure, in 1720, of the Credit Bank established by John Law in Paris (*Fig. 6*). The Dutchmen had been slow in taking shares and so saved their money. Several pieces bear the date *1720*, which was also that of the South Sea Bubble. This set is the usual bluish-toned porcelain with underglaze blue borders and engraved lines. Wholly Chinese specimens with similar subjects are also known, such as a plate inscribed *50 per cent op Delft gewonnen*, which also relates to the activities of John Law (illustrated in my *Guide to the Later Chinese Porcelain*, Plate 113*a*. See also an example of the same series, ANTIQUES, June, 1929, p. 487).

A large class embraces the imitations of the Japanese designs in the style supposed to have been invented by the potter Kakiemon and called by his name. These designs enjoyed a tremendous vogue in Europe during the second quarter of the eighteenth century, and were much imitated at the porcelain factories. Their motives, while not very common on delft, were constantly employed by the European enamelers of Oriental wares. The bottle in Figure 7 is (or was) a fine K'ang Hsi piece with copper-red

Fig. 11 — CUP AND SAUCER (c. 1734)
Chinese porcelain painted in colors at Delft, with the arms of England and Holland. Probably commemorating the marriage, in 1734, of William IV of Orange and Princess Anne of England.
From the Victoria and Albert Museum

Fig. 12 — DISH (*c. 1730*)
Chinese porcelain with underglaze blue borders, painted in colors at Delft. Inscribed on the back *GEORG II*.
From the British Museum

Fig. 13 — SAUCER (*c. 1750*)
Chinese porcelain, painted in China with design based on Lancret's *The Cherry Pickers*. (See also ANTIQUES for June, 1929, page 488.)
From the Victoria and Albert Museum

monsters, over which the Dutch enameler has added Kakiemon-style foliage and crude figures. Similarly, much of the decoration on the Japanese bottle in Figure 4 is adapted from the Kakiemon. Still more closely copied from the Japanese is the Chinese porcelain dish in Figure 9, which was, at one time, in the old Royal Saxon collection formed by Augustus the Strong (*1670–1733*), and bears the engraved inventory mark usually found on pieces from that source — *N:63*, with a small rectangle below.

These inventory numbers (known to collectors as the Johanneum marks) are accompanied by signs designating the category of the item as understood at the time. In this instance, the parallelogram below the numerals indicates the class known in the early eighteenth century as *Old Indian* or *Krack Porzellan*, terms which Doctor Zimmermann of Dresden tells me signify the Kakiemon type, though Franks conjectured that many pieces so marked were decorated in Holland, as this one undoubtedly was. One of the Fukien cups in Figure 3 bears the mark *N-92*, over an arrow. The latter was inscribed on porcelain called in the inventory "red Chinese porcelain."

Akin to the Kakiemon-style pieces and remarkable for their beautiful coloring, which includes a characteristic rather opaque glossy red, are some designs of parrots (*Fig. 10*), also found painted, but with much inferior effect, on delft *dorée*. These Kakiemon and kindred types date (in their European versions, at all events) from the 1720's onward. The same glossy red color is seen on certain armorial pieces painted in Holland (*Fig. 11*), *which are relatively few in comparison with the vast number done wholly in China in the course of the century*. The splendid dish with a horseman (*Fig. 12*), inscribed on the back *GEORG II*, shows the same red. Note the underglaze blue border and ring.

The largest class of this Dutch decoration, dating chiefly from the 1740's, appears on all sorts of wares besides Chinese,

Fig. 14 — BOWL (*c. 1747*)
Chinese porcelain painted at Delft. The fruit of the tree appears to be apples; possibly emblematic oranges are intended.
From the W. W. Winkworth collection

Fig. 15 — PERSIAN EARTHENWARE BOWL (*late eighteenth century*)
A Near-Eastern version of the "cherry-pickers" design. Compare saucer and bowl, Figures 13 and 14.
From the Victoria and Albert Museum

Fig. 16 — BOTTLES (c. 1745)
Japanese porcelain, painted at Delft

Fig. 17 — BOWL (c. 1745)
Chinese porcelain, painted at Delft

persons. Both made a "chinese copy" (small *c*, please, Mr. Printer) of their engraved model.

It may be asked what are the general criteria for distinguishing this Dutch and other European painting, on Chinese porcelain and often in Chinese style, from that actually by Chinese artists. Apart from slight but unmistakable differences of color, some of which have been mentioned, the outstanding characteristic of the Chinese work is its quality of line. The painting of arms, hands, and faces on the saucer in Figure 13 have an essentially Chinese rhythm and tautness, as of a coiled spring, which a European artist can never exactly reproduce. This may be due to training in calligraphy, or at least to the Chinese ideal of calligraphic quality in painting and drawing. The European artist tends to regard line merely as a means to an end, which is usually the "lifelike" rendering of a subject, with perspective and shadow, depth and volume; but with the Chinese porcelain-painter, line may be said almost to be an end in itself. Everything is stylized and two-dimensional; the masses enclosed by the lines matter less than the lines themselves and the patterns they achieve. Much of the forceful Dutch painting here figured would have seemed meaningless to the Chinese. It is not difficult to train the eye to sense the Chinese rhythm, which is in fact seen most clearly in the European subjects, where it is striking because of its unexpectedness.

[*A second article, on German and English decoration of Chinese porcelain, will be published in the March issue.*]

and was probably done at the workshop from which came the two Dutchmen who settled in England at Cobridge (otherwise Hot Lane) and began the charming Staffordshire enameling on salt-glazed stoneware, which exhibits many resemblances to that applied to Oriental porcelain. The mannerisms of the chief painters are easily recognizable: the pink and blue sky, the tufts of dotted herbage or bushes, the hooked grass, the warm brown-colored earth, and the trick of repeating the main subject in miniature on the lid are some of them. A favorite subject was that now usually known as "the apple-pickers" (*Fig. 14*). Mr. Winkworth has, however, suggested that the fruits are oranges with emblematical significance, and it is noteworthy that the date *1747*, when William IV of Orange became Stadtholder, occurs on some specimens, while his portrait and that of his wife Princess Anne of England are often found. The arms of the couple are, in fact, on the cup shown in Figure 11. A version of the "apple-pickers" design was copied in China and also, surprisingly enough, on Persian earthenware of the late eighteenth century; specimens of these are illustrated here for comparison (*Figs. 13 and 15*).

The first of them, however, derives from a well-known painting by Lancret, *The Cherry Pickers*, of which a fine example is owned by The Century Club in New York. Other favorite subjects were harlequins and characters from the Italian Comedy (*Fig. 16*), river-scenes — with wherries and horizontally dotted and dashed water — and ladies and gentlemen in gardens (*Fig. 17*). One delightful plate illustrated by Mr. Winkworth bears a Watteau scene with seated lovers beside a clipped hedge, which shows so much of the character of the Chinese painting in European style that it is tempting to regard it as itself copied from a Chinese version of a European subject. The dish painted with the Crucifixion here illustrated (*Fig. 18*), though undoubtedly Dutch work, shows the same character, which may, however (as Mr. Winkworth has suggested to me), be due to a similar uncomprehending method of attack on the part of both Chinese and Dutch artists, the latter being as a rule, for all their gifts, untutored and unacademic

Fig. 18 — DISH (c. 1730)
Chinese porcelain, painted at Delft.
Figures 16, 17, 18 from the Victoria and Albert Museum

German & English Decorators of Chinese Porcelain

By W. B. Honey

HOWEVER delightful much of the Dutch enameling described in my previous article, no great accomplishment or range of achievement may be claimed for it. On the other hand, among the German *Hausmaler* who occasionally employed Chinese porcelain were some artists of a marked individuality amounting even to genius. The great seventeenth-century masters of ceramic painting, such as Johann Schaper, Abraham Helmhack, and the "Monogrammist W. R.," never decorated porcelain. But, during the early eighteenth century, the Bohemian artists frequently used the bluish- or grayish-toned bowls and cups previously mentioned and familiar in Dutch work, for their black (*Schwarzlot*), red, or purple monochrome work, depicting landscapes with figures, *chinoiseries* (*Fig. 1*), or the fanciful baroque *Laub-und-Bandelwerk* of the period about 1725–1735 (*Fig. 2*). Theirs was an art with a distinguished ancestry in Netherlandish glass painting, and their work is often of great beauty.

Daniel Preissler (*1636–1733*) and his son Ignaz, at one time collectively known in ceramic history as "Preussler," worked at Friedrichswalde in Silesia near the Bohemian border, and at Kronstadt actually in Bohemia. The latter artist is recorded in contemporary correspondence as painting much Chinese porcelain, "particularly that with blue borders," which was bought for him in Prague by his patron, Count Kolowrat. The admirable plate shown in Figure 1 is noteworthy for the amusing way in which the artist has worked in his *chinoiserie* figures amongst the red flowers and foliage originally painted on it in China.

The highly gifted Ignaz Bottengruber of Breslau used Chinese porcelain with blue line-borders for some of his earlier pieces, such as a set of plates in the Schlesisches Museum at Breslau, with his usual bacchanalian subjects in iron-red monochrome, signed and dated *1728;* but subsequently he and his pupils, von Bressler and von Wolfsburg, painted chiefly upon wares from Meissen or Vienna. The Bayreuth *Hausmaler*, of whom

Fig. 1 — PLATE (*c. 1725*)
Chinese (K'ang Hsi) porcelain, originally painted in iron-red, with decoration in black added by Ignaz Preissler in Bohemia

J. F. Metzsch was the chief, used for some of their most important works a type of Yung Chêng porcelain of very fine quality. A bowl in the Victoria and Albert Museum, with figures in landscapes, one of the very few pieces signed by Metzsch, is extremely delicate Chinese porcelain, of the type with flanged rim to take a reversible saucer-shaped cover. A service of similar body was formerly in the Darmstädter collection in Berlin, with rich painting signed by Metzsch's aristocratic pupil R. C. von Drechsel. A similar bowl in the British Museum displays Bayreuth decoration imitated from *chinoiseries* of the type invented by J. G. Herold of Meissen (*Fig. 3*). The painting on the Ch'ien Lung tea caddy and tray in Figure 4 is also German, and has a border not unlike those on some of Metzsch's work, but the red flesh tones recall some Nymphenburg porcelain. This painting may therefore have been done in Bavaria after 1767, when a financial crash led to the dismissal of many painters, one at least of whom, named G. C. Lindemann, is known to have taken up independent decoration of foreign porcelain.

The Viennese painter Carl Wendelin Anreiter von Zirnfeld, who made history by helping to found the Doccia factory, is known by rare specimens of *Hausmalerei*, of which the beautiful signed cup shown in Figure 6 concerns us here as a piece of Fukien porcelain. The Saxon *Hausmaler* were naturally better able than other Germans to obtain Meissen porcelain and had no need of the Chinese product; but an instance of possibly Saxon work on the latter is provided by the not uncommon bowls, cups, and dishes with designs engraved through the black or brown glaze to the white body beneath (*Fig. 5*). This is undoubtedly glass-cutter's work, and was not improbably executed in the factory at Dresden founded early in the eighteenth century by Böttger's inspirer and coworker Tschirnhausen, where the former's red stoneware, as well as glass, was similarly decorated. Similar engraving, but in designs of a different character, is also found on some

Fig. 2 — CUP AND SAUCER (*c. 1725*)
Chinese (K'ang Hsi) porcelain with enamel painting in red added by Ignaz Preissler in Bohemia

Fulham stoneware. Also possibly Saxon is the decoration in raised gilding on the Fukien jug of Figure 7. This treatment is not unlike that found on some well-known specimens of Vienna porcelain and enamel boxes, identified as the work of the notorious wandering "arcanist" Christoph Conrad Hunger, as well as by the Meissen painter C. F. Herold, working for Fromery of Berlin. But it shows some points of difference, and may even be London work in a style that was widely favored, for it is found also on Saint-Cloud porcelain. There is a Bristol blue-glass plaque in the Schreiber collection with somewhat similar lacquer gilding — probably the work of a London jeweler.

Fig. 3 — BOWL AND COVER (c. 1735)
Chinese (Yung Chêng) porcelain, painted in Germany, probably by J. F. Metzsch at Bayreuth

ENGLISH enamelers came relatively late into this field. Though the English East India Company had long since shared in the export trade from China, it is not until about 1750 that we have evidence of English enameling shops likely to have used Chinese wares. The London account book of William Duesbury for 1751 to 1753, lately published in facsimile and transcription by Mrs. Everilda MacAlister, affords an extremely valuable record of the activities of one of the most influential figures in early English porcelain history, and is, in fact, indispensable for its study. But, though among the items recorded several references to "Chineys" men occur, no clue to actual specimens of Chinese porcelain decorated by Duesbury is discoverable. Apparently much of his

Fig. 4 — TRAY AND TEA CADDY (c. 1765)
Chinese (early Ch'ien Lung) porcelain, painted in Germany, perhaps at Nymphenburg by G. C. Lindemann

work was not enameled at all, but painted in oil color, which has long since been "cleaned away." The distinction between oil and enamel painting is evidently necessary, since in contemporary advertisements porcelain is "warranted true enamel."

As for another very noteworthy decorator, though we have no written evidence that he decorated Chinese porcelain, many actual pieces survive that may, with considerable probability, be associated with him, or rather, with his workshop. This man is John Giles, a London enameler of Kentish Town, with a showroom in Cockspur Street, and latterly in Berwick Street, Soho. In 1768 Giles advertised that he had "a great Variety of white Goods by him, Ladies and Gentlemen may depend upon having their Commands executed immediately and painted to any pattern they shall chuse." This white ware was chiefly Worcester china, much of which must bear Giles' decoration; but the part played by the artist in other directions is still undetermined. In my *Old English Porcelain* I suggested that a great deal of Bow china was probably decorated outside the factory, and cited the curious statement of Thomas Craft, a Bow hand, who, in presenting a Bow bowl to the British Museum, in 1790, observed that the painting on it was fired for him about 1760 by "Mr. Gyles."

Now certain cups of Chinese porcelain of which specimens are in the two London museums are, by tradition, said to have been decorated

Fig. 5 (above) — BOWL (early eighteenth century)
Chinese (K'ang Hsi) porcelain with design cut through the brown glaze by a European glass-engraver; probably Saxon work

Fig. 6 (left) — CUP (c. 1740)
Fukien porcelain, painted and signed by Carl Wendelin Anreiter, working at Florence

Fig. 7 (right) — JUG (c. 1720)
Fukien porcelain, decorated in gold. Perhaps Saxon

Fig. 8 — CUP AND SAUCER (c. 1760)
Chinese porcelain, painted in London, probably in the workshop of John Giles

Fig. 9 — CUP AND SAUCER (c. 1765)
Chinese porcelain, painted in London, probably in the workshop of John Giles

at Bow, though their treatment does not closely resemble any of the recognized Bow painting but, instead, is nearer to Worcester in style (Fig. 8). Can this confusion be due to the fact that they were decorated in Giles' workshop? On the Worcester side we have a chain of evidence starting with the appearance of the same type of "exotic birds" cn several makes of English porcelain. These "disheveled birds" appear on Bow, Worcester, Longton Hall, and Plymouth wares, and have sometimes been taken as evidence that the painter migrated to these places. It is more likely, as I have suggested in my book, that he merely worked for Giles, who obtained white porcelain from all four factories.

The Chinese saucer-dish of Figure 10 is painted in black washed over with green, and follows a style invented at Meissen and adopted also at Vincennes and Chelsea. I believe it to be by the same hand as a Worcester mug with a landscape, in the Schreiber collection (No. 521), in which the panel is outlined in a very curious way with red and black lines. Precisely similar red and black lines enclose a panel with a "disheveled bird" of the familiar type on a Plymouth dish in the Fitzwilliam Museum, Cambridge. This seems to show that all three were done in the same workshop. Another Chelsea-Worcester style of painting — "exotic" but not "disheveled" birds — on Chinese porcelain (Fig. 9), may be attributed to the same workshop, while the serrated gilt borders as well as the type of porcelain link these last with some delightful figure-painting referred to below. The serrated gilt borders are, indeed, very common on work from this source (that on the green and black dish — Figure 10 — is similar), and the quality of the gold is noticeably poor and thin and easily rubbed away. These are important points that help in the identification of the class.

Two other specimens that I believe to be of the same origin are here illustrated (Figs. 11 and 12). The first is on the earlier engraved porcelain familiar in Dutch and German work, and is, I think, by the hand of the painter O'Neale,

one of the few individual artists identified as a painter of early English porcelain. Similar work, with his signature, occurs on Worcester porcelain in the Frank Lloyd collection in the British Museum and elsewhere. The artlessly drawn but very charming horses, the trees with crossed branches, usually on the left, and the slender tufted trees on the right, the spiky "starfish" hands of the figures, and a group of red-brown rocks in the foreground are characteristic features of his work. Worcester pieces by him are said to be in the White House collection at Washington — a curious and diverse assemblage of ware.

The "O'Neale" in question is believed to have been a London miniature painter recorded as "Jeffrey Hamet O'Neal," and was probably identical with the "Mr. O'Neal" of "the China Shop," who exhibited miniatures at the Society of Artists in 1765, and with the "Mr. O'Neil, a painter," recorded as casually employed at Chelsea in 1770–1773.

The second specimen is a cup and saucer (Fig. 12) with charming figure-painting unmistakably by the painter of the teapot, which has a similar subject on the side not illustrated. On the evidence of the gilding these may all be regarded as products of Giles' workshop. Other Worcester styles of painting are seen on some pieces that received part of their decoration in China. The colored flowers on the steatitic vase and the cup and saucer in Figure 14 are examples of these, and are probably of the same origin as the work just described. The flowers on the teapot in Figure 13 are in another well-known Worcester style.

It seems possible that the Giles workshop at some time commanded the services of artists from various sources — from the London factories as well as from Worcester. There is a fluted Chinese saucer in the Schreiber collection (Fig. 15) painted in crimson monochrome, which has generally been attributed to the hand of the well-known Chelsea "fable-painter," but should rather, I think, be credited to O'Neale. The other cup and saucer in the same illustration are also Chinese, with charming painting in crimson and black, in

Fig. 10 — DISH (c. 1765)
Chinese porcelain, painted in black and green in London, probably in the workshop of John Giles

Figs. 11 and 12 — TEAPOT AND CUP AND SAUCER (c. 1765)
Chinese porcelain, painted by O'Neale, probably in John Giles' London workshop

Chelsea style but not certainly by a Chelsea hand. Chinese pieces are, however, occasionally found with decoration undoubtedly by Chelsea, Bow, and Meissen painters. (Since in illustrations these appear exactly like factory-work, there would be no point in showing examples here.)

Such pieces raise the question whether their decoration was done in the factories, or by the painters working at home "in their own time," or for Giles. We have still no conclusive proof that the Worcester-style pieces described above were done by Giles and not at the factory. Nevertheless the differences are marked enough for a provisional classification, and, on general grounds, more probably foreign wares would have been decorated at an independent enameler's establishment than at a factory.

Transfer printing, a characteristic English decoration, was seldom applied to imported Oriental wares, the glaze of which was probably too hard for successful results. Of two rare examples in the British Museum one bears a print of the well-known Worcester *Tea-Party* subject, while a similarly printed Chinese cup and saucer actually in the Worcester Works Museum (*No. 583*) bears the same print washed over in colors. This might

seem to be evidence for Worcester factory-decoration of Chinese porcelain. But the colored-over transfer printing is the one type of decoration hitherto attributed with confidence to Giles (see Mr. Hobson's *Worcester Porcelain* and his catalogue of the Frank Lloyd collection, p. 86), who is recorded as the purchaser of printed wares at the Worcester public sales. Further, there is, of course, no certainty that all the objects in the Works Museum are actually local products, since some are known to have been purchased for the collection. It is likewise probable that engraved plates could well have been obtained and used by Giles (the *Tea-Party* was engraved in many versions, one of which appears on Bow porcelain). The other specimen in the British Museum is imperfectly printed with a pastoral scene, somewhat in the early Bristol-Worcester

Fig. 13 (above) — TEAPOT (c. 1765)
Chinese porcelain, painted in colors, probably in John Giles' London workshop

Fig. 14 (left) — VASE AND CUP AND SAUCER (c. 1765)
Vase of Chinese soapstone porcelain with colored relief, and cup and saucer, Chinese porcelain with painting in opaque white, with flower-painting in colors added probably in the London workshop of John Giles

style of about 1750–1755, washed over in green in the manner of the dish in Figure 10, which we have attributed to Giles. A little jug in the Schreiber collection, with a Caughley-style print, formerly catalogued as Chinese, is now recognized as Bristol porcelain.

Another busy London decorating shop of the late eighteenth and early nineteenth centuries was conducted by one Baxter, father of the better known Thomas Baxter, whose figure- and flower-pieces are familiar on

Worcester and Swansea china. In 1810 Thomas Baxter painted a water color of his father's shop in Gough Square, Fleet Street, showing on the table pieces of porcelain apparently about to be decorated. Among these are fluted wares of late Worcester or Salopian type painted in underglaze blue such as could not have been fired in an enameler's kiln. They were evidently in Baxter's place to receive some

Fig. 15 — CUP AND SAUCERS (c. 1765)
Chinese porcelain, painted in crimson monochrome; one by O'Neale. Probably done in the London workshop of John Giles

kind of added decoration, which I believe to have been chiefly gilding. Chinese cups, dishes, and rectangular tea caddies (the last particularly numerous) are commonly found with arbitrarily placed bands and borders of hard, bright gilding, so precisely of the kind found on Salopian porcelain as to point to the same decorative source (*Fig. 16*). Also, in my opinion, Baxter's hand

to have been decorated at Bow, though twenty years too late in style, is one more instance of the untrustworthiness of such "evidence." There were other decorators in England in the early part of the nineteenth century, such as Allen of Lowestoft, Sims, Muss, and Robins and Randall of London — but there is no evidence that they decorated Chinese porcelain.

Lastly, as a dismal end to the tale of this interesting class of porcelain, must be mentioned the fittingly named "clobbered" decoration added in London to a great deal of usually indifferent Chinese blue-and-white during the second quarter of the nineteenth century. Spots and rough foliage of crude pink, yellow, red, and yellowish green were added in almost complete disregard of the blue designs which were often entirely covered up. The same treatment was sometimes accorded to Lowestoft and Worcester china.

Figures 1, 7, 10, 11, 14, 16, 17, 18 from the Victoria and Albert Museum; Figures 2, 3, 4, 5, 6 from the British Museum; Figures 8, 9, 13, 15 from the Schreiber collection; and Figure 12 from the A. E. R. Malcolm collection

Fig. 16 (above, left) — TEA CADDY (late eighteenth century)
Chinese porcelain painted in underglaze blue in the style of English transfer printing, with gilt borders added on the shoulder and lid, probably by Baxter in London

Fig. 17 (above, right) — CUP AND SAUCER (late eighteenth century)
Chinese porcelain painted with flowers in colors in China, with stripes in purple and gilding added, probably by Baxter, in London

Fig. 18 (right) — PLATE (1825-1850)
Chinese porcelain painted in underglaze blue, with over-decoration in colors ("clobbering") added in London. Only the quantity of this atrocious type of decoration that exists in London and the English provinces justifies its illustration here

is observable in the added decoration of similar gilding with purple stripes and wavy lines on the cup and saucer of Figure 17. The flowers here are Chinese work and show a characteristic brown enamel among the colors used. They are also touched with thin and delicate Chinese gilding, which it is instructive to contrast with the hard, bright, so-called "Salopian" gold on the same piece. That this cup and saucer are also by tradition said

IV American Market

In this section devoted to porcelain either made or decorated for the American market, all the articles with the exception of the last two are by Homer Eaton Keyes. Keyes had his own private collection of Chinese export and also possessed the good fortune to have two friends to consult with and advise him. They were the two most important collectors of this porcelain at the time—Edward A. Crowninshield and Henry F. du Pont.

Crowninshield was a direct descendant of the famous Crowninshield family of Salem, Massachusetts, whose ships were among the first to engage actively in the China trade of this country. His personal collection of American marine and related Chinese export porcelain derived in part from what his forebears had brought from China. In addition, there were important records, such as ship manifests, bills of sale, etc., which were retained in the family.

Henry F. du Pont became enamored of Chinese porcelain made for the American market early in his extraordinary collecting career. He began his collection of Americana in the early 1920s, including one of the largest and finest assemblages of American market porcelain, all of which is now included in the famous Henry Francis du Pont Winterthur Museum near Wilmington, Delaware.

In "Lowestoft, Exclusively American," Keyes draws a distinction between several kinds of pieces. Some are decorated with an exclusive American design, such as the bald eagle, the arms of the state of New York, etc. Others have decorations such as family initials, Masonic emblems, etc., which could just as easily have been suitable for the English market. This distinction, however, may be too finely drawn. Present-day collectors are likely to give greater weight to a sound provenance of original American ownership than to absolutely exclusive American design elements.

In a second article, "American Eagle Lowestoft," Keyes discourses on the variations of the American eagle decoration with sound conjectures as to the original source of the design. It seems perfectly fitting to him that Chinese artists should have been drawn to the symbols carried on United States coins, currency with which they became familiar in trade. Even Keyes, however, can not explain the curious bald eagle, illustrated in figure 4 on p. 121, which "is sprouting a Chinese pigtail."

In the following article, "State Arms on Chinese Lowestoft," Keyes discusses pieces decorated with the state arms of New York and Pennsylvania. He shows that pieces decorated with a lady leaning on an anchor and the word "Hope," or variations of this theme, are not to be considered as representing the somewhat similar arms of Rhode Island. These devices were used in various ways and times and bear absolutely no relation to the official arms.

When describing the variations in the decoration of the arms of the state of New York, Keyes points out that they fail to follow the details of the official version which includes a sun rising over the mountains within a shield, and the motto, "Excelsior." He was probably not aware that a few very rare pieces do exist with just such details included.

Keyes has included an illustration, p. 126, with the arms of the Commonwealth of Pennsylvania. In thirty-five years, this writer has never been able to locate an example for his own collection, and in fact has never seen another such object. The late Philadelphia dealer, Arthur J. Sussel, in the early 1920s sold a fifteen-inch punch bowl decorated with the Pennsylvania arms. The whereabouts of this bowl are unknown and this writer would appreciate hearing from any reader fortunate enough to know of its location.

Since the writing of the Keyes article in 1930, a tea set with the arms of New Hampshire has been found together with the original bill of sale for a New Hampshire individual. So, as of now, the arms of three states are known to have existed in export porcelain.

"American Ship Lowestoft" broadly covers marine porcelain in an informative way. Keyes comments on the scarcity of finely-decorated ship pieces, and expresses the opinion that, as time passes, exceptional pieces will hopefully surface, as indeed they have (see p. 50). One of the finer pieces, the "Grand Turk" punch bowl possessed by the Peabody Museum, Salem, Massachusetts, is illustrated and explained in this article. The story of its origins will delight the reader as it did Keyes.

In his article entitled "The Cincinnati and Their Porcelain," Keyes illustrates a plate from the well-known George Washington Cincinnati service. Examples from this service are the most important from a monetary standpoint, as well as from a collector's standpoint, as any produced for the American market. How General Washington commissioned Harry "Light Horse" Lee to purchase this set when the "Pallas" docked in New York is well documented by letters in the possession of The Mount Vernon Ladies Association and the Library of Congress.

Keyes raises the question as to why Cincinnati china was on the "Pallas" and mentions the fact that Thomas Randall sailed with Samuel Shaw on the "Empress of China" to Canton a few months earlier in 1784. For some reason he fails to note and explain that Randall was a business partner of Shaw and was aboard the "Pallas" on its return voyage. It would have been logical for Randall to have carried Cincinnati porcelain back with him.

The Cincinnati design shown in figure 2, p. 134, is, with one exception, the same as that shown on pieces made for Shaw, General Knox, David Townsend, Green, and William Eustis. Eustis had another service decorated with two small angels in blue enamel above and to each side of the emblem. All the sets with the design shown in figure 2 have the owner's initials in small gold script below the emblem. The Cincinnati pieces, simply, in Keyes' words, presented democratic American citizens with an opportunity "to own armorial china, handsome and exclusive enough to compare favorably with the services which graced the tables of the aristocracy of Europe."

A direct descendant of Stephen Decatur gives a history of "The Commodore Decatur Punchbowl" and similar bowls made for Philadelphia Naval Commodores Barry, Dale, Decatur, and Truxtun. All seem to have been commemorative presentation pieces. As the author notes in a caption to a detail of the portrait medallion on the bowl, "The extraordinary fidelity with which the Chinese artist has rendered the engraved portrait on a porcelain surface has probably never been equaled on any other piece of oriental Lowestoft."

At the end of the previous article is a short item about a duplicate of the Captain Samuel Morris punchbowl which had been celebrated in *Antiques* four years earlier, in 1932. It notes that J. A. Lloyd Hyde, author of *Oriental Lowestoft,* illustrated two other similar bowls. Within the past ten years this writer has come across yet three other bowls of this exact decoration and is of the opinion that very few decorated pieces can be considered unique, unless a specific decoration commemorating a one-time event was painted for a single individual.

For example, this writer owns a plate which has "Thos. Ross Remember the Chronometer" written across it in bold, gold script. Family tradition has it that Ross, a young man whose father was in partnership with Philadelphia merchant Robert Morris, sailed on one of the family ships. It was his duty to attend to the winding of the chronometer, and being of a forgetful nature, he overlooked this important duty. We don't know what his captain's reaction was but, later in Canton, Ross's shipmates presented him with this plate. It is certainly a one-of-a-kind item.

What may be a unique piece for an entirely different reason is described in the last article, "A Lost Set of Eighteenth-Century Oriental Lowestoft" by Harrold E. Gillingham. Armorial sets for American families are very rare. After the Revolutionary War most Americans eschewed anything that could be construed as indulging English aristocratic manners. There is ample evidence that this lost set with the family arms of Fuller was ordered and delivered. Benjamin Fuller was a ship owner and merchant who lived in Philadelphia. He died a wealthy man, but without children to form an aristocratic dynasty. A nephew living in Ireland inherited the service. Diligent searching there for an example has only turned up one badly damaged piece.

Lowestoft: Exclusively American

By HOMER EATON KEYES

IN A consideration of so-called "American Lowestoft," that is, Oriental porcelain decorated in the Far East at the behest of American customers, it is necessary to draw a fairly sharp line of distinction between items of an exclusively American significance and those whose national association is indicated solely by the addition of some specific emblem to a stock pattern. Insistence upon such a division may savor of hair-splitting, yet it is essential to a clear and reasonably scientific classification of the ware in question, as well as to an understanding of the relative desirability of the various types available to the collector.

We have already observed that the blue and gold designs emphasizing a mantled shield, upon which family initials are frequently emblazoned, were quite as popular in England as in the new Republic. Hence, except in scattered instances, it is impossible to determine whether an item of this pseudoarmorial type was brought into the United States in early Federal days, or has recently been obtained from among the ancestral treasures of some long-established English family.

Again, with certain notable exceptions, the American ship Lowestoft now so highly prized by collectors owes its citizenship in this country to the deft introduction of the Stars and Stripes at the stern of an essentially nondescript craft that, without its ensign, might pass as almost anything from a radio-equipped Noah's Ark to a Chinese junk. The more striking departures from this rule have already been cited in previous articles. One other, of unusually high quality and obviously deserving inclusion in the "ship-portrait" category, is shown in Figure 1.

In the ultra-exclusive American series, then, are to be reckoned a somewhat small series of ship items (ANTIQUES for June 1931); and, with them, a considerable number of single pieces and complete sets adorned with one or another of the many depictions of an unmistakably American eagle (ANTIQUES for

June 1930); those, likewise, bearing the arms of New York State, and of Pennsylvania; the Cincinnati porcelain as a whole; and the small but distinguished group that is now to be discussed.

First in honor, if not in excellence, of this group must be placed the Martha Washington set of porcelain, from which a broken two-handled covered cup and a saucer are shown in Figures 4 and 5. Their far from elaborate decoration reveals an almost childishly obvious symbolism. Surrounded by a laurel wreath, the initials M W are implanted on a gold background, emblematic of the sun in splendor, whose fifteen golden rays touch fifteen links of an indivisible chain, each inscribed with the name of a state of the Union. By way of its further reënforcement as a token of strength, the chain, in its turn, is surrounded by a blue and gold serpent, holding its tail in its mouth. The only other element of decoration is a pink ribbon scroll inscribed with the Latin motto *Decus et tutamen ab illo.*

Several tales relative to the origin of this Martha Washington service are adequately rehearsed and disposed of in Alice Morse Earle's *China Collecting in America.* According to one legend, the outfit was presented to the mistress of Mount Vernon by the French officers who had served with Washington during the War of the Revolution. Lafayette is likewise named as the donor. Not improbably, however, the credit should rightfully be accorded to a certain Captain van Braam, a Dutchman by birth, and a life-long friend of the first President.

Beyond reasonable question, both the making and the decorating of the service were accomplished in China, after a drawing and specifications supplied by the intending giver. We are unable to agree with the opinion expressed by Halsey and Tower, in *The Homes of Our Ancestors*, that, although the ware is Oriental, the enameled and gilded design was probably applied in France. The difficulties involved in routing the porcelain from China to the

Fig. 1 — SHIP-PORTRAIT PLATE (c. 1800)
While the name of the vessel does not appear, the careful accuracy of the drawing distinguishes this design among ship delineations on Chinese porcelain.
From the collection of Mrs. J. Insley Blair

Fig. 2 — MANTEL GARNITURE (1790–1800)
A design popular in America but by no means exclusive to this country. It is seldom that such garnitures, which originally consisted of five vases, survive today in their entirety.
From the collection of Mrs. Stanley W. Edwards

United States via the European continent, unpacking it for the French decorator, and then reforwarding it to its ultimate destination would have been serious. In view of the well-proved abilities of the Cantonese enamelers, such a course would have been quite unnecessary.

Whatever may be the artistic deficiencies of the Martha Washington service, its remains are excessively scarce, and, because of their associations, are virtually as precious as their weight in gold. Hence the collector should guard against mistaking the more or less plentiful late nineteenth-century reproductions of the pattern for original specimens. Of such reproductions, two

Fig. 3 — A CHINESE PORCELAIN TEA SET WITH AMERICAN ASSOCIATIONS (*c. 1800*)
The history of this tea service and the name *Maria Sturges* inscribed on each piece place the set in the American category, though the pattern is not specifically American in its implications.
From the collection of Ginsburg and Levy

editions on French porcelain appear to have been issued: one for the Philadelphia Centennial Exposition of 1876; another for the Chicago World's Fair of 1893. (*See Fig. 6.*) Three pieces representative of these late editions were included in the sale of the Frances Clary Morse collection at the old American Art Galleries in March of 1912. On this occasion, a plate from the 1876 series brought three dollars; a platter and a plate of 1893, three dollars and two dollars respectively. Similar items turn up from time to time, and, though their market price has lifted considerably since 1912, their purchase should not be permitted to exert a serious strain upon the purse strings.

Figs. 4 and 5 (right and below) — FROM THE MARTHA WASHINGTON SERVICE (*c. 1792*)
Covered cup and saucer; part of a set made in China and presented, about 1792, to Martha Washington. The date is fixed by the introduction of Kentucky among the group of states forming the endless chain of the border design.
From the Metropolitan Museum of Art

Fig. 6 (below) — FRENCH VERSION OF MARTHA WASHINGTON PLATE
One of the nineteenth-century imitations on French porcelain. Note rounded contours of chain links; separation of gilded rays; leafless wreath; and virtual elimination of serifs from small capital letters. The porcelain itself is likewise very different from the Chinese.
From the Koopman collection

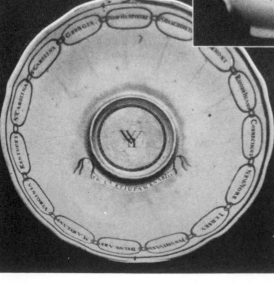

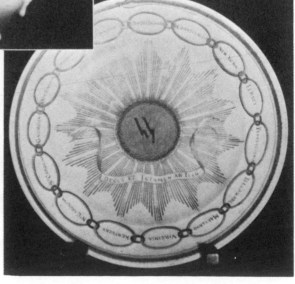

Fig. 7 — CHINESE PUNCH BOWL (*late eighteenth century*)
A gift from George Washington to Colonel Eyre. The decoration portrays the foreign warehouses at the mouth of the river near Canton, China. Among the flags displayed the American emblem is conspicuous. While American in association, this bowl does not qualify as a strictly American-market item.
From the Metropolitan Museum of Art

floral swags, and carrying, in a border medallion, the initials J R L. It is evidently to this very set, subsequently dispersed, that belonged the platter illustrated in Figure 8. We may doubt that many similar sets were produced. By the time they could have been ordered, produced,

Fig. 8 — WASHINGTON URN PLATTER
From a set made in China as a token of mourning for George Washington's death. Initials on the border medallion, *J R L.* *Collection of Mrs. W. Murray Crane*

In so far as we know, only one special-order pattern of Oriental ware other than the Martha Washington and some Cincinnati designs is associated with the first President, and that is the rare Washington urn. To be sure, Mrs. Earle mentions a Mount Vernon punch bowl bearing the initials G W and inwardly adorned with a frigate picture. She likewise tells us that Washington was wont to present Oriental punch bowls to special friends. Among these donations she cites a bowl said to have been given by the Commander-in-Chief to Colonel George Eyre in recognition of distinguished gallantry at the Battle of Princeton. Its surface is covered with a view of the foreign trading stations in Canton with various national flags flying before them (*Fig. 7*). The items named seem, however, to have been of stock type, American by adoption rather than by primary intent.

The Washington urn design, on the contrary, must have been invented expressly to touch a responsive chord in a people grieving over the death of its national hero. Mrs. Earle waxes enthusiastic concerning a set adorned with this design wrought largely in sober browns and gold, interspersed with

Fig. 9 (*right*) — MASONIC COVERED JUG OR FLAGON (*1790–1800*)
From the collection of Edward Crowninshield

shipped from China, and delivered to the American market, the gloom that they were intended to capitalize must have diminished, if not completely evaporated. Were it possible to penetrate the history of the service from which our illustration is taken, we should not improbably discover its

Fig. 10 (*below*) — MASONIC PORCELAIN (*1790–1800*)
The cup and saucer in the centre of the group display the American armorial eagle in conjunction with Masonic emblems. They are, therefore, to be recognized as exclusively American items. The other pieces would serve English quite as well as American requirements.
From the collection of Edward Crowninshield

source in a special command dispatched by the first vessel that cleared for the Far East from an American port after the fateful December 14 of the year 1799. As we shall see in a later chapter of these notes, the Washington urn has not escaped the attention of the imitator, and has been cleverly, if not quite convincingly, reproduced by one of the leading French makers of pseudo-Oriental porcelains.

There is ground for debate as to whether the American-market Masonic porcelain should be placed in the eagle category or given a separate classification. Masonic pieces without distinctive indications of nationality may be found both in this country and abroad — apparently the survivors of large quantities exported from China in the 1790's and early 1800's. Now and then to be encountered, however, are items upon which an American

eagle occupies a conspicuous place among the symbols of the fraternal order. In all such instances that have come to our attention, this fowl is of the armorial sparrow type considered in ANTIQUES for June 1930. There is no mistaking its patriotic implications, and no gainsaying the fact that its presence on a Masonic item adds immeasurably to the value of the latter in the eyes of the American collector. Apparently — though we make the statement with extreme caution — certain of the emblems of Masonry in which resided no mystic meanings, such, for example, as the T-square and compasses, the plumb line and triangle, were occasionally separated from the more esoteric insignia of the order and were distributed on articles of porcelain designed to signalize the trade of the cabinetmaker. Harry T. Peters, Jr., has a punch bowl, once owned by Duncan Phyfe, that exemplifies this practice. In addition,

however, to the implements usually associated with Masonry, its decoration includes a carpenter's tool chest. The piece is a curious and unusual item, and worthy of parenthetical mention at this point, despite the fact that its Americanism is attributable to personal association rather than to the inherent character of its ornamentation.

In previous discussions, we have considered the majority, if not all, of the known porcelain patterns of exclusively American

Figs. 11, 12, and 13 — COLONEL RICHARD VARICK'S CINCINNATI PUNCH BOWL (*c. 1788*)
Pictured here in three positions to reveal its entire decorative scheme, this bowl is the most notable item of Sino-American porcelain that has come to light. The decoration is a careful copy from the membership certificate of the Society of the Cincinnati engraved by Robert Scot of Philadelphia, who was subsequently appointed engraver to the United States mint.
From the collections of the Washington Association of New Jersey, at Morristown

significance that were produced in the Orient for export to the United States. We have also paid tribute to the highly individualized single pieces, such as jugs and punch bowls, that occupy an outstanding position in the purely American category. In the list of Cincinnati items, however, we have failed to note a uniquely magnificent punch bowl evidently made to special order for Colonel Richard Varick, one of Washington's military aides (*Figs. 11, 12, 13*). This bowl, now in the possession of the Washington Association of New Jersey, at Morristown, is eighteen inches in diameter. The decoration consists of an amazingly accurate copy of the certificate of membership issued to Colonel Varick by the Society of the Cincinnati and signed by George Washington as president of the organization.

These certificates were elaborate affairs, printed on vellum from a plate engraved for the purpose by Robert Scot of Philadelphia, subsequently engraver to the United States mint. Scot was a competent artist, who had been trained to his work in England. If he retained any prejudices of birth, he suppressed them in behalf of the distinguished patronage of the Cincinnati and produced a design not only exquisite in its lettering but with added pictorial adornments of a symbolism sufficiently bombastic to satisfy the most inflated patriotism. It is, of course, obvious stuff, but well executed. The American Cincinnatus, represented as a plumed knight, driving a plump and terrified Britannia and her lion into the sea; Fame trumpeting the message of victorious Liberty from the clouds; eagles amid thunderbolts; eagles bearing the emblem of the Society; clouds of war and clouds of glory pierced with swift shafts of light. All this drama of freedom, painted in full enamel colors, reappears upon Colonel Varick's bowl — a masterpiece of

Figs. 14, 15, and 16 — The General Morton Bowl (1812)
An important example of Sino-American porcelain; made to special order in China for presentation to the Corporation of the City of New York. Two views of the exterior and one of the interior, with its picture of New York, are shown.
From the Metropolitan Museum of Art

designed for presentation to an important civic body; its decoration signalizes its destined purpose; and its inscriptions not only fix its date but record its authorship.

On the exterior of this bowl appear the arms of the Union and of the City of New York, separated by vignette views of the town. The interior is occupied by a large picture of the Manhattan waterfront with shipping in the foreground, and an already serrate sky line in the distance: a faithful copy from an engraving by Samuel Seymour, after a drawing by William Birch. The date of the depiction is 1802, although the engraving was not issued until 1803. Only three extant copies of the latter are known.

The accompanying inscriptions on the bowl deserve to be quoted in full. That encircling the outer rim reads: *Presented by General Jacob Morton, to the Corporation of*

Chinese ceramic painting. Such a feat would have been impossible to any but an Oriental artist. It could not have been accomplished at all except for the clarity of Scot's engraving and the undoubted fact that Colonel Varick's own certificate was transmitted to Canton for the benefit of the Cantonese copyist.

To whom did he entrust the precious parchment? No record has yet been discovered to tell us. It is, however, worth noting that the date of the certificate is January 1, 1784. A month later the *Empress of China*, first American vessel to enter the Far Eastern trade, set sail from New York with Major Samuel Shaw as supercargo. We know that Major Shaw ordered not a little Cincinnati porcelain during his sojourn at the port of Canton, and though no mention of the particular transaction appears in his journal, it seems fair to assume that he procured the making of Colonel Varick's bowl. Why the New Jersey officer should have acquired a design far more magnificent in character and finer in execution than anything devised for Shaw himself, for General Knox, or even for George Washington, is something of a mystery. Perhaps, however, he was prepared to pay a higher price than the others. Perhaps as the historian William H. Richardson has suggested he received the piece as a token of regard from his Commander-in-Chief. In any event, this great punch bowl, despite a few cracks, must be accepted as the most important surviving example of American historical porcelain.

Almost as distinguished as the Varick example is the splendid punch bowl — now in the Metropolitan Museum of Art — presented by General Jacob Morton to the Corporation of the City of New York on the Fourth of July, 1812 (*Figs. 14, 15, 16*). In some respects it is preëminent in its class. It was specifically

the City of New York July the 4th 1812. Around the base we find the following: *This bowl was made by Syngchong in Canton Fungmanhe Pinxt.* The inner rim carried these words of sage advice from the donor: *Drink deep. You will preserve the City and Encourage Canals.* We may believe that the Corporation followed General Morton's admonition; for the interior of the vessel bears evidence of many stirring encounters with a silver ladle. Nevertheless, the fact that, in the course of more than a century, the

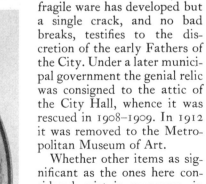

fragile ware has developed but a single crack, and no bad breaks, testifies to the discretion of the early Fathers of the City. Under a later municipal government the genial relic was consigned to the attic of the City Hall, whence it was rescued in 1908–1909. In 1912 it was removed to the Metropolitan Museum of Art.

Whether other items as significant as the ones here considered exist in museums, in the collections of historical societies, or in private possession, we cannot say. If they do, we shall welcome information concerning them for inclusion in a check list of American designs now in preparation. Unless such a list is reasonably complete, the time and effort involved in making the compilation would hardly be justified.

Fig. 1 — AMERICAN EAGLE TEA SET
Decorated with the armorial design listed below as the first form of Type I (*Fig. 2a*).
From the Edward A. Crowninshield collection

American Eagle Lowestoft

By HOMER EATON KEYES

AMERICAN collectors of Chinese Lowestoft are primarily interested in acquiring specimens of the ware which carry decorations of exclusive American significance. We have already pointed out that pieces edged with blue and displaying a pseudo-armorial shield are not properly included in this Simon-pure category; for such manner of ornamentation was virtually as popular abroad as in our own country. There are, however, a number of designs whose inspiration is beyond question. For example, the Cincinnati pattern, discussed in ANTIQUES for February, 1930, was made almost solely for American consumption, and at the instance of a highly restricted patriotic organization. It is the American-market Lowestoft *par excellence*.

Quite as obviously intended to appeal to the political susceptibilities of our ancestors, although, in so far as may be judged, quite unrestricted in its utilization, was the porcelain decorated with an eagle, either in crude approximation of the wide-winged bird of the United States arms, or rendered more or less independently of the armorial form.

It is unfortunate that we have no adequate record of the method of dealing between American mercantile agents and Chinese ceramic decorators. Captain Samuel Shaw, we know, personally sought out a capable Chinese artist, and strove with him in the delineation of a Cincinnati emblem that should be correct in detail and thus possessed of a genuine official significance. But concerning the genesis of the United States arms as a decorative motive on Oriental ware no information is forthcoming.

The point is perhaps of no great moment, except for the fact that the depiction of the Cincinnati emblem is accurate, whereas the contemporary Chinese rendering of the United States arms is quite otherwise. The design is armorial rather by implication than in fact: so much so as almost to force the conclusion that its making was initiated by the Chinese merchants rather than by their patrons, and that the ware itself never enjoyed any recognized status in American governmental circles. It was, in short,

turned out commercially for an uncritical popular market. Judging by the frequency with which specimens appear in salesroom and shop today, it must so far have fulfilled expectations as to be imported in large quantities, ordinarily in the form of tea services, and of individual pieces, such as tall mugs and vases.

On the whole, this armorial eagle is a rather sorry looking bird, far more closely resembling an English sparrow than the fowl of freedom. Usually painted in reddish brown or sepia against a sunburst background, and touched with gold, it is represented with one clawed foot grasping a bunch of arrows, while the other brandishes a leafless twig of laurel. Upon its breast reposes a shield, which may be treated in any one of three different ways: first, striped in approximation of the shield of the official arms of the United States; second, filled with a monogram or cypher; third, filled with a floral decoration. Occasionally this shield is colored, at least to the extent of displaying stripes of alternating red and white.

A variant of the sparrow eagle is depicted without a sunburst and with the shield in the red, white, and blue of the United States. Its laurel branch, instead of appearing as a leafless twig, burgeons with green. Moreover, it is clasped in the bird's left claw while the arrows are held in its right — a reversal of the normal order.

These various treatments are pictured in the accompanying illustrations (*Fig. 2*). In one of them, it is to be observed, the artist has rendered his bird in full gold rather than in sepia — a rather special bit of magnificence.

Whether or not it is possible to list the borders which occur in conjunction with this motive on Chinese Lowestoft, we cannot say; but we doubt that any rule was invoked. Invariably, however, such borders are narrow and far from elaborate.

Granting, as seems inevitable, that these armorial eagles were quite unofficial, and that their production lacked the careful oversight which ensured the satisfactory rendering of European coats of arms and of the Cincinnati emblem, we meet a somewhat difficult question. From what originals

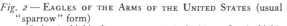

Fig. 2 — EAGLES OF THE ARMS OF THE UNITED STATES (usual "sparrow" form)
a, Striped shield; *b*, monogrammed shield; *c*, floral shield. Normally painted in brown, or sepia, and gold, though occasionally with shield in colors. The eagle of *b* is, however, in full gold. *d*, Variant eagle without sunburst, with colored shield, and with arrows and laurel reversed.
Ownership: a, from a coffeepot in the Rhode Island School of Design; b, from a pitcher in the Henry Forbes Bigelow Collection in the Boston Museum of Fine Arts; c, from a cup in the Henry Forbes Bigelow Collection; d, from a bowl loaned to the Metropolitan Museum

a.

b.

c.

d.

did the Chinese copyists derive their curious conception of the American arms? R. T. H. Halsey, in *The Homes of Our Ancestors*, suggests that United States coins carried to the Orient by American sailors may have served this purpose. On the whole, we are inclined to agree with him. As will be seen in the accompanying illustrations, the shield of the "sparrow type" eagle is different in shape from that utilized on the official seal. Again this type of eagle, when accompanied by a sunburst, is always depicted with wings drooping rather than broadly displayed as in the official form. It can hardly be mere coincidence that the spade shield employed by the Chinese decorators is precisely that which fronts the eagle on some American currency of the period; that an eagle with drooping wings occurs in Massachusetts copper cent and half-cent pieces of 1787–1788, and, further, that these Massachusetts pieces seem to be the only American coins on which the laurel appears on the left and the arrows on the right of the design, in the manner followed by the Chinese decorators. Nevertheless, closely as the droop-winged eagle on porcelain seems to follow the pattern of the Massachusetts coin, it should be observed that the latter is devoid of a sunburst. That element, or its semblance, first radiates on United States gold two and one-half dollar pieces of 1796 and on various silver coins from 1797 on, where, curiously, the wings of the accompanying eagle are displayed.

Perversely enough, the variant form of the sparrow type eagle (*Fig. 2d*), which follows the later coinage both in wing display and in the manner of holding the laurel and arrows, fails to exhibit any vestige of sunburst. Amid many contradictions, it is well to reserve judgment, particularly when the mental processes of eighteenth-century Chinese

porcelain decorators are involved in the problem. It is enough to know that the implications of these eagles are inescapable, and that the design proved generally acceptable.

But the true eagle hunter will not be fully satisfied with a collection of Lowestoft in which only these variant renderings of the bird occur. He will search for yet other examples, and, if persevering, he is likely to find them. Our own hunt, mercifully conducted with a camera rather than with a loaded pocketbook, has been rewarded by the discovery of no less than four distinctive birds in addition to those already discussed.

One of these, shown in Figure 4, is a striking and important version of the armorial type. Painted in blue and gold instead of the prevailing sepia, it is an animated specimen, whose surprised expression of countenance may be due to the sudden realization that its historically bald head is sprouting a Chinese pigtail. Among the Sino-American eagles of our acquaintance, this is the sole specimen carrying a scroll inscribed with the motto of the United States, and with its head surmounted by the official wreath of clouds and stars. It so closely follows the eagle of the Great Seal as to argue that it was copied from some document stamped with the correct form of that device. We believe it to be extremely rare.

Lowestoft eagles dissociated from the United States arms are curiously infrequent. But an exceptionally fine type, which we have found only on the pieces here illustrated, deserves a category of its own (*Figs. 5, 6, and 7*). Here we have an impressive flying bird with pinions outspread. Its talons grasp a trump of fame, its beak a scroll inscribed with the motto, IN GOD WE HOPE. Interrupting this motto appears a shield emblazoned with an anchor. About

Fig. 3 — THE ARMS OF THE UNITED STATES
As they appear on the Great Seal, for which the design was adopted in 1782. To this, most Chinese versions bear little resemblanec.

Fig. 4 — EAGLE OF THE ARMS OF THE UNITED STATES
A rare and fairly accurate version executed in blue and gold.
From a cup in the Russell Collection at the Rhode Island School of Design

the eagle's head shines a chaplet of stars — usually obliterated by wear.

Now exceptionally rare, this design may originally have had fairly wide currency, for its handling on the bowl and plate is materially different from that on the two vases, not only in the form of the eagle, but in the shape of the shield. Again, the inscription on the vases exhibits one of those curious errors of which Chinese decorators were frequently guilty in ornamenting European-market wares, although we have never before discovered them on pieces designed for America. The lettering on this scroll reads I E COE W F. HOPE, and was long accepted as revealing the names of Messrs. Coe and Hope, ship owners, until comparison with the similar bowl and plate proved the more pious intent of its enameled literation.

Those persons who are anxious to extend the list of State patterns on Lowestoft are likely to insist that this fine eagle, with its anchor and its use of the word *Hope*, has specific Rhode Island affiliations. On our own part, we harbor doubts. The symbolism as a whole is appropriate to American sea-borne commerce — triumphant, yet duly appreciative of divine interference in its behalf.

Another unusual eagle is that shown in Figure 8. Standing upon a laurel branch, it holds in its beak the chain of something

Fig. 5 — FLYING EAGLE ON BOWL AND PLATE
From the collection of Henry F. du Pont

Fig. 6 — FLYING EAGLE
Carrying a trump of fame, scroll inscribed IN GOD WE HOPE, and shield with anchor. Detail from bowl and plate shown in Figure 5. This is a rare type.

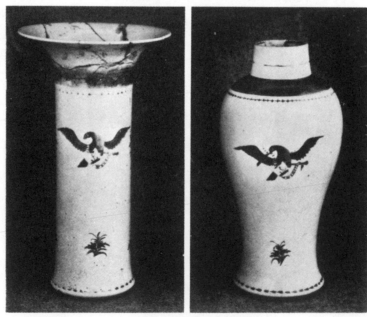

Fig. 7 — FLYING EAGLE ON VASES
The remains of what was once a set of four or five pieces constituting a garniture. The inscription on the scroll reads I E COE W E HOPE.
From the collection of Henry F. du Pont

very like a bottle ticket ornamented with a monogram. Here, we probably have nothing more than a general patriotic emblem, made subservient to the demands of a family designation. Nevertheless, the long-necked eagle suggests that of the silver dollar of 1794, though reversed.

The eagle of Figure 9 is open to some question. It may be a dove, and thus emblematic of matrimonial bondage rather than of national freedom. On the whole, however, its strut seems to entitle it to a place in the category of the undomesticated.

From the sole standpoint of appearance, the most thoroughly American among all the eagles of the Lowestoft aviary is that which adorns the teapot and sugar bowl of Figure 11. Its bald head, figured wings, and heavily feathered legs leave no room for mistake as to its identity. Whence it was derived, we cannot say, but we may be sure that whosoever ordered its making was insistent upon having a recognizably national bird and that he furnished an engraving or water color to the Chinese copyist. The bar on which the bird is poised suggests that the design as a whole may be a transcript of a family crest.

This brings our present list of American-market Chinese Lowestoft eagles to an end. But it is a list by no means closed. New types or distinct variants of those illus-

Fig. 8 — Bottle Ticket Eagle
Faintly suggestive of the eagle on the 1794 U. S. silver dollar.
From a cup in the Henry Forbes Bigelow Collection in the Boston Museum

Fig. 9 — Eagle of the Pigeon Type
Perhaps, after all, a matrimonial dove; but given the benefit of doubt.
From a teapot in the Essex Institute, Salem, Massachusetts

Fig. 10 — Crest with Phœnix
Obviously part of a European crest and inadmissible to the American category.
From an urn in the Boston Museum

trated and described are likely to turn up at any time. We should be glad to hear of them. For the moment, however, the summary appended to these notes must suffice. Of course, the designations employed are purely arbitrary; but they are, perhaps, descriptive enough to serve at least for a time.

To collectors who are ambitious to unearth still other types, we wish the best of luck. At the same time, we would offer a few words of caution. First, let it be remembered that eagles, or winged creatures of somewhat similar form, occur on European-market ware — frequently in conjunction with armorial designs. Such birds have no significance in the field of Americana. A specimen of the foreign breed is shown in Figure 10. It is part of a European crest, and better identified as a phœnix than as an eagle. But, whatever its name, it is an immigrant, quite disqualified for naturalization.

Secondly, it is reasonable to surmise that any concentration of interest upon eagle Lowestoft will set the wily Clobbers at work devising new types to lure the neophyte. And, since these fresh inventions will usually be cleverly painted on old pieces of ware, they are likely to disarm the suspicions of all but veteran buyers. In so far as we are aware, no eagle forgeries have as yet appeared on the genuine Chinese paste; but they are common enough on French imitations of Oriental ware — large vases, plates, and tea services alike. Generally they are wrought in blue and gold, and, though decoratively gorgeous, have no valid claim to inclusion in a collection of historical porcelain.

It had been our intention to picture the United States silver dollars of 1794 and 1798, and the Massachusetts copper cent of 1787, all of which coins may have furnished various Chinese decorators of porcelain with their conceptions of the American eagle. Just in time to save ourselves

Fig. 11 — Medallion Eagle
The most unmistakably American bald eagle of any in the series. Perhaps a crest.
From the collection of Mrs. J. Insley Blair

from suffering decapitation at the hands of the minions of government, we learned that — in the eyes of the law — portrayal of national currency is a crime only slightly less heinous than the bootlegging of pestiferous liquids, and, withal, considerably more likely to lead to dire consequences in so far as the perpetrator is concerned. Superior wisdom has doubtless reached the conclusion that real money in the hand is far too agile in its flight for observation and copying of its particular pattern by persons dishonestly inclined. Reproduced on the printed page, however, not only may it give rise to covetous and unholy thoughts, but it may afford opportunity to translate them into sinful deeds. Thus cavorts the law before the populace, wondering the while at the waning of its dignity.

We, therefore, refer the curious reader to the entirely adequate illustrations to be found in Guttag Brothers' *Coins of the Americas*, published in New York City in 1924, or to any of the other coin catalogues issued by various dealers.

Summary

Type I United States Armorial Eagle

1. Sparrow form with (*a*) striped shield; (*b*) monogrammed shield; (*c*) floral shield; (*d*) variant without sunburst, with colored shield, and with arrows and laurel reversed. In treatment, specific eagles of this type differ slightly according to the decorator.

2. Official Form
A fairly close approximation of the national arms.

Type II Flying Eagle
Only form known bearing trumpet, anchor, shield, and scroll inscribed IN GOD WE HOPE.

Type III Bottle Ticket Eagle
With monogram.

Type IV Pigeon Type Eagle

Type V Medallion Eagle
American bald eagle in oval medallion.

State Arms on Chinese Lowestoft

By Homer Eaton Keyes

WHETHER because of patriotism or a curious prejudice, American collectors of so-called Chinese Lowestoft exhibit a decided preference for specimens presumably made solely for the American market. We have previously stated that the blue and gold star border and its accompanying pseudo-armorial monogrammed shield are not specifically American in their implications. They merely exemplify a style current from 1790 to 1800, or thereabouts, and almost, if not quite, as popular abroad as in this country. There can, however, be no mistaking the strictly limited purport of the porcelain decorated for members of the Society of the Cincinnati (ANTIQUES for February, 1930, p. 132), and of that carrying a version of the arms of New York State.

Why or how the arms of New York were specially selected as a decorative motive by Chinese porcelain painters, we have no means of learning. Official sanction for their employment in this way seems to have been quite lacking. The pattern is not specifically mentioned in contemporary advertisements or discussed in known private correspondence or personal diaries. We do, nevertheless, note two circumstances that may have some bearing upon our enquiry.

In the first place, as they appear on Chinese porcelain, the New York arms display certain important departures from the contemporary official form. The nature of these departures is clearly demonstrated in Figures 2 and 3, where the New York seal of 1778 is reproduced opposite a typical version from a Chinese teapot. In both we have the figures of Liberty and Justice standing on a scroll and supporting a shield surmounted by a half globe upon which perches an eagle. In the Chinese version, however, the eagle, instead of defying the universe, somewhat tentatively waves a branch of laurel — while the rising sun, domi-

nant in the official shield, yields place to a rose, or sometimes to a cypher or monogram.

Not content with these changes, the ingenious Chinese omitted the all-important word *Excelsior* from the scroll, and in addition introduced two entirely superfluous shields.

The care that was exercised to ensure an accurate copy of the Cincinnati emblem, and the fidelity with which English and Continental arms were normally reproduced are here notable for their absence. It seems fair to conclude, therefore, that the employment of the New York arms as a decorative motive on Oriental porcelain represents a commercial experiment on the part of Chinese merchants rather than the fulfilment of some specific foreign order. Otherwise, glaring discrepancies between original and copy would hardly have been tolerated.

While, of course, no more than a surmise, this idea finds further justification in the fact that the first American vessel to engage in the Chinese trade sailed from the port of New York, and doubtless carried papers bearing the official seal of the State. In such case, the design might easily have become available to Chinese copyists and have been adopted by them as a semistock pattern. That it was somewhat widely accepted as a general ornamental motive is indicated by its occurrence, now and again, on porcelain made for the English market.

Yet, however profoundly we may doubt the official status of New York armorial porcelain, we may not question the essential validity of the design or its derivation from an official model, no matter how free the resultant translation. The history of the arms themselves and a sufficient consideration of their interpretation by Oriental ceramists will be found in ANTIQUES for January 1929. To repeat the discussion is unnecessary. It will suffice to offer a few illustrations showing how portrayals of the arms varied

Fig. 1 — Chinese Teapot with Arms of New York State
Differing in minor details from the design shown in Figure 3.
From the collection of Edward A. Crowninshield

Figs. 2 and 3 (left and right) — Arms of New York State
Left, from a photostat of the seal used in 1778.
Right, from a Chinese teapot. The latter's omissions and alterations indicate its lack of official significance

Fig. 4 — Chinese Mug
with Arms of New
York State
A rather exception-
ally fine specimen, in
which, however, the
eagle closely resem-
bles a dove.
*Formerly in the col-
lection of Edward A.
Crowninshield*

according to the in-
dividual whim, or
skill, of different
decorators.

So rare is porcelain
of this type, and so
highly prized by col-
lectors, that, of late,
it has been inge-
niously imitated. The
counterfeits are, for
the most part, genu-
ine pieces of old Chi-
nese ware, from
which a simpler form
of decoration has
been removed to
make room for a
forged depiction of
the arms. They are,
of course, quite
worthless, but they

times of crisis. The
choice of these obvi-
ous and timeworn
symbols indicates but
little imaginative
power on the part of
the General Court.
It has resulted in no
end of confusion
among collectors of
porcelain. Many have
jumped to the con-
clusion that any and
every piece of ware
upon which appears
an anchor, foul or
unfouled, and the
word *Hope* — with or
without the plump
contemplative female
who stands for that
optimistic state of

Fig. 5 — Chinese Cup
and Saucer with
Arms of New York
State

are often so clev-
erly executed as to
deceive anyone but
a connoisseur.
Hence, it will be
well to exercise
caution in embrac-
ing casual finds.

The interest dis-
played in New York
State porcelain and
the high prices that
specimens of it have
brought quite natu-
rally have set col-
lectors to searching for items
associable with others of the
early states.

As pointed out in the article
published in Antiques for
January, 1929, the official seal
of Rhode Island represents an
anchor. To this simple emblem
were added, about 1664, an
entwining cable and the sur-
mounting word *Hope*. Why this
device was selected by the
General Court of the Province,
we are not informed. Hope, to
be sure, was a necessary ingredient of life in early Colonial
days, and the anchor was a
common emblem of stability in

Fig. 6 — Many Anchors and, Perhaps, Hope
From an English set of Chinese armorial porcelain bearing the arms of Carr and Martin. Obviously
there is no Rhode Island relationship here.
Formerly in the collection of Sir Algernon Tudor-Craig

Fig. 7 — Chinese Bowl with Hope in a Shield
Blue Canton border and unusually well painted decoration, which can
have no more association with Rhode Island than has the knob of Figure 8.
From the Ginsburg and Levy collection

mind — must in
some way be con-
nected with the
State of Rhode Is-
land. On this point
it will be well to
quote the words of
Howard M. Chapin,
Librarian of the
Rhode Island His-
torical Society.
Says Mr. Chapin:

Several Lowestoft
plates are decorated with
a Classic female figure,
holding in her right
hand an anchor, and
resting her left elbow on
a shield, the entire device
being surrounded by or-
namental borders and
four foul anchors. Inasmuch as the Rhode
Island arms from 1660 to 1893 were a
foul anchor with the motto *Hope*, those
who rush in where angels fear to tread
hastily conclude that, since the foul
anchor and the word Hope were the
emblems of Rhode Island, this alleged
figure of Hope with an anchor must of
necessity be emblematic of Rhode
Island. They forget that these are devices occurring in innumerable ways
and places quite unrelated to the old
Plantation. A female figure in flowing
robes holding an anchor is often used
on English signboards for the *Hope and
Anchor* or the *Hope* tavern, alehouse, or
shop, as the case may be. In fact Pepys
spent Sunday, September 23, 1660, at
one such *Hope* tavern:

"To the Hope and sent for Mr.
Chaplin, who with Nicholas Osborne
and one Daniel come to us, and we

drank of two or three quarts of wine, which was very good; the drawing of our wine causing a great quarrel in the house between the two drawers which should draw us the best, which caused a great deal of noise and falling out, till the master parted them, and came up to us and did give us a long account of the liberty he gives his servants, all alike, to draw what wine they will to please his customers; and we eat above two hundred walnuts."

With specific reference to the plate recently ascribed to Rhode Island, it is not at all certain that the female figure upon it represents Hope. In the second place, it has never been customary to represent Rhode Island by the female figure of Hope with an anchor. Furthermore, the shield on which the Classic lady rests her elbow is not the shield of Rhode Island; nor has it any association with Rhode Island.

The foul anchor is an emblem of the British admiralty, as well as of Rhode Island. It is also used, in some cases, as emblematic of the United States navy, and of various commercial interests, and even of commerce in general. Indeed it is more likely that the female figure on this plate represents Commerce personified than that she represents Hope.

Mr. Chapin's observations are confined to a plate described some time since in an auction catalogue as having "Rhode Island State Coat of Arms" decoration. Part of the set from which this plate was derived is illustrated and described on page 40 of Sir Algernon Tudor-Craig's *Armorial Porcelain of the Eighteenth Century*, where we learn that the arms are those of Carr with Martin, and that, in the four border panels, are scenes representing the four quarters of the globe (*Fig. 6*). Sir Algernon speaks of the figure as representing Hope, but the implications of the panels might permit her to be called Commerce.

Nevertheless, a female figure draped over a huge anchor and gazing wistfully seaward is usually Hope, and she recurs again and again, as Mr. Chapin observes, not only on English tavern signs, but upon printed English tableware and even on English

Fig. 9 — Chinese Tankard with Ship and Hope
Hope frequently appears on wares of nautical import. In this instance the accompanying ship bears an American flag. The central monument has a singularly funerary aspect.
From the collection of Mrs. W. Murray Crane

Fig. 11 — Rare Chinese Cup Bearing Pennsylvania Arms
Decorated with a careful transcript of an early version of the design.
From the collection of Mrs. J. Insley Blair

enamel mirror knobs (*Fig. 8*), where by no stretch of imagination could she symbolize Rhode Island. In the exceptionally fine Chinese bowl of Figure 7, we find the lady occupying a shield surrounded with an intricate rope device, ribbons, and flowers — no doubt a mariner's gift to his lady love, and pointing far more clearly to the state of matrimony than to the Commonwealth of Rhode Island.

Another Chinese piece (*Fig. 9*), a mug adorned with something closely resembling a funerary monument, whose supports are an American vessel and a shield portraying the pensive Hope, bears little more reference to Rhode Island than to Charon's ferry on the Styx. Hope, one may recall, hangs eternal over the memorial devices of the late eighteenth century. Perhaps, indeed, this mug is a kind of memorial to one lost at sea. Its decoration was apparently something of a stock affair. We know of one instance where it appears quite as in the illustration, except that the ship moored to the monument flies the British flag instead of the American emblem. On the whole, we doubt that such a thing exists as a Rhode Island armorial Lowestoft pattern of Chinese manufacture.

Of Chinese ware carrying the arms of any other states than New York, we have seen but one specimen — a cup in the collection of Mrs. J. Insley Blair of Tuxedo Park, New York (*Fig. 11*). On this we find a depiction of the arms of Pennsylvania so finely and accurately executed as to argue official sponsorship for its production. As for its date, the absence of trappings on the horses suggests a period as late as 1805, in which year Pennsylvania unharnessed her gallant steeds for a vacation of seven decades. Yet the cup may well be a souvenir of Pennsylvania's venturings in the Orient before the close of the preceding century. There should be others, but we are not aware of their existence.

Fig. 1 — PUNCH BOWL PORTRAYING THE "GRAND TURK" (*1786*)
Presented to the officers of the *Grand Turk* of Salem, on that vessel's first visit to China. *Diameter: 16 inches.*
From the Peabody Museum, Salem, Massachusetts

American Ship Lowestoft

By HOMER EATON KEYES

IT IS not difficult to account for the popularity of Chinese porcelain decorated with ship pictures — either in the days when it was an article of commerce, or at the present time, when it enjoys the special esteem of collectors. Its symbolism is agreeably obvious and its associations are essentially direct and human. Just as the eighteenth-century sea captains whose vessels touched at the port of Liverpool, England, were wont to possess themselves of the local creamware bowls and pitchers adorned with painted or transferred depictions of their craft, so those navigators who voyaged to the Far East readily

Fig. 2 — DETAIL FROM THE INTERIOR OF THE "GRAND TURK" PUNCH BOWL
It is probable that the ship pictured was borrowed from an English engraving, and is, therefore, not a true portrait of the *Grand Turk* herself

Fig. 3 — PLATE PORTRAYING THE "FRIENDSHIP" (*c. 1820*)
Painted in colors by a Cantonese artist. The wide, elaborate border in colors and gold corresponds with the late date; though the reserve medallions recall an earlier type of *famille rose* decoration.
From the Peabody Museum

succumbed to the allure of porcelain objects, which, perhaps first made to compete with Liverpool models, were offered in the shops of the Chinese merchants.

It need hardly be stated that the ships pictured on porcelain were seldom individualized. In the majority of cases, national significance was bestowed upon them by the simple device of attaching an appropriate flag. Occasionally, the Liverpool custom of adding the vessel's name was adopted. In the better grade of decorations, further, it is possible to guess at the approximate period of naval architecture represented — though this by no means always coincides with the period when the painting was executed. Usually, however, the depiction is not only generalized; it is reduced to the lowest possible terms of artistic effort. If a captain or owner yearned for a more accurate portrait of his vessel, he could find in Canton plenty of native artists capable of satisfying his requirement with an oil painting minutely faithful to every mast, rope, spar, and porthole of the subject. The small size of porcelain decoration normally precluded such fidelity to differentiating detail — at least where cost was a consideration.

So it is that, among the vessels on ship Lowestoft, we shall ordinarily look in vain for individualizing features other than the national flag, which, no doubt, was usually painted to order on stock pieces already decorated with a quite neutral merchant craft. As we shall presently observe, some of these versions were technically much better than others — a circumstance too often overlooked by American collectors so intent upon capturing a craft flying the stars and stripes as to be indifferent to other considerations.

But there are exceptions to every rule, even

Fig. 4 — Plate with Ship in Perspective (c. 1800)
The position of the vessel is unusual in Chinese porcelain decoration. For reasons unknown and of doubtful validity, this craft has been called the Constitution.
Formerly in the Edward Crowninshield collection

Fig. 5 (above) — Teapot with Ship and Pseudo-Armorial Design (1790–1800)
Probably a ship officer's gift to his prospective bride. The doves symbolize domestic bliss; the ship, the hazards of the sea.
From the collection of Mrs. Frank L. Hinckley

Fig. 6 (left) — Plate with Marital and Maritime Symbols (1790–1800)
Other pieces of similar design occur, except that on them the ship is shown flying the British flag.
Formerly in the Edward Crowninshield collection

that of ship porcelain. Now and again a specimen turns up that is so distinguished from the rank and file, either in apparent verisimilitude or in elaboration, as to require no external documentary evidence in proof of its having been painted to special order. The Dutch-market *Vryburg* plate of 1756, illustrated on page 109 of Antiques for August, 1929, is of this type. So too — in the category of American items — is the fine *Grand Turk* bowl now preserved in the Peabody Museum at Salem, Massachusetts.

The well-known history of this bowl is recited at some length in Robert Peabody's *Log of the Grand Turks* (published by Houghton Mifflin Company, 1926). It will be recalled that the ship *Grand Turk*, owned by Elias Hasket Derby of Salem, was the second American merchantman to enter into direct trade with the Orient. She sailed from her home port in December of 1785, more than a year after the *Empress of China* had ventured from New York on a similar errand.

Apparently the enterprising officers of the first expedition had made a favorable impression upon the Oriental merchants, and had thus prepared a pathway of good will for the later American voyagers.

In any event, we learn that, after Mr. Vans and Captain West of the *Grand Turk* had finished their business at Canton and were about to set sail for home, they went ashore to pay a farewell visit to Pinqua, the Chinese merchant through whom their various negotiations had been transacted. After the formality of tea drinking had been disposed of, the old merchant summoned his servants, who thereupon appeared, bearing a porcelain bowl. This, the American visitors were surprised and delighted to observe, "was beautifully decorated with a painting of the *Grand Turk* under full sail and bore the inscription 'Ship *Grand Turk* at Canton 1786.'" Pinqua begged the acceptance of the bowl as a souvenir of pleasant acquaintanceship. Needless to say, his request met with prompt compliance.

The accompanying illustrations of this historic bowl (*Figs. 1 and 2*) are sufficiently clear to relieve us of any necessity for describing the piece, or for discussing the high quality of its decoration. As ship painting on porcelain goes, the portrayal of the *Grand Turk* is on a par with that of the earlier *Vryburg*. Nevertheless, it may not be accepted as a completely faithful likeness drawn from a study of the vessel herself. More probably it was borrowed directly from an engraving of the British ship *Hall*, which serves as frontispiece to Hutchinson's *Naval Architecture*, a book first published in London in 1777. The same design, furthermore, reappears on a plate dedicated to the American frigate *Alliance*, which, in 1788, Robert Morris of Philadelphia converted into an East Indiaman and sent forth on a single voyage to the Orient.

Less distinguished as decoration, but perhaps more authentic as a portrait, is a far later piece of Chinese porcelain (*Fig. 3*) — a plate upon which is depicted the ship *Friendship*, apparently furling sail as she drops anchor and fires a salute to announce her arrival in port. The *Friendship* was built in Portland in 1815, and owned by the Silsbees of Salem. The plate in question is said to have been purchased in China about 1820. Not improbably, the design was taken from a painting supplied by the owner or captain of the vessel. The border must be viewed as a stock ornament applied by another hand than that which portrayed the *Friendship*. Its selection, however, may have been due to the fact that the symbols interwoven throughout the pattern are supposed to be portents of health, wealth, and happiness.

Another American ship item that departs materially from the ordinary type is illustrated in Figure 4. Here the vessel is shown in perspective, a rare method of presentation either on Chinese porcelain or in the somewhat stereotyped oil-painted ship portraits of the period. The workmanship is careful, and the border decoration of shells and seaweed appears to be an adaptation of a late eighteenth or early nineteenth-century English pattern. Why it has been assumed that the ship itself represents the sturdy old frigate *Constitution* is anyone's guess. The correctness of the identification would best be doubted until sustained by incontrovertible evidence.

In the instances so far cited, a ship constitutes the chief, indeed the only, element of special ornamentation of the porcelain. There exists, however, a number of pleasing pieces on which we find the nautical symbol subordinated to others of a more personal significance. Such practice is exemplified by the teapot of Figure 5, which, without much doubt, was acquired as a mariner's present to his bride. The decoration is of the pseudo-armorial type — a mantled, monogrammed shield, surmounted by the usual emblems of domestic bliss. The addition of the ship clearly indicates the occupation of the man of the family.

Figs. 7-9 — STOCK PATTERN SHIPS (*1790–1800*)
Varying considerably in technical quality and in the treatment of rigging, but all reduced to little more than a stylized symbol.
Formerly in the Edward Crowninshield collection

Not improbably a similar significance attaches to the more elaborate design illustrated in Figure 6, where Hymen's altar, an American ship, and a pseudo-armorial shield are somewhat confusedly combined. That this association of marital and maritime symbols appealed to the English as well as to the American heart is indicated by similar articles on which the moored vessel flies the British flag.

The usual type of ship Lowestoft is adequately illustrated in Figures 7

129

through 10. Mrs. Little, in an article on American early trade with the Orient, has pointed out (ANTIQUES for January, 1929, p. 31) that the models from which these designs were borrowed may have been the vessels engraved on bills of lading and other maritime documents easily available to the Cantonese decorators (*Fig. 11*). As most of these engravings were rather nondescript affairs, we need not be surprised to learn that the painted copies in no wise improved upon them. Some of the latter picture a ship in full sail, some reduce the craft to a bare skeleton. In quality, they exhibit a wide diversity, explicable only on the ground of varying cost. When old Pinqua ordered the *Grand Turk* bowl, he knew where to find a competent artist whom, in all likelihood, he stimulated to conscientious effort with the promise of adequate reward. Most

Fig. 10 — ENLARGEMENT OF SHIP PAINTING ON PORCELAIN
The swift, calligraphic strokes with which the sails and ropes are indicated may be easily studied in this magnified version of a design hardly more than two and one half inches high. The summary treatment of the ship's hull and of the water is likewise worth observing.
From a mug in the collection of Henry F. du Pont

to be viewed as the rarest and most desirable known specimen of American ship Lowestoft. Yet two other items, which we have reserved for concluding comment, are equally deserving of eulogy. One of these is a covered, barrel-shaped, porcelain flagon of the early nineteenth century, belonging to Mrs. J. Insley Blair of Tuxedo Park, New York (*Figs. 12–14*). It is here reproduced in the three views necessary for unfolding its full panorama of an American brig, at one moment proceeding under full sail upon an untroubled sea, at another, almost beam-ended by the tumultuous waves of a heavy storm. This dramatic treatment is carried out with great care in full color, and may be accepted as recording the actual experience of a brave craft that encountered the Pacific Ocean in a far from pacifistic mood. Somewhere, even today,

seamen would have been neither so critical nor so generous as the Chinese merchant, and they seem to have fared accordingly.

An unfortunate feature of the ordinary Chinese ship delineations on porcelain is the ease with which such handiwork may be imitated by the modern forger. The deft touch apparent in the finest among even the highly generalized portrayals is today probably beyond imitation; but the coarser forms may be approximated by almost any experienced decorator. Hence it is advisable to examine a specimen of the characteristic ship Lowestoft with a good deal of care; first, to determine whether its surface betrays signs of the removal of an earlier decoration preliminary to applying a ship design, and, secondly, to make sure that the nationality of the flag has not been altered to satisfy the American demand for native ships. To what extent genuine old pieces, originally almost undecorated, have latterly been elaborated with ships or with state emblems it is impossible to say. Experience should, however, have taught collectors not to accept either ship or state "Lowestoft" on the sole basis of a pedigree that has not been subjected to exhaustive scrutiny.

From the dual standpoint of history and type, the *Grand Turk* punch bowl is, perhaps,

Fig. 11 — BILL OF LADING ENGRAVING (*enlarged*)
Eighteenth-century bills of lading and other ships' papers were frequently adorned with a small engraving of a ship. Such engravings may have been copied by Chinese decorators of porcelain.
From a bill of the sloop "Experiment," 1785, in the Metropolitan Museum of Art

the print or painting from which this panorama was derived may still survive; for it is almost a foregone conclusion that any Chinese pictorial design of this character on porcelain is a direct transcript from a pattern supplied by the Occidental customer.

Still another flagon, virtually duplicating the one in Mrs. Blair's collection has recently been acquired by Charles Woolsey Lyon of New York.

It will, perhaps, be observed that, after the beginning of the nineteenth century, borders on Chinese porcelain decorated for the foreign market become increasingly elaborate. The influence, first of the European Empire style and later of the luscious Victorian mode, seems to have been felt quite as strongly in the Orient as in Europe. Presently the finely penciled reedings and delicately enameled floral swags of the eighteenth century are supplanted by broad belts of gold interwoven with rich leaf and flower forms. We see obvious signs of this change in Mrs. Blair's covered flagon. The process is carried very nearly to its ultimate on a magnificent ship bowl owned by Mrs. James Richardson of Providence (*Fig. 15*).

Though of relatively late date — about 1830 — this bowl may be reckoned among the supreme examples of ship Lowestoft to

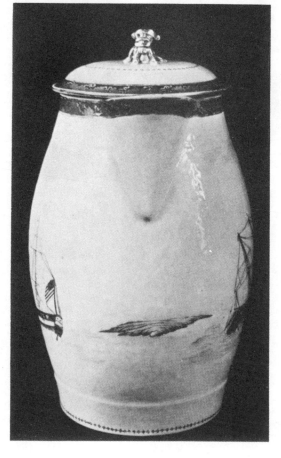

Figs. 12–14—A SHIP-DECORATED FLAGON
(*c. 1810*)
Three views showing a panoramic picture of
a brig in fair weather and in foul.
From the collection of Mrs. J. Insley Blair

be found in America. It comes to its present owner by inheritance from her great-grandfather, Henry Eckford, an American naval architect, who, about 1830, accepted service under the Turkish government as director of naval construction. At the close of his term, he received from the Sultan a token of esteem in the form of a huge punch bowl and two flagons of Chinese porcelain. In form, the flagons of this set are almost identical with Mrs. Blair's ship flagon; and their handles, though slightly different in position, show the same elaborate foliation at the point of attachment (*Fig. 16*). Their painted and gilded borders are, however, wider and more gorgeous. The borders of the accompanying bowl repeat those of the flagons, but are interrupted by two large medallions, in one of which occurs the recipient's monogram, *H E* in gold, in the other a painted-in-ink picture of a shipyard with a great vessel nearing completion on her ways. The interior of the bowl, below the

floriated rim, portrays a group of gold-red Chinese carp. In accuracy of delineation and in exquisiteness of miniaturelike technique, the ship medallion of this nineteenth-century bowl is not surpassed by similar Chinese work of any period. Although, by 1830, Chinese export porcelain as a whole had begun to betray evidences of degradation, wealth could still command skilled and patient artistry such as, of old, had distinguished the wares of the Orient.

In this instance, the vessel portrayed is no commonplace modern craft, but a magnificent eighteenth-century East Indiaman, with storied after-cabins rising like the gabled end of a Dutch mansion framed in carven scrolls, and topped with a resplendent pediment. Here, again, we must assume that the Chinese artist had recourse to the illustrations in some western treatise on naval architecture; but we may be thankful that, in his selection of a model, he was guided by other considerations than those of being up-to-date in his design.

As we review the field of American ship Lowestoft, we may well experience some surprise at its paucity of really outstanding specimens. In the

131

Fig. 15 — SHIP-DECORATED PUNCH BOWL (*c. 1830*)
Presented by the Sultan of Turkey to Henry Eckford, an American naval architect. A magnificent example of Chinese ship porcelain.
Below is another view of the bowl, showing the monogram — *HE* in gold — and, on the interior, a gold-red Chinese carp.
From the collection of Mrs. James Richardson

aggregate, the number of surviving pieces of the stock variety is doubtless large. Some of these items will surpass others both in fabric and in decorative technique; some, again, will exhibit peculiarities of treatment that, in separating them from the common run, will materially enhance their value in the eyes of collectors. As a whole, they offer the student ample opportunity to exercise his connoisseurship as well as to satisfy his appetite for unusual variants, which may, indeed, deserve a special catalogue.

But it is a far cry from even the finest of the stock items to such monumental examples as the *Grand Turk* bowl, the *Friendship* and the *Alliance* plates, the exciting flagons of Mrs. Blair and Mr. Lyon, and the shipyard bowl belonging to Mrs. Richardson. These constitute a group apart — an exclusive and obviously superior class of their own. Yet it is difficult to believe that all the candidates qualified for admission to this select circle have been discovered and recorded. Of the swarm of American vessels that, between 1784

Fig. 16 (left) — FLAGON (*c. 1830*)
One of a pair accompanying the punch bowl (*Fig. 15*) given by the Turkish Sultan to Henry Eckford.
From the collection of Mrs. James Richardson

and 1830, engaged in the Chinese trade, far more than a scant half dozen must have been specifically immortalized on Oriental porcelain, and the souvenirs preserved despite the hazards of storm and shipwreck, and the subsequent vicissitudes of domestic life ashore. Hence we may still hope that, out of unsuspected obscurity, American ship bowls, or plates, or flagons will, from time to time, emerge to flaunt decorative glories exceeding the richness of any hitherto revealed. Such thrilling resurrections may occur in New England, but it seems more logical to look for them farther to the south in districts whose contribution to the lore of American Lowestoft has thus far seemed disproportionately small in comparison with the measure of their erstwhile participation in commerce with the Far East.

Fig. 1 — CINCINNATI PLATE (*c. 1785*)
    The border shows a stock pattern border in underglaze blue. The flying figure of Fame supporting the emblem of the
Cincinnati is painted in enamel colors over the glaze. It seems not unlikely that this design represents a compromise between Shaw's ambitious conception discussed in the text and the very limited capabilities of the Chinese decorator. It
is this Fame type of porcelain with the wide blue border which appears to have been used by Washington. There is no
sufficient reason for believing that it is either earlier or later in date than the simple emblem type.
From the Metropolitan Museum of Art

The Cincinnati and Their Porcelain

By HOMER EATON KEYES

PERHAPS the most notable Chinese porcelain of armorial type made for the American market is that decorated with the emblem of the Cincinnati. By the same sign, specimens of this porcelain are those most earnestly sought and jealously treasured by American collectors. Concerning the history of this Cincinnati porcelain, however, no two writers agree; and, since disagreement seems to be the order of the day, we may as well present our own version of the matter.

First, as to the Society itself: At the suggestion of Major-General Henry Knox, presented in the form of a circular letter sent out from West Point under date of April 15, 1783, just prior to the disbanding of the Revolutionary Army, the officers of that army formed themselves into a society, whose basic intent was the maintenance of the friendly personal associations established during the war. Recalling the fact that, after strenuous years of campaigning, they were about to return to the peaceful pursuits of civil life, the founders viewed themselves as spiritual descendants of that hardy old Roman, Lucius Quinctius Cincinnatus, who, half a millennium before the Christian era, had turned from plow to sword and back again to plow with epoch-making alacrity. Hence the name which the group of American and allied officers adopted for their organization.

General Knox had been explicit, not only in formulating the purposes of the Society and in outlining a scheme for its national development, but in defining the symbolism of the insignia "by which members shall be known and distinguished." With only slight modifications, the General's ideas, in whose formulation he had, no doubt, been materially assisted by his aid, Captain Samuel Shaw, were adopted by the officers assembled at the "Cantonment of the American Army, On Hudson's River," May 13, 1783.

It was then and there agreed that the order, or emblem, of the Society should be a medal of gold, suspended by a deep blue ribbon two inches in width and edged with white — "descriptive of the Union of America and France." The obverse of this medal was to depict Cincinnatus receiving a sword and "other military ensigns" at the hands of three senators. In the background, the great Roman's wife was to be visible at her cottage door; near by, a plow and instruments of husbandry: encircling the whole, the motto, *Omnia relinquit servare Rempublicam.*

The reverse was to display a rising sun, a city with open gates, and vessels entering the port, while in the foreground, Fame should crown Cincinnatus with a wreath inscribed *Virtutis Præmium;* below, joined hands supporting a heart, with the motto *Esto Perpetua:* the whole complication surrounded by the inscription, *Societas Cincinatorum instituta A. D. 1783.*

In their enthusiasm for loading their new emblem with

Fig. 2 — CINCINNATI TUREEN (*c. 1785*)
A simple sprigged type of Chinese porcelain upon which has been imposed the official emblem of the Society of the Cincinnati in enamel colors and gold. Below this, the initials *S. S.* indicate the original ownership of Samuel Shaw. Probably brought to America by the *Empress of China* on her return from her first voyage to the Orient, in 1784–1785. General Washington's possession of the Fame type of porcelain, while his subordinate officers utilized the more restricted design, indicates the contemporary estimate of the relative importance of the two patterns.
Loaned to the Boston Museum of Fine Arts by Henry Forbes Bigelow

Fig. 3 — CINCINNATI TEACUP (*c. 1785*)
Of the same type as the tureen shown above, but taken to show the reverse side of the medal, whose obverse appears on the soup tureen.
From the United States Museum, Washington

expressive symbols, the founders of the Society failed to realize that a really adequate fulfillment of their grandiloquent notions would necessitate a medal almost as large as a dish pan. But, after all, their function was to initiate: the task of wrestling with the preparation of a working drawing was left to Major Pierre Charles L'Enfant, who lost no time in executing the commission. However, in rendering his report, together with sketches, in June of 1783, the Major urged that a round or oval medal could be but a commonplace affair, since in Europe such things were looked upon "only as a reward for artists and artisans" or as the badge of a religious or commercial group. Accordingly, he recommended that the emblem take the form of a bald eagle, a bird peculiar to America, and distinguished from the eagles of other countries by its white head and tail. He further advised that the originally proposed medal designs — in gold or enamel — should be affixed to the breast and back of this bird, whose body should be of gold, while the head and tail might be of silver or enamel, or set with diamonds. The addition of laurel and oak leaves, he seemed to feel, would be effective.

With the fact that Major L'Enfant submitted an alternative design, we are not here concerned. The one which we have described at some length was officially accepted, and the Major was sent to Paris to supervise the cutting of a die and the stamping of a sufficient number of medals to meet the immediate requirements of the Society.

Shortly after the issuance of this first edition, the die was lost; and thereafter, when further emblems were

Figs. 4 and 5 — INSIGNIA OF THE CINCINNATI (1784)
Obverse and reverse views. The history of the design, with an explanation of its symbolism, will be found in the text. The photographs, somewhat larger than the emblem itself, were taken from one of the few surviving contemporary specimens, which was originally owned by Jabez Bowen of Providence. Eagle, medal, and supporting decorative elements are of gold without a trace of enamel. *From the Philip Flayderman collection*

required, they were made more or less according to the fancy of the State Society immediately interested. Until within recent years, the result has been an unfortunate diversity in the designs produced. The insignia here illustrated are, however, from contemporary originals made, quite probably, early in the year 1784.

The founding of the Society of the Cincinnati caused a great deal of foolish consternation among the American public. Since right to membership in the organization was to be inherited by male

Fig. 6 — ENAMELED INSIGNIA OF THE CINCINNATI (*1784*)
A contemporary specimen, given by General Washington to his aid, Colonel Tench Tilghman. It is now owned by Colonel Oswald Tilghman, President of the Society of the Cincinnati in the State of Maryland.
Photograph by courtesy of T. S. Clay

with various paraphernalia ornamented with that mystic emblem. Here, in short, arose the opportunity for American citizens to own armorial china, handsome and exclusive enough to compare favorably with the services which graced the tables of the aristocracy of Europe. Little time was lost in procuring a supply. As to the means employed in the furtherance of that end, two distinct traditions exist, both of them erroneous.

One tradition holds that a set of this porcelain was presented to Washington, in 1780, by a group of French officers; the other, that it was a gift provided by subscriptions from the entire membership of the Society.

Alice Morse Earle, in her *China Collecting in America*, cannily observes that a Cincinnati set could hardly have been conceived in 1780, when neither the Society nor its badge were in existence. She likewise notes the fact that there is no minute in the records of the Society regarding a unified movement to present anything whatsoever to

offspring in direct line of descent, suspicious folk thought that they perceived an attempt to foist a class of nobility upon a free and democratic republic. While this idea was probably sheer nonsense, there can be little doubt that the members of the Cincinnati thought well of themselves as men somewhat apart from the common herd, and that they were as eager to acquire their new badges and to have them emblazoned on their household gear as a college freshman to don a fraternity pin and to surround himself

General Washington. So much for the traditions. Mrs. Earle proceeds to emphasize the very strong probability that the President purchased all of his Cincinnati china on his own account in the open market, or that he used some such means of augmenting an inadequate supply already in his possession.

A letter which she quotes almost proves her contention. Another document, of which she may have been ignorant, appears to settle the matter. The quoted letter, addressed to Colonel Tench Tilghman, was written from Mount Vernon, under date of August 17, 1785. Five days earlier the Baltimore *Advertiser* had announced the arrival of the ship *Pallas*, commanded by its owner, Captain O'Donnell, with a most valuable cargo, whose sale at auction was scheduled for the first of October. Besides tea, fabrics, "elegant paper hangings," spices, and "japanned tea-chests," the following amazing array of porcelain was specified:

Table-Sets of the best Nankin blue and white Stone China; white stone and painted China of the second Quality in Sets; Dishes of blue and white Stone China 5 and 3 in a Set; Stone China flat and Soup Plates; Breakfast Cups and Saucers of the best blue and white Stone China in Sets; Evening blue and white Stone China Cups and Saucers; Ditto painted; *Ditto with the Arms of the Order of Cincinnati*; Bowls — best blue and white Stone China in Sets; blue and white Stone China Pint Sneakers; Mugs — best Stone China in Sets; small Tureens with Covers; Wash-Hand Guglets and Basons.

It was in response to the promptings of this advertisement that Washington wrote to Colonel Tilghman: "If *great bargains* are to be had, I would supply myself agreeably to an enclosed list," which is as follows:

A sett of the best Nankin Table China
Ditto — best Evening Cups & Saucers
* A sett of *large* blue & white China
Dishes say half a dozen more or less
* 1 Doz *small* bowls blue & white
* 6 Wash hand Guglets & Basons
6 Large Mugs or 3 mugs & 3 jugs
A Quart^r Chest best Hyson Tea
A Leaguer of Battavia Arrack if a Leaguer is not large
About 13 yards of good blu: Paduasoy
A ps of fine muslin plain
1 ps of Silk Handkerchiefs
12 ps of the Best Nankeens

* With the badge of the Society of the Cincinnati if to be had.

18 ps of the second quality or coursest kind for servants
G. Washington

17th August 1785

Fig. 7 — WASHINGTON'S DIAMOND INSIGNIA OF THE CINCINNATI
Presented to General Washington, President General of the Society, by French naval officers who were members of the organization. It is said that this elaborate decoration was paid for with a sum of money originally tendered to Washington as a cash offering, which the General promptly declined. It is now a carefully guarded possession of the Society of the Cincinnati.
Photograph by courtesy of T. S. Clay

Those pieces marked with an asterisk he expressly states are, if possible, to bear the badge of the Cincinnati. It is apparent, therefore, that at this time Cincinnati china was already being made in the Orient, and that Washington was acquainted with its aspect. How was it then that the *Pallas*, second American vessel to make the voyage to and from China, should have had this ware on board, and have advertised it as something already familiar? The answer is perhaps discoverable in the journals of Captain Samuel Shaw, who served as supercargo on the *Empress of China*, which preceded the *Pallas* to the Orient by a few months, and returned to her home port, New York, quite six months ahead of the Baltimore vessel.

Captain Shaw had acted as secretary of the meeting at which the Society of the Cincinnati was instituted. With him, on his subsequent voyage to the Orient, was Captain Thomas Randall, one of the military aids of Major-General Knox, first Secretary of War of the United States. Captain Shaw's journal contains the following entry, which supplies an illuminating supplement to Mrs. Earle's quotations:

There are many painters in Canton but I was informed that not one of them possesses a genius for design. I wished to have something emblematic of the order of the Cincinnati executed upon a set of porcelain. My idea was to have the American Cincinnatus, under the conduct of Minerva, regarding Fame, who, having received from them the emblem of the order, was proclaiming it to the world. For this purpose I procured two separate engravings of the goddesses, an elegant figure of a military man (The Count d'Estaing at the taking of Granada) and furnished the painter with a copy of the emblem which I had in my possession. He was allowed to be the most eminent of his profession, but after repeated trials was unable to combine the figures with the least propriety; though there was not one of them which singly he could not copy with the greatest exactness. I could therefore have my wishes gratified only in part. The best of his essays I preserved as a specimen of Chinese excellence in design and it is difficult to regard it without smiling. It is a general remark that the Chinese, though they can imitate most of the fine arts, do not possess any large portion of original genius.

Here, then, without much doubt, we have the true history of the Cincinnati porcelain. Its design was apparently of Shaw's own devising. Originally intended as an elaborate composition which should include Fame, Minerva, and George Washington in an important allegorical group similar to those with which we are familiar on Liverpool ware, it was, perforce, contracted either to a simple representation of the order of the Cincinnati, or to a single flying figure of Fame, dangling the emblem like a censer, and trumpeting to the universe.

The Handbook of the American Wing of the Metropolitan Museum states, on what authority we know not, that a set of this china was brought by Captain Shaw to General Washington, and another set by Captain Randall to General Knox. The latter set, of which a cup and saucer are preserved in the Museum, carries the General's initials. There was, of course, no reason why the owner of the ship *Pallas*, which was anchored at the port of Canton during much of the stay of the *Empress of China*, should not have been permitted to have Captain Shaw's design repeated for the benefit of members of the Cincinnati less distinguished than the President of the United States and the Secretary of War, and hence less capable of commanding the services of special agents to satisfy their wants.

Shaw likewise secured some of the Cincinnati china for his own use. The Boston Museum of Fine Arts shows a tureen from this lot. It is of modestly sprigged porcelain with a narrow wave border. As is often the case with the Cincinnati pattern, Fame is omitted and only the emblem of the Society appears as a decoration. In this instance the initials of the owner, *S. S.*, are inscribed below the emblem, and serve to identify its ownership (*Fig. 2*).

The plates of Cincinnati porcelain usually ascribed to the Washington set have the wide, blue, butterfly border frequently found on Chinese porcelain. In the centre appears Fame equipped with brown wings and trumpet, and clad in a light green robe from which streams a pink scarf. The emblem of the Society, attached to a long, light

Fig. 8 — MAJOR-GENERAL BARON VON STEUBEN
From a portrait by Ralph Earle. Baron von Steuben, one of the founders of the Society of the Cincinnati, is shown wearing the eagle pendent from his left coat lapel, the position prescribed by the rules of the Society.
Photograph by courtesy of T. S. Clay

blue ribbon, depends from her outstretched hand (*Fig. 1*).

Precisely how many pieces remain from the various sets of the Cincinnati Chinese porcelain that were brought to America, is quite beyond telling. Mrs. Earle gives the names of various public institutions and private persons, who, some thirty years since, were known to possess one or more items. But thirty years — a long period in the life of a collection—accomplish many shifts and changes. Suffice it, then, to say that specimens of Cincinnati porcelain are excessively rare and seldom appear in the open market. In consequence, various ambitious folk have endeavored to enlarge the visible supply by classifying in the Cincinnati category all porcelain showing the figure of a winged Fame or Victory. The absurdity of such a procedure should be patent. Cincinnati porcelain may occur without this figure, which, after all, is merely an incidental motive; but *it may not occur without the emblem of the Society*. If this emblem is missing, no host of trumpet-blowing goddesses supplies compensation. Under such circumstances, indeed, these damsels are an almost certain indication that the ware which they adorn was made for European rather than for American consumption.

The same reasons which prompt the mis-identification of such porcelain likewise prompt the too-ready assumption that all porcelain decorated with an eagle is associable with the Society of the Cincinnati. This is a serious error. Several types of eagles, as we shall later see, appear on Sino-American porcelain of the early Federal period. The great majority of these birds carry a shield upon their breasts and are, quite obviously, Chinese versions of the arms of the United States. Aside from lacking the distinguishing seal of the Cincinnati, they are quite different in form and pose from the dignified fowl of the Society emblem — and they are infinitely more common.

Note. — To T. S. Clay, Assistant Treasurer of the Society of Cincinnati in the State of Georgia, I am indebted for much of the information in the above article.

The Commodore Decatur Punchbowl

By Stephen Decatur

IT HAS been stated on various occasions that the oriental Lowestoft punchbowl which belonged to Commodore Stephen Decatur, Sr. *(1751–1808)* was a gift from the United States Government. Such a pedigree would be very pleasing, if it were true. Unfortunately, it is not. No existing records even suggest that such a present was ever made by the government to a naval officer. Probability argues against the likelihood of any official procedure of the kind. If, however, family tradition may be accepted, the bowl was tendered to the Commodore by a group of "admiring friends" in Philadelphia, possibly a club or a society of some kind. Since nothing inherently questionable mars this tradition, it is quite possibly valid, although, of course, the Commodore may have had the bowl made to his own order.

In a recent article (see ANTIQUES for February 1936) were mentioned two punchbowls of similar porcelain which originally belonged respectively to Commodore Richard Dale and Commodore John Barry. Their date is 1786–1787. On each is depicted a full-rigged ship copied by the Chinese artist from the frontispiece of Hutchinson's *Naval Architecture (1777)*. Dale's bowl carries the owner's initials. That of Barry is inscribed *John Barry, Esqʳ: Alliance, Commander.* Both pieces are probably commemorative; that of Barry certainly so, since he was the commander of the frigate *Alliance* in the famous engagements toward the close of the Revolution which made him our first Commodore.

Decatur's bowl is likewise commemorative, for it celebrates the capture of the French privateer *La Croyable* by the U. S. S. *Delaware*. Its exterior exhibits four decorations, one for each quarter. First of these is a painting, in enamel colors, of the *Delaware* in pursuit of the French vessel. The portrayal of each craft is said to be accurate; but since, at the time, *La Croyable* was designated as a schooner and the painting represents her as a full-rigged ship, we must cherish doubts. The representation of the *Delaware* may well be reasonably correct. She was a converted merchantman, formerly the ship *Hamburg Packet* of Philadelphia, which had been purchased by the government and altered into a 22-gun sloop-of-war, at the commencement of the quasi-war with France in 1798. Under the command of Decatur, she was one of the first vessels of the navy to get to sea, and on

July 7, 1798, captured *La Croyable* off Egg Harbor, New Jersey, after a long chase. Thus the French privateer was the first prize of the war and the first vessel to be captured by the Navy of the United States after its establishment. Undoubtedly the painting was copied from a drawing or sketch sent to China for the purpose.

Fig. 1 — THE COMMODORE DECATUR PUNCHBOWL (*c. 1800*)
Made and decorated in China for Commodore Stephen Decatur and commemorating the capture of the French privateer *La Croyable* by the United States ship *Delaware. Capacity*, 3 gallons. *Owned by Stephen Decatur*

Fig. 2 — DETAIL OF SHIP MEDALLION ON THE DECATUR BOWL

On the next quarter of the bowl, a profile of Decatur is executed in black within a circular border of gold and enamel colors. This portrait was copied from the engraving of the Commodore by Saint-Memin. It is a remarkably accurate piece of work, testifying to the extraordinary skill of the Chinese copyist. On the side of the bowl directly opposite this portrait appear the entwined initials of the Commodore in gold. The remaining quarter is occupied by an adaptation of the Arms of the United States, showing the flying eagle and the shield in colors. It is a particularly fine rendering of this decoration, so rare and highly prized on Lowestoft.

The exact date of the bowl is unknown, but the piece was in Decatur's possession by 1805 and, of course, cannot be earlier than 1799. A reasonable conjecture may fix the date as 1800. Late in 1799, Commodore Dale was given leave of absence from the navy and made a trip to China in command of the merchant ship *Canton.* Apparently this was the only voyage to the East made by a Philadelphia captain during the period in question (see *Transactions*, Connecticut Academy of Arts and Sciences, Vol. 28). As Decatur was also a Philadelphian, it seems probable that Dale obtained the bowl for his fellow townsman on this cruise.

Accompanying Decatur's bowl is a silver ladle with a wooden handle, and, as well, a receipt for making Fish House punch, the latter endorsed as having been presented to the Commodore by the Governor of the State in Schuylkill. The quantities given in this receipt suffice to fill the bowl comfortably after the ice has been added. The receipt, which differs in details from that published in ANTIQUES for February 1936 (*p. 58*) is as follows:

Five lbs. white sugar, 4 pints water; mix well and crush the sugar fine. Then add: 1 qt. brandy, 2 qts. best rum, 1 qt. lemon juice (lime juice better). Mix all well. Then add 3½ qts. water. Then add 2 wine glasses of peach brandy. One half hour before using, put in 8 lbs. of ice — one or two lumps. The above will last for years in bottles or demijohns.

At the time of the misunderstanding with France, the rank of captain was the highest in the Navy. But a captain in command of a squadron was addressed by the courtesy title of commodore. Philadelphia boasted of four such officers, Barry, Dale, Decatur, and Thomas Truxtun. As the first three owned punch-bowls of oriental Lowe-stoft, there is a strong likelihood that Trux-tun was similarly

Fig. 3 — DETAIL OF PORTRAIT MEDALLION ON THE DECATUR BOWL: SAINT-MEMIN'S ENGRAVED PROFILE OF DECATUR
The extraordinary fidelity with which the Chinese artist has rendered the engraved portrait on a porcelain surface has probably never been equaled on any other piece of oriental Lowestoft. The nearest approach to it are the contemporaneous portraits of Washington to be found on two jugs surviving from a group of four fashioned in China to the order of Benjamin Chew Wilcocks. It is by no means unlikely that Wilcocks, a Philadelphia merchant frequently resident in China from 1800 to 1829, was instrumental in obtaining the Decatur bowl

answering to any such specification. If one ever existed, it disappeared long ago. Nevertheless, a Chinese bowl without significant decoration is owned in one branch of the family. Truxtun may well have acquired it on his own account when he went to China about 1791 in command of the *Canton*, the same ship later taken out by Dale. It is possible likewise that some of the other Philadelphia captains — there were five or six of them at least — may have possessed commemorative bowls. If so, some of them

blessed, especially as, like Dale and Barry, he made a voyage to China. If the Decatur bowl was a presentation piece, it seems almost certain that Truxtun would have been similarly honored. However, diligent search has failed to locate a Truxtun bowl may eventually come to light. Incidentally, it is strange that thus far no trace has been found of a commemorative punch-bowl belonging to a naval officer from any other city than Philadelphia. Why this happens to be so, I know not.

Duplicate Punchbowls

IN CONNECTION with his entertaining article *Punch and Punchbowls* published in ANTIQUES for February 1936, Doctor Samuel W. Woodhouse, Jr., illustrated an uncommonly handsome oriental Lowestoft bowl, originally owned by Captain Samuel Morris, president of the Gloucester Fox Hunting Club of Philadelphia, and still cherished as an heirloom in the Morris family. Publication of this item, hitherto considered unique in its decorative motives, has brought ANTIQUES photographs, here reproduced, of what appears to be an exact duplicate of the Morris bowl. The recent find has no recorded pedigree prior to its purchase in Boston as a wedding gift for the present owner, John L. Winston of New York City. As may be seen in the accompanying pictures, one side of it carries a medallion portrayal of a horseman encouraging his mount toward a barrier. A balancing medallion on the opposite side exhibits man and beast at full gallop. While less extensive in their scenic depiction than many hunt bowls turned out by painstaking Chinamen,

the Morris and Winston examples represent as high a grade of animal painting as oriental hands ever achieved on foreign-market porcelain. In this respect they deserve to rank with the fine bowl from which three medallions, enframing flat racing and portraits of a hunting dog and of a stag, are illustrated in J. A. Lloyd Hyde's *Oriental Lowestoft (plate XIX)*. In none of these ceramic paintings is the oriental touch conspicuous. Instead, the artist seems not only to have captured the European mode of expression but to have absorbed something of its spirit as well. A similar genius for effacing native characteristics is evident in the decoration of other late eighteenth- and early nineteenth-century Chinese porcelains, as well as in paintings on canvas and glass executed by Chinese artists after occidental originals. It may, not unjustly, be urged that this kind of proficiency is a symptom of general decadence in the Chinese arts. Such, indeed, may be the fact: in the domain of art, as in the garden, the moment of perfect flowering but briefly preludes the hour of going to seed.

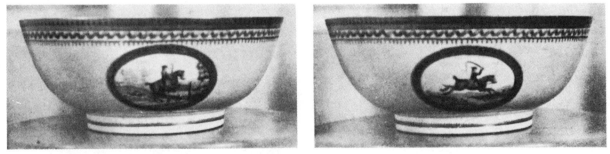

Fig. 1 — PORCELAIN HUNTING BOWL: ORIENTAL LOWESTOFT (*c. 1800*)
Apparently an exact duplicate of an example published in ANTIQUES for February 1936 (*p. 59*). Two other bowls with similar if not quite identical decorations are pictured in J. A. Lloyd Hyde's *Oriental Lowestoft (plate XVIII)*. It is logical to infer that a number of such pieces were made in China at the same time, either to the order of an English porcelain merchant, or to that of a singularly perspicacious Chinese agent

A LOST SET OF EIGHTEENTH-CENTURY ORIENTAL LOWESTOFT

By HARROLD E. GILLINGHAM

A COLLECTOR is always concerned with the pedigree of his acquisitions and is particularly pleased when he is able to discover where and by whom they were originally purchased. When such identifications are applicable to armorial Lowestoft porcelain, they cause double rejoicing. In the present instance, however, I propose to tell about a set of this ware whose armorial decoration has been determined and the order for whose purchase is fully recorded, yet of which, at this writing, but one surviving piece is known.

Philadelphia merchants sent many ships to China during the decade immediately following the War for Independence. The first of these Philadelphia vessels, the *United States*, Thomas Bell master, cleared from the Quaker City port March 22, 1784. (See *Log and Journal of the Ship United States*, *Pennsylvania Magazine of History and Biography*, July 1931.) Others soon followed, each to return laden with rich cargoes of Chinese goods, including Canton ware and the specially ordered porcelain now popularly known as oriental Lowestoft.

Thomas Truxton (*1755–1822*), already distinguished as a privateer during the Revolutionary War, won further laurels in 1799, when he defeated the French frigate *L'Insurgente*. He was, furthermore, part owner of the 250-ton Philadelphia-built ship *Canton*, which he commanded on three voyages to China. On the second of these journeys, he sailed, December 8, 1787, carrying with him a letter from Benjamin Fuller, a local merchant of some standing, requesting the Captain to purchase chinaware "of the most fashionable kind" for Mrs. Fuller. To avoid possible mistake Fuller carefully specified his requirements (see next column).

In addition to the chinaware listed, and some silk and satin goods for his wife, Benjamin Fuller also ordered considerable china "for merchandise," and later wrote Captain Truxton to have it all "enameled which I am informed will suit this market much Better than Blue and White." We may wonder what Mrs. Fuller wanted with a "Genteel & Elegant" two-gallon punchbowl, but self-interest has been known to govern the choice of gifts between married couples.

The "Coat Armorial" which Fuller wished reproduced on his personal service of porcelain was *argent, three bars gules, with a canton in the upper left corner also gules*. According to the heraldry records, the proper crest was a cock in natural colors. Despite Fuller's demand that the bird be rendered in silver, the one remaining specimen of his set shows it in the correct manner. The description of the arms as quoted is confirmed by the seal attached to Fuller's will, filed in Philadelphia, and by the device carved on the marble tombstone that marks the spot where the merchant and his wife repose in Christ Church Burying Ground, Philadelphia. Mrs. Fuller lived but two years to enjoy her porcelain after its arrival in Philadelphia. She died in 1791, to be followed eight years later by Benjamin.

In relation to the present study Benjamin Fuller's lineage is of some importance. He was an Irishman, the son of Benjamin Fuller and Ann Baxter (married in 1716, according to the register of St. Bride's Parish Church, Dublin, Ireland). The merchant himself was born, we may surmise, about 1723, for in a letter of August 18, 1790, he speaks of "being in a few weeks 67 years old." Precisely when he came to Philadelphia is not revealed; but we learn from the printed records that he was a ship owner in 1755. Apparently from that time he prospered in the mercantile and ship-

ping business, maintaining his store first on "Water-street a little below the corner of Walnut-street and next door to Mr. William West's"; and later moving to 162 South Front Street between Spruce and Union Streets, where in addition to his other pursuits he conducted an "Insurance Office." (*Marine Insurance in Philadelphia, 1721–1800*, Philadelphia, 1933, by the present writer.)

In a letter to Mrs. Judith Sober of Barbados he tells of having retired to the country early in the summer of 1775 "in Order to be out of the Way of the then impending troubles — Where I remained until the British Forces evacuated Philadelphia in 1778 . . . having suffered the loss of the Greater part of my Fortune by the unhappy Contest." This suggests that his sympathies were somewhat on the Tory side. Fuller no doubt was financially embarrassed by the depreciation of the Continental currency, for we find in his correspondence many references to dealing in "Hard Money," "Spanish Milled Dollars," and "Mexican Pillared Dollars." In one communication he remarks, "I have ever been particular in my directions not to meddle with Paper Money on

---

Inclos'd you have Bill of Loading for Seven hundred Spanish Mill'd pillor'd Dollars to your Address which, on your arrival in China at Canton, you will please to lay out or invest in the undermentioned Articles, and ship them on Board the Ship Canton (under your Command) for my Acct. . . . Mrs. Fuller begs your attention to the few articles design'd for her own use. . . . Inclos'd you have my Coat of Arms, which I request you to have put on every piece of China mentioned in the following List intended for Mrs. Fuller's own use — Small or large in proportion to the size of the Piece of China. . . .

For Mrs. Fuller —
    A Sett of China for Tea & Coffee viz.[t]

12 Tea Cups and Saucers
12 Coffee   do
 1 Tea Pott & Stand
 1 Coffee Pott & Stand (2 Quarts)
 1 Milk Jug Top and Stand
 1 Sugar Bason Top and Stand
 1 Slop Bason & Stand
 1 Butter Plate
 1 Tea Cannister & top
        Breakfast Sett
12 Large Cups and Saucers
 1 Tea Pott & Stand
 1 Milk Pott Top & Stand
 1 Sugar Bason Top & Stand
 1 Slop Bason & Stand
 1 Butter Plate
    The following of the most ⎫
    fashionable kind which I ⎬
    believe are nearly square ⎭
12 Table Soup Plates
18 Table Plates
18   do   smaller
18   do   small
12 Dishes (in a nest) Different Sizes
 2 Large Tureens ⎫
    Genteel   ⎬ with Stands
 6 Smaller do   ⎭
    (Three different Sizes)
 1 Gallon Punch Bowl
 1 Two Gallon do Genteel & Elegant

All this China of the most fashionable Kind and must have my Coat Armorial on each Piece — Small or large in proportion to the Size of the piece — The Best Nankeen China light Blue & White except the Coat of Arms which must be of the Colours there pictur'd — The Crest and Field to be a Silver Colour

my Accts. but sell my property for Gold or Silver only." Other correspondence is similar in tenor.

In nearly all of his orders to London and Canton, Fuller included some special requisition for his wife. Thus in a letter to Bristol, November 13, 1773, he called for "Two genteel Cases for knives and forks, such as you would choose for yourself. One to contain Twelve Table knives and forks and Twelve Spoons; the other to hold Twelve desert knives and forks—The knives and forks for each Case you are to buy, Ivory handles and of the best kind & newest fashion, the Spoons I already have." Again in 1785 he asked Captain Truxton — on his first trip to China — to expend the eighty dollars provided for "two pieces of Black Sattin of the first Quality; Two Fanns & Two Green Umbrellas & two genteel Rich China Punch Bowls, one three Quarts the other four Quarts — If there should be an over Pluss he will please to lay it out in Table China or in any articles suitable for the use of a Lady upwards of Sixty. . . . If you bring any China please to have it of the Best Ninkin and edged with Gold."

It will be observed that the requests were always for the *best* of its kind. Evidently Fuller's house was quite splendidly furnished.

Fuller's "hard money" policy and his acumen in other directions brought him a neat fortune, which, following his death, was distributed according to the generous terms of his will. To relatives, friends, servants, the Pennsylvania Hospital, and Christ Church he bequeathed in all over fifteen thousand "Spanish milled Dollars." To a nephew, Joseph Fuller Doyle, he gave 10,000 acres of land in Kentucky (purchased from Benjamin Wynkoop *et al.* in 1792), and five thousand Spanish dollars. To another nephew, Abraham Fuller, went "1500 spanish milled dollars, having already given him 1000 pounds on March 2d. 1795 as will appear by my books. *I also devise him all my china ware marked with my Arms, and no other.*" This last sentence tells us precisely who was the second owner of the great set of china ordered in 1787. This second owner, Abraham Fuller, was the son of Benjamin's deceased brother Joseph (perhaps the Joseph Fuller of Violet Hill, County Dublin, whose will was filed in Dublin in 1783). From Benjamin's letter books we learn that for more than a year the merchant kept urging his sister-in-law, Mary Fuller, to leave Ireland and come with her children to Philadelphia. On Sunday, May 22, 1785, he had the happiness of welcoming the widow, her son Abraham, and her daughter, "Matty." Concerning the boy, he presently wrote, to John Thornburgh, a linen draper of Cork, "Aby is a sweet Youth and if Providence

FIG. 1 — SMALL "ORIENTAL LOWESTOFT" TRAY *(1787)*
The decoration portrays the arms of Fuller. Without reasonable doubt this tray once belonged to a large set of porcelain whose purchase in Canton was ordered by Benjamin Fuller, Philadelphia merchant.
Photograph by courtesy of Doctor Francis William Lamb

but grants me a few Years of Life, he will never repent his coming to America." Having no children of his own, Benjamin hoped that this twelve-year-old nephew might become to him as a son and eventually take over the business. But in this he was disappointed. His sister-in-law, Mary, returned to Ireland about 1793 and — according to Benjamin's receipt book — was followed two years later by Abraham, then in his twenties. Though the merchant's ambitious plans for his nephew were frustrated, his generosity was not impaired. Abraham left Philadelphia with 1,000 pounds in cash and credit, given him by his uncle. This donation, acknowledged by Abraham as "in full of all he purposes to give me," was, as already noted, amplified in Benjamin's will. We may not doubt that the "Coat Armorial" china was shipped to Abraham Fuller in Ireland.

Enquiries among museum curators and private collectors in the United States have failed to bring forth even a single piece of this set. On the other hand, M. S. Dudley Westropp of the National Museum of Dublin, who has assisted me in my search, has found just one — a badly damaged small tray or tea-caddy stand. However, this fragment preserves intact and unmistakable the "Coat Armorial" of Benjamin Fuller. The border of this tray, painted in underglaze blue, is of the so-called "Nanking type." The rest of the decoration is applied, as usual, over the glaze in gold and colors. Doubtless the latter work was done by enamelers in Canton.

Through the courtesy of Doctor Francis William Lamb a photograph of this tray has been obtained. The piece has been in Mrs. Lamb's family for many, many years, and, while Mrs. Lamb has known it since her childhood, she has been unable to learn what became of the rest of a once large service. Her home, Woodfield House, near Clara, County Offaly (late King's), Ireland, was long ago damaged by a fire. Perhaps at that time the China was destroyed. However, we are fortunate in retrieving this one small memento to complete the story of Benjamin Fuller's oriental china adorned with his "Coat Armorial."

In this connection, however, we must admit a bare but hopeful possibility. Circumstances may have prevented the shipment of the complete Fuller set to the nephew in Ireland. If so, a piece of it may today be lurking unrecognized in some American collection. Again, granting that none of the outfit remained in the United States, parts of it may in time have drifted from Ireland to England, there to await ultimate identification.

FIG. 2 — BENJAMIN FULLER'S ARMS
Reconstructed from an imperfect impression on the seal of the merchant's will and the carving on his tombstone. The bearings are precisely those shown on the armorial tray

V Patterns and Designs

The five articles in this section do not cover all the classifications of patterns and designs found in Chinese export porcelain. Ship decoration, American eagle, and state and American market pieces have already been discussed. As no articles on Jesuit or religious decoration or on Lotus Leaf, Tobacco Leaf, or Imari designs, to mention a few, have appeared in *Antiques* over the years, this anthology suffers to that extent. Yet, there is much here, much more than most readers will want to sample.

Possibly the largest and certainly the most important classification, namely armorial decoration, is represented first by a fine article, "Chinese Armorial Porcelain," by an outstanding scholar and authority on the subject, the late Sir Algernon Tudor-Craig, K.B.E., E.S.A. Sir Algernon was the author of *Eighteenth-Century Armorial Porcelain,* published in 1925 and until recently the collector's main reference source.

The editor's note preceding this article explains how armorial porcelain may be used as a fool-proof means of accurately dating the various borders and decorations, as well as the china itself. A coat-of-arms is the specific arms, or property, of only one individual and not, as many Americans erroneously suppose, the arms of all members of that family. The vital statistics of an individual, when he was born, married, died, as well as other important events in his life, can often be used to establish the date of the porcelain, and, concurrently, to rather precisely categorize the use of certain types of borders and other decorations.

Tudor-Craig illustrates and describes various pieces and shows how such pieces can be dated. Because of his English background, he may be excused one slip when he ventures into identifying a piece supposedly with American arms. He illustrates in figure 12, page 147, a plate with the arms of Chase and identifies these as those of Samuel Chase of Maryland, a signer of the Declaration of Independence. Actually, they are the arms of Sir Richard Chase, Sheriff of Essex in 1744, who died in April of 1758. Samuel Chase was distantly related but used as his arms those of his mother's family, Townley.

Tudor-Craig's early book has been superseded by the new, definitive work on the subject, *Chinese Armorial Porcelain* by David Sanctuary Howard. Howard spent fourteen years on his book which lists over 3,000 services and illustrates 2,000; in addition, it lists over 900 mottoes with the names of the families.

Collecting armorial examples of Chinese porcelain is better enjoyed and appreciated if the collector has some basic knowledge of heraldry to enable him to identify the original owners and their histories. As heraldry is an exact science, a study of it may appear a formidable subject. However, Jane Boicourt in her "Introduction to Heraldry" outlines in a concise manner the principal points to a working understanding of this interesting subject.

In the following article, "Collecting Armorial Export Porcelain," Horace W. Gordon explains how the collector, with the aid of certain specific books, can go about identifying the arms found on individual pieces. With the advent of Howard's book such instructions are made largely, but not entirely, obsolete.

Probably the most popular of all export designs is the so-called Fitzhugh which is found in colors of blue, green, orange, sepia, black, gold, mulberry, apricot, yellow, and combinations of these colors. In addition, Fitzhugh borders are occasionally used with an armorial device in the center.

There has always been a great deal of conjecture as to the origin of the word "Fitzhugh," a term more popularly used in America than in Great Britain. It has even been suggested that Fitzhugh was a mispronunciation of Foochow, a Chinese seaport, an explanation that appears far-fetched, to put it mildly. J. B. S. Holmes in his article, "Fitzhugh and Fitz Hughs in the China Trade," does an excellent research job and seems to tie the name firmly to the Fitz Hugh family of England, three members of which were active in the China trade toward the end of the eighteenth century. In a recent conversation, David Howard told this writer about tracking down an English service with the Fitzhugh design which is still in the hands of descendants of the original eighteenth century Fitz Hugh purchaser. Holmes relates that he found at least one piece still in family hands.

The final two articles on Canton, Rose Medallion, and Mandarin patterns bring into focus material on later export ware which has become increasingly popular *and* expensive in recent years. Considered of lower quality by many experts, it has been harshly judged and too little understood. Hiram Tindall and Carl L. Crossman have performed pioneer work in this field, and today's collectors of later export are greatly in their debt.

"The Canton Pattern" by Tindall describes this pattern as well as the Nanking and Fitzhugh designs. As is often the case, the terms *Canton* and *Nanking* are used interchangeably. Canton, Nanking, Fitzhugh, Rose Medallion, Mandarin, and Cabbage Leaf designs are technically all Chinese export porcelain, but china with these designs is usually referred to by these specific names. This may be an unconscious effort or desire on the part of dealers and collectors to retain the term "Chinese export" for those pieces of finer quality made in the eighteenth century.

"Canton varies in quality," Tindall notes, "more than the other wares." It was certainly made as early as the late eighteenth century, but the majority of the ware reached America in the nineteenth century. Much of it was used by one generation and discarded. It was, in Tindall's words, "everybody's porcelain; it graced the tables of the most prominent citizens, and it was found in many humble homes."

Rose Medallion and Mandarin ware, as Carl Crossman explains in his article, derived from the *famille rose* designs made popular in the mid-eighteenth century. The range of color and extent of decoration, however, burst forth into a new array not seen before. Crossman states that the patterns "reached the peak of their popularity in the 1820s and 1830s, [and] by 1850 designs were so crude that they do not merit study" today. Many fine pieces of an earlier date, however, merit not only study but connoisseurship.

Chinese Armorial Porcelain

Some Eighteenth-Century Borders

By Sir Algernon Tudor-Craig, K. B. E., F. S. A.

Note.— The following notes on the borders used on Chinese armorial porcelain produced for the English market, should be viewed as a collateral contribution to the more general discussion of Chinese European-market porcelain, which is now appearing serially in Antiques under the entitlement of *Lowestoft: What Is It?*

Armorial designs provide the most authentic obtainable evidence as to the date of the specimens of Chinese porcelain upon which they occur. Incidentally they serve to establish the limits of time within which a given border or type of border was in general use in the decoration of such porcelain. Familiarity with different types of borders and their dates is, in its turn, useful in determining the approximate period of specimens of the pictorial, or non-armorial, Chinese porcelain which, during the eighteenth century, was made in such quantity for European consumption. Hence the special significance of Sir Algernon Tudor-Craig's notes. Sir Algernon, it may be observed, was an expert in heraldry before he undertook the study of armorial porcelain. His statements as to the dates indicated by heraldic devices may, therefore, be relied upon as representing final authority. — *The Editor.*

THE subject matter of this article is based entirely on specimens of Chinese porcelain in the writer's collection, enameled with British armorial bearings, the details of which indicate, without possibility of contradiction, almost the exact date of the porcelain itself. There can no longer be any doubt that practically all the so-called "Lowestoft" armorial services to be found in the United Kingdom were manufactured and decorated in China, during the eighteenth century, for the English market; and that the decoration, which, in the early part of that century, was decidedly Chinese, gradually developed a European character more in accordance with the taste and instructions of the prospective British buyer.* A study of the development of the various borders used may, therefore, prove of service to collectors who are interested in this class of porcelain, surely a

Fig. 1 — Arms of Johnston Impaling Lovelace (*1693–5*)
Decoration in underglaze blue. *Khang-hsi.*

*See Antiques, Vol. XIII, p. 384 *et seq.*

Fig. 2 — Early Eighteenth-Century Types
(*Left*) Arms of Stanley Impaling Granville (*c. 1710*). *Famille verte* and *rouge-de-fer.*
(*Centre*) Arms of Parsons Impaling Crowley (*c. 1720*). *Rouge-de-fer* circle and blue dragons.
(*Right*) Arms of Lethieullier (*c. 1720*). All underglaze Nankin blue.

Fig. 3 (Left) — ARMS OF LORD SOMERS (*1720*) Red, blue, and gold Imari design.

Fig. 4 (Right) — ARMS OF THOMAS PITT, LORD LONDONDERRY (*c. 1720*) Golden floral border, with panels in colors.

Fig. 5 (Below) — ARMS OF HARRIES (*c. 1730*) Border all in gold. *Yung-tcheng.*

most instructive one, telling us, as it does, its own date and history.

Figure 1 illustrates a jardinière, the date of which, from the arms, can be proved to be 1693–5 (*Khang-hsi period*). It is decorated entirely in underglaze Nankin blue, and is believed by the writer to be the earliest piece of Chinese armorial porcelain in existence. The crudeness of the drawing of the arms, with helmet and crest above, should be noted as indicating that the Chinese artist had little or no idea of what he was trying to represent. The top border also is of interest as an early specimen of the fine blue diaper with inset panels charged with scrolls.

During the next twenty-odd years of the Khang-hsi period, up to 1723, most of the services sent to England have this diaper and panel decoration in *famille verte*, *rouge-de-fer*, or underglaze blue, the small panels bearing miniature views, utensils, or flower sprays; while the backs of the rims in every case are enameled with three or four flower sprays in colors similar to those appearing on the front (*Fig. 2*).

Another type of border used during this early period was in brilliant reds and blues, copied by the Chinese from the Japanese Imari designs (*Fig. 3*). Several very handsome services of this design are still in existence, notably those made

Fig. 6 (Above) — ARMS OF BENNET, EARL OF TANKERVILLE (*c. 1735*) Panels in puce.

Fig. 7 (Left) — ARMS OF PAYNE (*c. 1730*) Sepia diaper circle, panels in color, sprays in *famille rose*.

Fig. 8 (Right) — ARMS OF GIBSON IMPALING GREEN (*c. 1730*) Panels in *famille rose*. Diaper, green, pink, and black.

146

Fig. 9 (*Left*) — ARMS OF HOLT, QUARTERLY (*c. 1740*)
  Scenery in color and sprays on rim.
(*Right*) — ARMS OF MATTHEW IMPALING BYAM (*c. 1745*)
  Raised white floral border, brown and gold circles, *famille rose* centre.

for James, Duke of Chandos — "the Princely Chandos" — for Lord Somers, Lord High Chancellor of England, and for Doctor Walker of Lancaster. Figure 4, from a service made, *circa* 1720, for Thomas Pitt, Baron of Londonderry, is also of this period, the gold floral border being apparently a forerunner of a similar border (*Fig. 5*) prevalent during the Yung-tcheng period (*1723–1736*). This is again varied with charmingly designed panels of scenery (*Fig. 6*), the color of which, in this case, is in puce.

During this period the diaper work assumed a more open trellislike appearance, and is more often found carried out in sepia,

Fig. 10 — ARMS OF HESKETH (*c. 1750*)
  Gold diaper and spearhead circles, with *famille rose* sprays.

as in Figure 7, the borders being finely enameled in *famille rose* flower sprays. In Figure 8, an example is seen where the whole of the border is in alternate green, pink, and sepia diaper, with inset panels. During this Yung-tcheng period, the flower sprays virtually disappeared from the backs of the rims, and are found only in very rare instances.

About 1740, or early in the Kien-Lung period (*1736–1795*), services begin to show signs of European taste, the centres being decorated in sepia or colors, with pastoral scenes, exotic birds, or mythological subjects, while the armorial ensigns are relegated to the border and alternated with flower sprays (*Fig. 9, left*).

The border shown in Figure 9, *right*, which dates about 1745, is very distinctive and unusual. It consists of raised white flower sprays between two floral circles in gold and brown, while the centre is decorated with an exquisitely designed basket of flowers in *famille rose*, the arms again showing on the rim.

From 1745 to 1760 the gold spearhead, or chain, border, either twice repeated or with a gold diaper rim, manifests itself (*Fig. 10*) and is common to the majority of serv-

Fig. 11 — ARMS OF WATSON (*c. 1755*)
  Small *famille rose* sprays and gold chain.

Fig. 12 — ARMS OF CHASE (*c. 1760*)
  Red, blue, and gold diaper, with gold spearheads.

Fig. 13 — PART OF THE DINNER SERVICE OF HORATIO WALPOLE OF WOOLTERTON, NORFOLK (*c. 1765*)
Brilliant underglaze blue of Japanese design, scrolls on back of rim.

ices of that period, which also begin to show small sprays, in *famille rose*, all round the border, the dishes and many of the plates being octagonal in shape instead of circular as heretofore (*Fig. 11*).

One of the most beautiful of such services, still in fine condition, is that bearing the arms of Samuel Chase of Maryland, a Signer of the Declaration of Independence. Its date is about 1760 (*Fig. 12*). It will be seen that, in addition to the Chippendale Rococo shield, it has the gold spearhead circle, while the whole of the border is in brilliant red, blue, and gold diaper.

Another service of peculiar interest, and of about this date, is that made for Horatio Walpole of Woolterton in Norfolk (*Fig. 13*). It is of the finest quality porcelain, with decoration in exquisite Nankin blue, evidently copied from a Japanese design, the back of each rim bearing scrolls in the same color; while, oddly enough, the armorial bearings are also shown on the back, probably owing to the fact that the design on the front would hardly allow their insertion there.

Fig. 14 — ARMS OF GOURLAY (*c. 1760*)
Gold scrolls and scallop-shells.

Between 1750 and 1770 a stock pattern border of gold scallop-shells joined by thin gold scrolls (*Fig. 14*), appears to have been used, as the writer knows of several services with this design, but with different arms in the centre. Another favorite design at this time is found on what is called "journey china," represented by a panel of shipping on each side and a building in the centre, the arms being on the base of the rim, and the crest on the top of it. This pattern is said to represent the Chinese port of departure (Canton), the port of arrival (Lowestoft, or, more probably, Deal), and the ware's final resting place in the home of the owner.

A border of great attractiveness, shown in Figure 15, dates about 1775, and is in a beautiful rose-pink diaper, a design much copied in after years by two or three of the English factories, notably New Hall and Lowestoft. From this date onward to the year 1790, the large majority of services made for the English and American markets had underglaze blue borders, beginning with a wavy diaper design about 1780 (*Fig. 16*), and then, about 1790, showing a stock pattern in deep blue spearhead circles (*Fig. 17*), sometimes varied with silver-gray, the arms in the centre being in correct colors on a spade-shaped shield.

About 1790–1800 (*Kea-King period*), appeared the design so dear to the American collector — a blue rim powdered with gold stars and painted over the glaze, the centre showing blue and gold sprays of flowers, or a shield on a draped mantle displaying the arms, or cypher, of the owner.

Fig. 15 — Arms of Lennox (c. 1775)
Rose-pink diaper border, painted over the glaze.

became Fitzhugh and thus remains to this day.

This porcelain is found either in blue, green, or rust red, and carries a wide spearhead border in one of these colors. The centre displays four large peonies grouped round a shield, or a starlike circle surrounding a crest or other simple design. When the color is neatly outlined in gold, this porcelain can be most attractive.

After the year 1800 the Chinese trade in porcelain tableware would seem to have greatly declined, doubt-

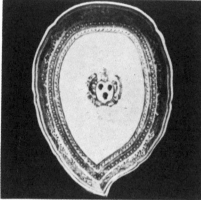

Fig. 16 — Arms of Canning (c. 1780)
Wavy floral border in underglaze blue.

Last, but not least in interest, we find, about 1800, the Fitz-hugh pattern (*Fig. 18*), so called in America only, owing to the fact that an old sea captain, trading from Salem, Massachusetts, to China, used to buy large consignments of this

less owing to the fact that English and Continental factories had sprung up to meet their own local demands. Chinese manufacturers, therefore, reverted to native designs, enameling their porcelain all over with richly dressed mandarin figures, and with Chinese battle

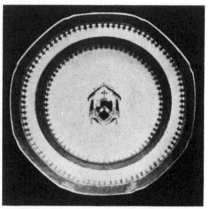

Fig. 17 — Arms of Meriton (c. 1790)
Underglaze blue border, arms in colors.

porcelain at Foochow and return with it to his home port for his wife to sell during his next trip. She, dear lady, apparently did not hold with such outlandish names; so Foochow

and domestic scenes. Examples of this late porcelain are frequently over-decorated, and cannot compare with the charming efforts of the eighteenth century.

Fig. 18 — Arms of Denison
Fitzhugh pattern in underglaze blue.

Introduction to heraldry

THE STUDY OF HERALDRY takes one back to the tournaments of the Middle Ages: A new knight is making his appearance; a herald steps forward, "blasons" (blows the trumpet), and proclaims the knight's arms. Today we continue to speak of "heraldry" and refer to a description of arms as "blazoning."

The main function of arms was to serve as a rallying point in battle, when it was obviously desirable to have some vivid and unmistakable insignia on one's shield and flag. Arms were also important in a day when documents had to be signed with a seal, and they served as distinctive ornaments on tombs and dwellings and all sorts of small objects. By the thirteenth century arms had been adopted by most of the leading families of Europe.

Armorial emblems (*bearings*) are arranged on an escutcheon, which for a man takes the form of a shield. In the case of a woman it is a diamond-shaped lozenge, though a small shield (*pretence*, or *inescutcheon*) may be used within a larger one for the arms of a married heiress or co-heiress. In the case of a husband and wife both entitled to arms the shield may be divided vertically, with the husband's arms on the left and the wife's on the right. Their son might then divide the escutcheon into four quarters, with his father's arms on the upper right and lower left and his mother's in the other two sections. This quartering might continue to be subdivided, so that coats of arms sometimes become very complex.

The jargon of heraldry looks rather frightening at first, but if you master the basic terms the rest will come in time. First of all, a thing is not properly referred to as "right" and "left" but as *sinister* and *dexter*—designations which come from the position of the shield carried by the knight. *Dexter* refers to the side under his right arm, which appears *left* to the spectator, and *sinister* to the part under his left arm, which appears on the *right*. Therefore, *dexter* means *left*, and *sinister* means *right*.

Color plays an important part in armorial bearings. The *tinctures*, as they are called, include two *metals* and five *colors*. Since it is often necessary to reproduce arms in black and white, a system was worked out at the beginning of the seventeenth century for indicating metals and colors by lines and dots:

METALS. Gold (*or*), dots on a white ground. Silver (*argent*), plain white.

COLORS. Blue (*azure*), horizontal lines. Red (*gules*), perpendicular lines. Black (*sable*), cross-hatched vertical and horizontal lines. Green (*vert*), diagonal lines from upper left to lower right. Purple (*purpure*), diagonal lines from upper right to lower left.

There is a rule that one must not place a metal on a metal, or a color on a color, so that if one has a shield of *argent*, the bearings must be in *azure, gules, sable, vert,* or *purpure*, not in *or*.

In addition to metals and colors, there are various furs. *Ermine* is represented by three sable dots (standing for ermine tails) on a field of argent, and there are two variants—*ermines*, with silver spots on a black field, and *erminois*, with black

spots on a gold field. The fur known as *vair* represents skins sewed in layers, alternately blue and white.

Next to the *tinctures*, the most important things to learn are the standard patterns into which the shield is divided. The ones most used, and therefore called *ordinaries*, are as follows: (Much of the material here, and elsewhere in this article, is from Bolton's *American Armory*.)

CROSS. A common bearing from early times, of which there are many forms.

CHIEF. The top third of the shield.

FESS. A horizontal band.

PALE. A perpendicular band. When a shield is divided *per pale* with a husband's arms on the dexter side and the wife's on the sinister, the husband's arms are said to be *impaling* those of the wife.

BEND. A band diagonally from *dexter chief* (upper left) to *sinister base* (lower right). *Bend sinister* is just the opposite. A thin bend sinister not touching either side of the shield is called a *baton*.

CHEVRON. A bend and a bend sinister springing from the lower side and meeting.

SALTIRE. A bend and a bend sinister intersected, to form a diagonal cross.

There are many other patterns not used so often and therefore called *subordinaries*. These include the *pile*, a triangle with its base against the *middle chief* (upper middle part) and pointing towards the base of the shield; the *bordure*, a border around the outer fifth of the shield; the *quarter;* and the *canton*, a square in *dexter chief* (upper left) which is smaller than a quarter.

These ordinaries and subordinaries alone are enough to constitute a *heraldic blazon*, as, for instance, a *chief* of *or* against a field of *azure*. Many of the oldest armorial bearings, in fact, are of this simple type. But as anyone knows who has looked at coats of arms at all there is a bewildering array of other bearings, or *charges*.

Among these the most striking are the heraldic beasts. The lion usually appears *rampant* (standing on his left hind leg, his forepaws raised, the right higher than the left). Then there is the leopard *passant* (walking with his left paw raised, either *guardant*, full-face, or *reguardant*, turned back), and strange creatures, like the griffon (part lion and part eagle), and the wyver (a dragon with small wings). The eagle also appears, with spread wings to distinguish him from the falcon whose wings are folded. The rest of the assorted birds, fishes, and other devices are often a play on words referring to the name of the owner.

The shield is the main feature of a coat of arms, but there are other less vital parts—the helmet, with a *wreath* above it supporting the *crest;* the ornamental drapery called the *mantle* or *lambrequin;* and the *motto*, which usually appears on a scroll under the shield. All of these together make up an *achievement of arms.*　　　　　　　　　　　—JANE BOICOURT

Heraldic decorations courtesy the Encyclopaedia Britannica.

Fig. 1. Charger with the arms of Brydges, Duke of Chandos, impaling Willoughby *(c. 1715)*. Diameter, 18½ inches. The rim is decorated with an Imari design in red, blue, and gold. A light floral design in underglaze red appears on the back of the rim, a feature not found after 1723. *All photographs by the author from his own collection.*

Collecting armorial export porcelain

BY HORACE W. GORDON

TOWARDS THE END of the seventeenth century a vogue was started by prominent families in England and on the Continent for export porcelain dinner services decorated with their coats of arms. This demand grew until it reached a peak in the latter part of the eighteenth century and terminated abruptly shortly after the start of the nineteenth. Armorial services were often very large, sometimes running to five hundred pieces; the invoice for the Peers service in the British Museum specified 524 pieces.

Orders for these sets were given to representatives of the East India Company and taken to Canton. The china was manufactured in Ching-tê Chên, where most of the decorating was probably done, especially that in underglaze blue, though there is evidence that some of the enamel decoration was done in Canton. The coats of arms were copied from drawings sent out by the purchaser.

The advanced collector may succeed in finding specimens with arms from a number of European countries, but the vast majority of pieces one comes across bear English, Scottish, or Irish arms. It is therefore best to confine oneself at first to this branch of the subject.

In my experience, the identification of most armorial

Fig. 2. Plate with arms of Wheatley. Diameter, 8 inches.

Fig. 3. Octagonal plate with arms of Booth quartering Lloyd, Wilkinson in pretence. Diameter, 8 inches.

Figs. 2, 3, 4, 5. Armorial decoration of the mid-1700's. From 1736 to 1755 the mantling of the arms is characterized by flowing scrolls, and the decoration of the rim is plainer, with scattered flowers or graceful gold scrollwork. Borders of thin gold cable chain design or gold spearheads are found around the rim, the plate well, or both, with a half-inch border of running gold leaves on some of the larger round platters or chargers.

Fig. 4. Charger with the arms of Baker. Diameter, 15 inches.

Fig. 5. Platter with the arms of Jervis in a six-part quartering. Length, 17 inches.

Fig. 6. Saucer with the arms of Gosling impaling Newcombe. The spade-shaped shield surrounded by floral sprays and the garlands of flowers on the border are often seen on armorial porcelain of the period from about 1755 to 1770.

Fig. 7. Cup and saucer with arms of Osborne, and teapot with arms of Dumbar impaling Byle. Plain shields with no mantling were the fashion about 1790. The teapot has no other decoration except a narrow border around the top. The cup and saucer have a narrow dark blue border with small gold stars.

Fig. 8. Platter with the arms of Ibbetson. Length, 17 inches. The wide border in underglaze blue is the general type referred to as a Fitzhugh border, introduced about 1795, which may consist either of a fret design or the pattern composed of honeycomb, circles, and stylized butterflies seen here.

used by the Cheyney, Pede, and Uvedale families. With these names you may turn to Burke's *General Armory* and find that the description of the arms of the Cheyney family exactly matches the arms on your piece.

If the arms bear a motto, as they often do, the work of identification is usually hastened appreciably. Alphabetical lists of mottoes, with the names of the families using them, are to be found in *Fairbairns' Crests, Burke's Peerage,* and Sir Algernon Tudor-Craig's *Armorial Porcelain of the Eighteenth Century.* The latter is an invaluable reference book on all aspects of the subject.

Armorial decoration often affords the collector the opportunity to establish the date of his piece within relatively close limits. For instance, in the Duke of Chandos service, illustrated here, the arms of Brydges, Duke of Chandos, are shown impaling those of his second wife, Cassandra Willoughby, whom he married on August 4, 1714. Since he died in 1744, the service must have been made between these dates, and probably shortly after his marriage.

One of the first things that the collector of armorial porcelain should do is to acquire a rudimentary knowledge of heraldry. Burke's *General Armory* contains a brief history and an explanation of heraldic terms, and there are a number of other readily available sources of information. A knowledge of heraldry is not only necessary for the identification of arms but will be useful to the collector in other ways. If one knows, for instance, that a metal, color, or fur is never placed on another metal, color, or fur, one would be justified in questioning the authenticity of a piece where the coat of arms shows a red lion rampant on a blue field. Some unscrupulous individuals have taken pieces of export porcelain with blank spaces and executed armorial designs which represent no authentic arms, a practice which goes back to the latter part of the 1800's.

A special class of armorial porcelain is that bearing state seals or the American eagle. Because of their scarcity, such pieces command a relatively high price, and blank pieces have been widely painted with these insignia. The novice collector who may be tempted by such pieces should assure himself that the dealer is qualified to pass on their authenticity. Some of the export porcelain made for the American market displays "arms" which were the invention of a family desiring the prestige of armorial bearings. Pieces decorated with a shield enclosing initials in gold or blue and drapery in blue, gold, or ermine are perfectly good Oriental export porcelain but not truly armorial.

Collecting armorial export porcelain has many advantages. It is not so plentiful that you will be surfeited with the amount available, but neither is it so scarce but what diligent search will turn up a piece here and there. Best of all, the cost is within the means of the average collector. If he is satisfied with specimens which are slightly chipped or cracked or which have been mended, the cost is modest indeed. On this point many collectors are willing to overlook small nicks, chips, or age cracks because of the vastly greater selection available.

Unlike some porcelain, where different patterns tend to clash when placed together, all armorial pieces seem to complement each other and blend harmoniously, since the designs are all rather similar. And the history of the different family arms makes each item a conversation piece and a source of unending interest.

porcelain can be accomplished with the aid of a few books generally available in the larger libraries. The quickest way is to use Papworth's *Dictionary of Coats of Arms,* where the various arms are listed according to the devices used. After ascertaining the names of the families using the arms in question, Burke's *General Armory* may be consulted. Over sixty thousand English, Irish, and Scottish families are listed here, with a description of the arms in exact heraldic detail. Further information about the family can generally be found in *Burke's Landed Gentry* or *Burke's Peerage.*

One may also go about the problem of identification from the crest. *Fairbairns' Crests* shows over two thousand different crests, with the names of the families using each. For example, a hat with two plumes is found to be

Fitzhugh and FitzHughs in the China Trade

BY J. B. S. HOLMES

ONE OF THE MOST PLEASING patterns of China Trade porcelain is that commonly known, particularly in the United States, as Fitzhugh—a name whose derivation has been shrouded in mystery. The literature usually suggests that it is a possible mispronunciation of the place name Foochow, or else that this porcelain may have been named after some unknown Englishman.

In the first instance, it has always seemed to me that Foochow as a source was rather farfetched. That city does not appear to have been identified with porcelain making, and it was not opened as a trade port until the 1840's, well after the trading in Fitzhugh porcelain had reached its peak. If we discount the city of Foochow as a source of either porcelain or the Fitzhugh name, there remains that unknown Englishman. Therein lies a story that begins in London, reaches into Surrey, and ends in Wales in a FitzHugh family home and a porcelain plate in the Fitzhugh pattern.

Page from the China Diary of William FitzHugh, British East India Company supercargo at Canton from 1775 to 1791.

In the summer of 1964, I visited the library of the India Office Records, off Whitehall Street in London, to inspect the papers and ship's manifests of the defunct British East India Company in a search for information about blue and white Canton porcelain. Unfortunately these papers simply describe all porcelain as chinaware, but the short visit was not a total loss. I discovered that the China Diaries—almost daily reports to London by the Canton agents of the British East India Company—had been signed by three supercargoes named Bevan, Raper, and—FitzHugh! My time at the library was limited, so I wrote for further information as to when FitzHugh was at Canton. In reply I learned that, even while I was studying at the library, a present-day FitzHugh was also there doing research on the family history. This was T. V. H. FitzHugh of Ottershaw, Surrey, who is presently writing a biography of his ancestor Captain William Fitz-Hugh.

Through Mr. FitzHugh I have been able to collect information about not one but several FitzHughs who were active in the Canton trade, information that it has taken him years to assemble. He was also kind enough to put me in touch with his cousins Colonel and Mrs. Edmund FitzHugh of Plâs Power, Wales.

The FitzHugh family connection with China starts with a Captain William FitzHugh, who first sailed his ship to the Orient in 1703. He reached Chusan in 1704, but there is no record that he ever got to Canton. Captain William had two sons, Thomas and Valentine. Thomas was born in 1728 and died January 1, 1800. He was employed by the British East India Company and first sailed as "writer" (junior clerk) to the supercargo on the ship *Sandwich* bound for Canton in 1746. He continued in the China trade, becoming supercargo and eventually senior supercargo for the company's China service, attached to various ships (the British did not establish a permanent shore staff at Canton until 1770).

In 1767, Thomas retired from the China service but remained with the British East India Company in London. In that year he married Mary Lloyd, whose family lived at an estate in Wales called Plâs Power. Thomas and Mary settled in Portland Place, London. However, in 1779 the company again sent him to Canton, this time as president of the Canton factory, as their trade establishment was known. The staff there consisted of supercargoes and writers who lived at the Canton factory during the shipping season and were required by the Chinese to live in Macao the rest of the year. Thomas remained in Canton as president until 1781.

During this stay Thomas was entrusted with the delicate task of settling huge and long-standing debts owing to the company by the hong merchants—a task in which he was not entirely successful. He also shipped porcelain back to England, both for his private account and for friends, a privilege granted by the company to their senior employees. A reproduction of one page of the

China Records shows some of his transactions during the year 1780-1781. He returned to England in 1781, rounding out his career as a director of the British East India Company.

Thomas' son, Thomas II, was in Canton from the late 1780's until well into the 1790's. This son returned to England and inherited the estate of Plàs Power from his mother's family, the Lloyds, in 1816. There do not seem to be any records of shipments of chinaware to England by Thomas II.

William FitzHugh, son of Valentine and grandson of Captain William, was at Canton as a supercargo from 1775 to 1791. It was this William who signed the China Diary which I discovered so recently. He served part of the time under his uncle, Thomas I. William shipped two chests of chinaware on the *Hillsborough* in 1778, two boxes on the *General Coote* in 1789, and ten boxes on the *Hindostan* in 1791.

Thus three FitzHughs were prominently connected with Canton at the very period in which the China Trade was thriving and at or near the time when the United States entered that trade. It seems reasonable to conclude that the Fitzhugh pattern derived its name from one of these three.

The Edmund FitzHughs have inherited at Plàs Power, where the family has lived continuously since 1816, a large blue and white dish or round platter, sixteen inches in diameter, in the pattern known as Fitzhugh, with a post-and-spear border. All subsequent generations have been rather proud of the roles Thomas I and Thomas II played in the Canton trade and have carefully preserved the mementos of China brought back by these two. For this reason, they feel that the Fitzhugh platter is not likely to be one remaining piece of an entire set in this pattern, but more probably represents a gift to either Thomas, perhaps commemorating some event or service rendered in Canton. (Incidentally, the family did not know the pattern of the platter as Fitzhugh; this name for it seems to be much more common in the United States than in England.)

Of the three FitzHughs at Canton, Thomas I seems to me most likely to have earned such an award. On his death it could have passed to Thomas II, at Plàs Power. If so, this platter may be the first piece of porcelain decorated in this pattern. It is easy to imagine that American merchant captains, arriving in Canton for the first time

in 1784, were at a loss to select from among the many porcelain patterns available. Might not the hong merchants, or the English-speaking neighbors at the British East India Company factory, have suggested the pattern presented to or purchased by Thomas FitzHugh I, late of Canton?

J. A. Lloyd Hyde (*Oriental Lowestoft*, 1964; p. 72) describes the Fitzhugh pattern as follows: "The *Fitzhugh pattern* has a trellis-work border with four split pomegranates showing the fruit inside, and butterflies with wings spread. In the center of the pieces appear four separate groups of flowers and emblems, martial or otherwise, surrounding a medallion or an oval monogram. *Fitzhugh pattern* china is most frequently in blue, but it occurs also in sepia, gold, brown, pink, black, and bright green . . ." However, it should be noted that the characteristic central design is found not only with the border described here, but also with the post-and-spear type which appears on the FitzHugh platter—certainly an earlier design than the butterfly-and-pomegranate border. One of the earliest examples of Fitzhugh known to me, a blue and white set made for Thomas Middleton of South Carolina and imported in the 1780-1790 period, combines the post-and-spear border with the four-section center and the Middleton arms. I should like to suggest, therefore, that the term Fitzhugh pattern be reserved for pieces showing the "four separate groups of flowers and emblems" in the center without regard to the design of the border.

Blue and white platter in Fitzhugh pattern with post-and-spear border (sometimes called a Nanking border); diameter 16 inches.
Cf. Phillips, *China-Trade Porcelain*, upper illustration on p. 221.
Collection of Colonel and Mrs. Edmund FitzHugh.

Reverse of Fitzhugh platter shown above.

The Canton pattern

BY HIRAM TINDALL

Fig. 1. Saucer, Fitzhugh pattern, c. 1810. Diameter 5¾ inches. *Collection of the author; photograph by Helga Photo Studio.*

CANTON is a confusing term. It has designated porcelain from the city of Canton, and the poorer quality of common blue-and-white China Trade wares in general. It has also been used interchangeably with the term Nanking (or Nankeen or Nankin), and to define a particular pattern of China Trade ware. It is in this last sense that Canton is chiefly used today and it is in this sense that I use it in this article.

Just after the Revolution, when America began trading with China directly, one of the major imports was porcelain. The more common blue-and-white wares eventually began to be designated according to three major patterns: Nanking, Fitzhugh, and Canton. Canton also designated a mediocre quality of porcelain, just as Nanking denoted the best quality. The Essex Institute in Salem, for example, once had a piece labeled "Nanking china in the Fitzhugh pattern."

It is by the borders that one may easily distinguish the three patterns. Both Canton and Nanking have at the extreme outer edge a narrow white rim, then a wider blue band which is diapered. Inside this band Canton has a border of short diagonal lines contained by a continuous scalloped line. In place of the diagonals and scalloped line, Nanking has an intricate network of small spears and posts. The diapering of the Nanking border is much more delicate than it is on the average Canton piece. The Fitzhugh border (Fig. 1) is the most elaborate of the three. It consists of geometrically arranged flowers, fish scales, butterflies, diapering, and Chinese symbols. There are many variations of all of these border designs.

The central decoration of Canton and Nanking is similar. It is sometimes called the "island," "island and bridge," or "willow" design. It consists of a river, islands, a bridge (usually with three arches), teahouses, willow and pine trees, mountains, rocks, boats, and clouds. On Canton there is usually a figure or the suggestion of a figure at a window of one of the teahouses. On Nanking there is often a single figure with an upraised umbrella on the bridge. The landscape in both patterns is arranged to conform to the contour of the piece (Fig. 2). English willowware is derived from these two patterns. Although Canton, Nanking, and Fitzhugh were made for export only, almost all the elements comprising the borders and the central decorations are found on domestic Chinese porcelain and in Chinese art.

The central decoration of Fitzhugh varies, but it always consists of four geometric sections grouped around a central medallion. Sometimes the medallion is replaced by a monogram or other decoration; sometimes it is left blank. Often the Fitzhugh central decoration is used with the Nanking border. Both the Nanking and Fitzhugh borders are used with other central designs. The Fitzhugh pattern, most common in blue, was also produced in green, orange, and on rare occasions brown and other colors.

Canton varies in quality more than the other wares. Some of it is as fine as the better trade porcelain (see Pl. II), but some is coarse, pitted, carelessly decorated, and marred by all kinds of imperfections. William Milburn wrote in 1813, "There is an infinite variety of this sort of china, both as to form, coloring, workmanship and price."[1] In 1821 John Prince Jr., of Salem, instructed Benjamin Shreve, ". . . purchase me a dining-set of China dark-blue, with 2 or 3 extra 20 inch dishes—all free from knobs & specks."[2] The color of Canton varies from faded light blue or gray-blue to an almost navy blue. The surface texture varies from orange peel to eggshell to smooth and glassy. Much Canton was not only made of the least refined clay and decorated by the least skilled painters but was also given the least favorable position in the kiln and thus was vulnerable to damage by ash, flames, soot, and less well-controlled heat. The reticulated fruit-basket tray shown in Figure 3, for example, was badly warped in the kiln.

It is often said that after the first quarter of the nineteenth century the quality of Canton deteriorated. While this may be partly true, there is much evidence that from the beginning Canton was produced in various qualities and in different shades of blue. In 1794, in discussing "30 to 40 Dining Setts of common blue and white China," the supercargo of the *John Jay* was instructed to obtain "5 Setts of rather better Quality. . . ."[3] In 1815 Joseph Minturn wrote from New York to William Bell in Canton that he preferred waiting to having porcelain of inferior quality, and that "I think it handsomest when the white is principally covered by the Blue, and the Blue dark."[4] In the same year Ropes, Pickman and Company wrote to Benjamin Shreve in Canton regarding porcelain to be brought back on the *New Hazard*, "Let the China be

Pl. I. Cider flagon, Canton pattern, c. 1800. Height 7 inches. The foo-dog finial is rare on Canton-pattern ware. *Author's collection; Helga photograph.*

Pl. II. Tea set, Canton pattern, 1800-1825. Height of teapot, 4 inches. *Author's collection; Helga photograph.*

Fig. 2. Two helmet-shape cream pitchers, Canton pattern, c. 1800. Height of pitcher at left, 4 inches; of that at right, 5 inches. The pitcher at the left is crudely shaped and poorly proportioned. The pitcher at the right is of the finest quality. The decoration on both is adapted to the contours. *Author's collection; Helga photograph.*

Fig. 3. Reticulated stand for a fruit basket, Canton pattern, c. 1825. Length 9¾ inches. The rim was warped in the kiln, probably by excessive or uncontrolled changes in temperature. *Essex Institute; photograph by Richard Merrill.*

smooth, the cups & saucers in particular not thick & clumsy. . . . The blue & white Dining sets should be of uniform shade & same pattern. They are often put up without attention to these particulars. The bottoms of Plates, Dishes etc. are apt to be very rough. . . .''[5]

Dating much Canton with certainty is almost impossible. It was known to have been imported from the last quarter of the eighteenth century throughout the nineteenth, and into the twentieth century. The frequent allusion in early orders to common quality, best quality, light blue, dark blue, and roughness make it dangerous to judge age by color or quality; texture and form are safer criteria. Canton inscribed *China* may be assumed to have been made after 1894, when Congress passed a regulation which stated that all imports must be ''marked, stamped, branded, or labeled in legible English so as to indicate country of origin.''[6]

Pl. III. Tea caddy, Canton pattern, c. 1790. Height 6 inches. The shape, texture, color, and decoration combine to make this a fine example of a rare form. *Peabody Museum, Salem; photograph by Mark W. Sexton.*

Pl. IV. Covered dish, Canton pattern, c. 1835. Length 12, width 9¼ inches. This unusual form is topped by a peach-pit finial, the most common finial on Canton-pattern wares. *Author's collection; Helga photograph.*

Fig. 4. Plate and platter with cut corners, Canton pattern, 1790-1800. Diameter of plate, 7¾ inches; length of platter, 18¾ inches. These are two of fourteen pieces of Canton-pattern ware at Mount Vernon believed to have been used by General and Mrs. Washington. The platter is of much finer quality in all respects than the plate. *Mount Vernon Ladies' Association.*

Fig. 5. Teacups and saucers, Canton pattern. The cup and saucer at the left are c. 1785, those at the right c. 1835. Diameter of the left-hand saucer, 5½ inches. *Author's collection; Helga photograph.*

Fig. 6. Hot-water plate, Canton pattern, c. 1840. Diameter 9 inches. The form is common in both dinner plates and in serving dishes. The latter often have lids. *Stratford Historical Society, Stratford, Connecticut, gift of Adelaide de Groot; photograph by Nancy Hugo.*

Fig. 7. Trencher salt, Canton pattern, c. 1825. Length 3¾ inches. Few of these have survived. Flaked glaze, as here, is commonly found on the edges of pieces that were used regularly. *Essex Institute; Merrill photograph.*

Fig. 8. Sauce tureen with tray, Canton pattern, c. 1825. Length 8½ inches. The passion-flower finial appears in Canton-pattern ware only on tureens, which were made in both small and large sizes (see Fig. 13). *Peabody Museum, Sexton photograph.*

Fig. 9. Candlesticks, Nanking pattern, c. 1850. Height 9½ inches. Although the border is lacking, the figure on the bridge classifies these as Nanking. Note that the figures face each other, indicating that this is a true pair. *Author's collection; Hugo photograph.*

However, there is every reason to believe that great quantities came in after that date bearing only gummed paper labels identifying the country of origin.

The Canton pattern is less complicated than Nanking and Fitzhugh and was probably quicker and less costly to make. Most Canton was made at Ching-tê Chên and shipped by water six-hundred miles south-southeast to the port of Canton. Long before the industrial revolution the Chinese used the assembly line, and Canton was a product of this method. Father d'Entrecolles, a Jesuit missionary to China, wrote in 1772, "It is surprising to see with what Swiftness these Vessels run thro' so many Hands. Some affirm that a Piece of *China* by the time it is bak'd, passes the Hands of seventy Workmen. . . ."[7] Painting of the familiar blue decoration on the unglazed piece was also accomplished by the assembly line method, so that each component of the design was rendered by a different artisan.[8] The decoration of the more elegant forms was usually much more carefully executed than that on plates of all sizes. When the decoration was dry, the piece was glazed except for the bottoms of platters, oval vegetable dishes, mugs, and some other pieces; the rims on which pieces sat; and the under lip of lids and the surfaces upon which they rested. The porcelain was then fired and exported.

In addition to the profits realized from its sale, Canton served as ballast on the ships importing it. Boxes of porcelain were arranged in the hold to form a platform on which were loaded tea, silks, and other items that might be damaged by bilge water. The average vessel carried two hundred to two hundred and fifty boxes of porcelain.[9] Fortunately, many records of the China Trade have been preserved. The most frequently mentioned porcelain is common blue-and-white, and from the amount of Canton that survives today it is safe to assume the bulk of these common wares was Canton.

Canton was everybody's porcelain; it graced the tables of the most prominent citizens, and it was found in many humble homes. Some of George Washington's Canton is

Fig. 10. Cut-corner bowl, Canton pattern, c. 1840. Diameter 9½ inches. *Stratford Historical Society, de Groot gift; Hugo photograph.*

Fig. 11. Mug, Nanking pattern, c. 1825. Height 4¾ inches. The form is rare in the Nanking pattern although common in the Canton pattern. The twisted-strap handle is also found on covered custard cups, tea and coffee pots, sugar bowls, and cider flagons. *Peabody Museum; Sexton photograph.*

at Mount Vernon (Fig. 4) and in museums. Shards dug at Mount Vernon are mostly of "underglaze blue and white canton"[10] and their number suggests that Canton was used in greater quantities than any other porcelain there.

Early Canton tea and coffee pots were made in the lighthouse and drum shapes; creamers were of the helmet type and teacups were actually tea bowls (Fig. 5). Later, several additional types of creamers and teapots were produced, as were now-obsolete forms such as bakers, pudding dishes, butter boats, and milk pots. Certain forms are especially desirable today because of their rarity, quality, or decorative value (see Figs. 6-13, Pls. I, III, IV). Among these are helmet creamers; cider flagons with foodog finials; candlesticks; garden seats; fine quality reticulated fruit baskets with handles; cut-corner bowls; and mugs with twisted handles.

In 1845, the firm of W. R. and A. H. Sumner of Boston sent a large order for porcelain to its representative in Canton with the instructions that "such of the articles as are to be found in the hands of the manufacturers when this order arrives in Canton precisely conforming to the order in respect to shape, size, color and quality are to be immediately forwarded. The other articles are to be made precisely according to order as early as possible and forwarded as soon as made."[11] Thirty-nine of the seventy-seven listings were for Canton, including the two that follow:

12 doz. Blue and White Canton China handled Tea Cups and Saucers form and size of Tea Cup & Saucer sent marked No. 2, but of the figure and quality of the plate marked No. 6. Handles to be like those on Coffee Cup marked No. 3, but to be suitable size for the tea cup.
12 doz. Blue and White Canton China unhandled Tea Cups and Saucers form & size of Tea Cup & Saucer sent marked No. 2. but of the figure and quality of plate marked No. 6. without handles.[12]

This order shows that even late in the China Trade, porcelain was still being made to order in China and was still

163

sometimes ordered in large quantities. It also destroys the myth that handleless teacups belong only to the early period.

Alice Morse Earle was one of the first to consider Canton seriously. In her *Collecting China in America* of 1892 she wrote of Canton that "it has been crushed grievously under foot in Salem attics; has been sold ignominiously to Salem junkmen. . . ."[13] This has now changed. Canton is no longer crushed under foot nor sold to junkmen. It has come to be respected as it should be and is deservedly displayed by leading museums.

[1] William Milburn, *Oriental Commerce* (London, 1813), Vol. 2, p. 503.

[2] Jean McClure Mudge, *Chinese Export Porcelain for the American Trade* (University of Delaware Press, 1962), p. 76.

[3] *Ibid.*, p. 81.

[4] *Ibid.*, p. 76.

[5] *Ibid.*, p. 75.

[6] United States Statutes at Large, Vol. 28, Ch. 349, Section 5.

[7] John Goldsmith Phillips, *China-Trade Porcelain* (Cambridge, Massachusetts, 1956), p. 9.

[8] *Ibid.*

[9] Mudge, *Chinese Export Porcelain*, pp. 71-72.

[10] James Hunter Johnson, "Ceramics at Mount Vernon, Part 1—Chinese Export Porcelain," *Daughters of the American Revolution Magazine*, Vol. 101 (April 1967), p. 374.

[11] "Canton and Nanking Ware sent to China in 1845," *Old-Time New England*, Vol. 6 (January 1936), p. 100.

[12] *Ibid.*, p. 102.

[13] Alice Morse Earle, *China Collecting in America* (New York, 1892), p. 184.

Fig. 12. Channel-lip pitcher, Canton pattern, c. 1850. Height 3½ inches; from extreme of lip to handle, 5¼ inches. This is the most common shape for Canton-pattern pitchers, which are found in many sizes and qualities. *Author's collection; Helga photograph.*

Fig. 13. Tureen with boar's-head handles and helmet finial, Canton pattern, c. 1840. Length 13 inches. This form is found in many sizes of Canton ware (see Fig. 8). *Stratford Historical Society, de Groot gift; Hugo photograph.*

The Rose Medallion and Mandarin patterns in China Trade porcelain

BY CARL L. CROSSMAN

THE CHINA TRADE porcelain patterns which we know as Rose Medallion and Mandarin have been ignored by serious collectors, who have always considered them to be end-of-the-trade designs of poor quality and execution. Although Rose Medallion and Mandarin are somewhat later in date than many of the more familiar Western-market porcelains decorated with ships, eagles, landscape vignettes, and so forth, the patterns were in actuality made much earlier than most people believe. Some of the pieces of the first quarter of the nineteenth century are of extraordinary quality and beauty, and are certainly as fine as other export porcelains made in that period.

Rose Medallion is usually a multicolor enamel overglaze decoration of birds, flowers, butterflies, and Chinese figures arranged in four or more panels around a center medallion containing similar designs (Fig. 1). The area between the panels is filled with rose-color tree peonies

Fig. 1. Rose Medallion teapot, c. 1830. This piece is typical of the Rose Medallion of good quality exported from 1815 to 1835. *Collection of Mrs. O. V. Porter.*

and green tendrils on a gold ground. When the basic elements of this pattern are used together but are not arranged in panels, the pattern created is often referred to as "elements of Rose Medallion" or "Rose Canton."

Mandarin pattern differs from Rose Medallion in that the predominant decorative element is one or more figures, within a border of flowers, fruits, and butterflies similar to those on Rose Medallion but usually on a gold ground (Fig. 2). In some early pieces the border lacks the gold ground, but this should not be used as a definite guide to dating. The names Rose Medallion and Mandarin are, of course, modern and are applied on the basis of dominant motifs in the decoration. To some degree they are interchangeable, since they employ such similar motifs in an almost infinite variety of combinations that the patterns overlap and cannot always be differentiated.

Rose Medallion and Mandarin were designed by the Chinese exclusively for the export market and were not intended for home consumption. However, the patterns were derived from the eighteenth-century Chinese floral and figural designs of the *famille rose* porcelains and from the eighteenth-century Chinese-style porcelains made for export to Western markets. When first introduced, Rose Medallion and Mandarin were not the fully developed patterns we think of today. In the late eighteenth century, elements of their designs were used sparingly

Fig. 2. Mandarin pitcher, c. 1830, with a border characteristic of the best examples of the pattern. *Porter collection.*

and sometimes in combination with borders, initials, monograms, and crests of Western derivation which had been in demand throughout the eighteenth century. By 1800, examples representing the full development of Rose Medallion and Mandarin had appeared, usually beautifully executed and of fine quality. The patterns reached the peak of their popularity in the 1820's and 1830's; by the late thirties, however, the quality had declined, and although the patterns continued to be in demand throughout the century, by 1850 designs were so crude that they do not merit study.

Throughout the development and full flowering of the Rose Medallion and Mandarin patterns, there was a continual recombination of the Chinese motifs with various designs of Western inspiration. Basically Chinese patterns were sometimes specifically redesigned or adjusted by the artisans to harmonize with the particular Western design which was to be added, and in many cases great care was taken to effect a striking combination of motifs. Through study of the porcelains decorated with this type of design, in which Chinese and Western motifs are blended, one can most easily trace the development and tentatively date the patterns of Rose Medallion and Mandarin.

In studying the development of both patterns, it is necessary not only to recall the eighteenth-century *famille rose* porcelains but also to examine the export porcelains with Chinese motifs made in the second half of the eighteenth century. The saucer in Figure 3 is an example of the latter type, exported to Europe and later to America, from about 1760 to 1795. Though strictly Chinese in appearance and choice of ornament, it shows Western overtones in the shading and in the penciled quality of the vignette, which is not unlike the Western landscape vignettes and mythological scenes based on engravings. The colors here are exactly those of Rose Medallion and Mandarin, and the drawing is comparable to that found on early pieces in the two patterns, although the saucer lacks the breadth of handling characteristic of Rose Medallion and Mandarin.

The vegetable tureen in Figure 4, made for De Witt and Marie Clinton in 1796, represents an important phase in the development of the patterns, and in its colorings and use of figures can be considered a forerunner of many of the Mandarin designs. The center decoration is compositionally identical to the landscape centers on Canton and Nanking wares, although here the landscape is in full color over the glaze rather than in blue under the glaze. The fleur-de-lis border around the edge of the cover is of the French type, introduced in export porcelains of the eighteenth century. The small figures spaced around both cover and tureen represent Chinese gods upon clouds, and are executed and colored very similarly to the figures found on Mandarin. The presence of this type of decoration on a piece of this early date suggests that perhaps

Fig. 3. Saucer with polychrome overglaze decoration, c. 1770. Made for export markets, this type of decoration was based on that of eighteenth-century Chinese *famille rose* porcelain and was the prototype of China Trade Mandarin porcelain. *Author's collection.*

Fig. 4. Vegetable tureen from the dinner service made for De Witt and Marie Clinton in 1796. This piece, with its Canton-type landscape in full color on the glaze, is an important forerunner of many Mandarin designs.

Fig. 5. Chinese export urn, c. 1810, one of a pair of so-called Marieberg type, decorated with elements of the Rose Medallion pattern. *Photograph by courtesy of Mink Hill Farms.*

the full-color Chinese-type designs of Rose Medallion and Mandarin were in demand at the end of the eighteenth century—some twenty years before the generally accepted date for the appearance of this porcelain on the export market.

Figure 6 is the well-known plate depicting the ship *Friendship* of Salem, Massachusetts. One of the few ex-

amples of export china bearing an actual ship portrait rather than a design based on a Western ship engraving, it is also rare in its combination of Chinese border and Western center decoration. Instead of the simple border of grape leaves or daggers which would have been typical with the Western ship portrait, the purchaser of the plate chose to have a well-developed multicolor four-panel Rose Medallion border. It is of very fine quality, with panels containing motifs reminiscent of eighteenth-century *famille rose* porcelains. This combination on a plate known to have been exported in 1821 firmly dates the highly developed Rose Medallion pattern in the first quarter of the nineteenth century.

The platter in Figure 7 is a well-documented piece of the Rose Medallion family. Although it lacks the paneling, its design is of the Rose Medallion (or Rose Canton) type. Brought from China in 1831, the service from which it came was a wedding gift for Mr. and Mrs. Frederick Hall Bradlee of Beverly, Massachusetts. The decoration is simpler than that of most examples of this pattern, since it lacks the gold ground in the borders and has a green inner border which is more European than Chinese. The gravy tureen from the same service is of a shape derived from a Wedgwood creamware pattern of 1774 but is squatter and less graceful than the undocumented tureen of similar shape in Figure 8, which may therefore be somewhat earlier. The Western-type border here may be of English derivation, while the flowers and fruit are in the best Rose Medallion style. Possibly exported about 1815, the tureen is unusual in its combination of Western and Chinese motifs with a specifically ordered initial but is another instance of the use of Rose Medallion motifs with Western designs after 1800.

A more impressive example of a Western device combined with a polychrome pattern is the plate in Figure 9. It is of the Mandarin pattern, but the figures in the center have been arranged to allow for the large and ornate crown studded with three-dimensional drops of paint in imitation of jewels. The Spanish inscription below the crown reads *Exmo Sor Marques de Almendares.* That a member of the nobility should acquire, obviously on special order, a service of this kind indicates the esteem in which the pattern was held. The simplicity of the border, lacking a gold ground, and the fine execution of the figures and crown place the plate in the early nineteenth century. The integration of the Western crown and inscription and the Chinese Mandarin motifs indicates that in this instance the latter had not been previously made up as a stock pattern, but rather that the entire design was planned as a unit.

The large well-and-tree platter in Figure 10 shows the use of an English crest—that of the Hamilton family—with a basically Chinese design. The decoration is of excellent quality, with well-drawn figures of larger size than usual. The groups of Chinese symbols and *objets d'art* interspersed with the figures are often found in borders of the Mandarin pattern, and the figures are dressed in the same manner as those on fine Mandarin porcelains that may be dated in the first quarter of the 1800's. For example, a Mandarin wash service at Gore Place, Waltham, Massachusetts, is known to have been among the household furnishings of Governor Gore who died in 1827, and thus may have been purchased in the early 1820's or even earlier. The service displays the same simplicity of style and design as the Hamilton platter.

The urn in Figure 5 is of the type often called Marieberg. It was copied from vases—originally inspired by a Scandinavian silver model—made at the royal Swedish porcelain manufactory at Marieberg. The shape was often used, especially for the American market, after 1785 and until about 1815. Called also pistol-handle urns, examples were generally painted with simple landscape vignettes or scenes from European engravings within oval medallions. The bases were almost always marbleized and the handles often gilded. On the unusually fine pair of which one is illustrated, Chinese landscape vignettes are framed by the medallions and repeated on the covers, the daisy borders around the rims are distinctly European-inspired, while the body decoration is made up of the elements of Rose Medallion. The presence of these latter motifs on urns of this period indicates that the pattern was becoming popular at the turn of the eighteenth century.

The figures are very similar and the groups of *objets d'art* are identical. The borders, although slightly different, also lack the gold ground. The Hamilton platter may be compared likewise with pieces at the Adams National Historic Site in Quincy, Massachusetts. John Adams, who died in 1826, left in his estate a wash basin and ewer of Mandarin with figures identical to both the Hamilton and Gore pieces but with more ornate borders on gold backgrounds.

The most important piece of Mandarin porcelain of the nineteenth century is the large punch bowl made in 1832 which is now owned by the Bostonian Society (Fig. 11). Of extraordinary size, it is one of the few examples of

Mandarin to bear not only a dedication indicating to and from whom it was given, but also a finely painted view of Canton in the interior center. The two figural panels on the outside of the bowl are similar to those on Mandarin bowls and plates previously discussed. The heavy borders around the inner and outer rims are characteristic of the pattern and are identical to those on fine Mandarin bowls made between 1815 and 1835. The interior sides are covered with a continuous court procession including figures, animals, and vehicles against a landscape background. It should be borne in mind that the Western parts of this design, as in the other special-order pieces illustrated, could not have been added to a previously

Fig. 6. An actual portrait of the ship *Friendship* of Salem decorates this plate made at Canton in 1821. The border is of the fine early Rose Medallion type. *Peabody Museum.*

Fig. 7. Rose Medallion platter and tureens brought from China in 1831 as a wedding present for Mr. and Mrs. Frederick Hall Bradlee of Beverly, Massachusetts.

168

Fig. 8. Gravy tureen, c. 1815, with Rose Medallion flowers and fruits and Western-inspired border and initial. Shape based on a Wedgwood creamware model of 1774. *Author's collection.*

decorated Mandarin bowl: the entire design had to be planned and executed as a whole.

The inscriptions on this bowl and the story behind them are as interesting and unusual as the view of Canton. In a shield on each side are the words *From/The Commander and Ward Room Officers/of the/U. S. Ship Peacock/To/Dwight Boyden—Tremont House/Boston/ 1832.* At this time Boyden was the manager of Tremont House, the hotel designed by Isaiah Rogers about 1828 and considered the first "modern" hotel in America. It was a popular gathering place for old salts of the War of 1812, such as Mad Jack Percival, sailing master aboard the *Peacock,* which fought the last major battle of that war. The bowl must have been given Boyden by the *Peacock*'s officers on some special occasion—or perhaps as an appeasement for the carousings of the group. The bowl was frequently used throughout the nineteenth century, as its current condition indicates.

Rose Medallion and Mandarin dinner services and odd pieces with initials, monograms, coats of arms, and crests were also made for prominent families of Philadelphia, New York, Boston, and Newport, as well as for innumerable European families. Although Rose Medallion and Mandarin are generally thought to have been ballast types of export china, like Canton and Nanking—stock patterns bought in great quantity—the examples shown here indicate that these patterns were indeed used on special-order pieces and must have been highly regarded by those who commissioned them. Rose Medallion and Mandarin porcelain of the best quality, with or without Western motifs, deserves the consideration of collectors as much as the familiar custom-designed China Trade porcelain of the late eighteenth and early nineteenth centuries.

Fig. 9. Plate in the Mandarin pattern made for the Marqués de Almendares. Spanish market, early nineteenth century. *Author's collection.*

Fig. 10. Well-and-tree platter in the Mandarin pattern with crest of the Hamilton family. English market, early nineteenth century. *Author's collection.*

169

Fig. 11 (*two views*).   Mandarin punch bowl with interior center decoration of the hongs, or factories, at Canton. American market, 1832. *Bostonian Society*.

Index

Index